GEORGE HENRY LEWES
as Literary Critic

GEORGE HENRY LEWES

as Literary Critic

Alice R. Kaminsky

SYRACUSE UNIVERSITY PRESS

Syracuse, New York

FIRST EDITION

ALICE R. KAMINSKY

Alice R. Kaminsky is Associate Professor of English at the State University of New York, College at Cortland. *George Henry Lewes as Literary Critic* is the culmination of a fifteen-year interest in Lewes that began with the author's doctoral dissertation for New York University in 1952. She received her M.A. from N.Y.U. in 1947 and her B.A. from Washington Square College of N.Y.U. in 1946. Professor Kaminsky edited *The Literary Criticism of George Henry Lewes* for the Regents Critics Series and has published a number of articles on Lewes and other nineteenth-century English writers.

Library of Congress Catalog Card Number: 68-54067

Manufactured in the United States of America

To
JACK and ERIC

Preface

Since this is the first book length study of the critical thought of George Henry Lewes, it may be considered a pioneer effort to resuscitate his reputation as an important literary critic. His interesting life still awaits definitive biographical treatment. A.T. Kitchel notes in the foreward to *George Lewes and George Eliot: A Review of Records* that the book is not a "real biography;" she is primarily interested in Lewes' relationship to George Eliot. G. Haight's invaluable *George Eliot Letters* contains many of Lewes' letters, but this work and Haight's new *George Eliot: A Biography* show his basic concern with George Eliot. Through the years Lewes has been discussed in articles, dissertations, and special sections of books, but no published work exists which attempts to survey and evaluate his total critical contribution.

After carefully scrutinizing all of Lewes' writings, I have found them to contain a coherent and relevant theory of literature. This book attempts, therefore, to integrate the ideas expressed in his many works in order to reveal how his general philosophic position is related to his theory of criticism, and to show how the theory is applied in relation to the poem, the novel, and the drama.

I wish to express my thanks to those who have helped me to complete this study which has occupied me for many years: Professor Robert B. Doremus of the University of Wisconsin, who by now may have forgotten that he very kindly sent me his two-volume dissertation on Lewes' dramatic criticism; Professor Gordon Haight of Yale University, who as reader for *PMLA* approved my article on Lewes in 1955, thereby encouraging me to continue my study of Lewes; Professor Paul A. Olsen of the

University of Nebraska, who by asking me to do an edition of Lewes' criticism for the Regents Critics Series led me to rethink and refine some of my ideas; the Research Foundation of the State of New York for awarding me a Summer Research Fellowship in 1966, which enabled me to put this book in its present form; Professors Francis Mineka and William Sale of Cornell University, and Professor Van A. Burd of the State University College at Cortland for their support of this project in letters which enabled me to obtain the fellowship. I am particularly grateful to Professor Mineka for taking the time to read my manuscript and for his penetrating criticisms.

I also wish to thank the following: the Beinecke Library at Yale for granting me permission to reprint some of the material I examined in their Lewes collection; *PMLA* for giving me permission to reprint my article "George Eliot, George Henry Lewes, and the Novel," and Macmillan for allowing me to reprint "The Philosophy of George Henry Lewes," *Encyclopedia of Philosophy*.

Finally I must speak of what I owe to my husband, Professor Jack Kaminsky of the State University of New York at Binghamton, whose knowledge of Lewes' philosophy has been of inestimable aid to me and without whose encouragement this book would never have been completed.

Alice R. Kaminsky

June, 1968
Cortland, New York

Contents

List of Abbreviations

A	*Aristotle: A Chapter in the History of Science*
BFR	*British and Foreign Review*
BQR	*British Quarterly Review*
CPS	*Comte's Philosophy of the Sciences*
FC	*Foundations of a Creed*
FR	*Fortnightly Review*
GE	*The George Eliot Letters,* ed. Gordon S. Haight
HP	*The Biographical History of Philosophy*
MFO	*Mind as a Function of the Organism*
PBM	*The Physical Basis of Mind*
SP	*The Study of Psychology*
WR	*Westminster Review*

GEORGE HENRY LEWES
as Literary Critic

1

G. H. Lewes
A Nineteenth-Century Littérateur

In literary history reputations are won, lost, and rewon in unpredictable patterns that would confound the powers of a Tiresias. A few weeks after George Henry Lewes died, several prominent Victorians dined together and talked about Lewes: "Morley . . . put him very high as a philosopher, Huxley as a physiologist; Arnold thought him strongest as a dramatic critic. Both Morley and Harrison seemed to think that he would appear a more considerable person to posterity than he did to his contemporaries."[1] In his own age, Lewes was esteemed for certain solid achievements. His *Biographical History of Philosophy* was a great success, read by thousands, and translated into German, Hungarian, and Russian. His *Life of Goethe* earned him great literary acclaim as well as financial remuneration. As he told Francis Espinasse, he contributed to all of the important reviews of his time, "except the d——d old *Quarterly*."[2] He edited at different intervals such influential magazines as the *Leader*, the *Cornhill*, and the *Fortnightly Review*. Carlyle praised him as the "prince of journalists."[3] A man of remarkable talent and versatility, Lewes was during his lifetime journalist, editor, critic, novelist,

1 Sir Mountstuart E. Grant Duff, *Notes from a Diary: 1873-1881* (London, 1898), II, 88.

2 Francis Espinasse, *Literary Recollections and Sketches* (New York, 1893), 276.

3 *Ibid.*, 282.

dramatist, actor, biographer, scientist (physiologist and zoologist), philosopher, and psychologist. Yet such are the vagaries of fame that the modern world remembers him primarily for his connection with George Eliot. However, his writings do not deserve the oblivion to which they have been consigned. Judged from the perspective of our century, he merits recognition as a critic of considerable importance.

George Henry Lewes was born in London on April 18, 1817, the youngest of three sons of John Lee Lewes. His grandfather was Charles Lee Lewes, the comic actor who achieved fame for his performance of the part of young Marlow in *She Stoops to Conquer.* John, or "Dandy Lewes" as he was called, was also an actor; he published his father's *Memoirs* after his death and two volumes of his own mediocre poetry.[4] He must have died some time before 1825, for in that year his wife, Elizabeth Ashweek Lewes (1787–1870), married a Mr. John Willim (1778–1864), a retired captain of the 18th Native Infantry Regiment in Bengal. Lewes evidently had a strong affection for his mother. His brother Edward died at sea in 1855, and Lewes helped support his widow Susanna and son Vivian. His oldest brother, Edgar James, died about 1836.[5]

Very little is known about Lewes' boyhood. His extant *Journals* and *Diaries* offer no significant revelations about his youth.[6] However, he attended schools in London, Jersey, and Brittany, and Dr. Burney's school at Greenwich. His departure from Greenwich, in 1833, apparently terminated his formal education, and his actual preoccupations from 1833–1835 have been vaguely surmised. He seems to have drifted desultorily from the position of a clerk in a notary office, to work in the counting house of a Russian merchant, to an interest in science and study of medicine. He supposedly gave up medicine because he could not stand the spectacle of human suffering. During this period, he formed a friendship with the Leigh Hunts. They and their friends exerted

[4] John Lee Lewes (ed.), *Memoirs of Charles Lee Lewes* (4 vols.; London, 1805).

[5] GE, II, 216; V, 83, 109 n. 1. See also A.T. Kitchel, *George Lewes and George Eliot: a Review of Records* (New York, 1933), 7.

[6] Beinecke Library, Yale University, *Diaries* 1869-1876, 8 volumes; *Journals,* X, July, 1856-March, 1859; XI, April, 1859-January, 1866; XII, June, 1866-May, 1870.

an important influence in encouraging his intellectual growth. A member of that group wrote about Lewes' interest in philosophy, religion and art, his wit, ambition, and astonishing facility in language; at the age of twenty he already seemed a "promising man of parts, a mixture of the man of the world and the boy."[7] In 1838 he went to Germany as a tutor and remained there for a year, returning in 1840. Back in England, on February 18, 1841, he married Agnes Swynfen Jervis (1822–1902), the beautiful nineteen-year-old daughter of Swynfen Jervis of Darlaston Hall, Chatcull, Staffordshire, M.P. for Bridport.[8] The Leweses had four sons: Charles Lee (1842–1891), Thornton Arnott (1844–1869), Herbert Arthur (1846–1875), St. Vincent Arthy (1848–1850). From 1843 to 1847 Agnes helped supplement the family income by writing articles which Lewes submitted to the magazines under his name.[9] Lewes and his wife frequently visited the big house in Queens Road, Bayswater, where the Phalanstery, an experiment in cooperative living inspired by Fourieristic principles, was carried on by the Hunt-Gliddon circle.

This circle consisted of John Gliddon and his wife Jacinta, the daughter of Leigh Hunt; her brother, Thornton Hunt and his wife Kate, the sister of John Gliddon; Samuel Laurence and his wife Anastasia, a cousin of the Hunts; and several unmarried sisters. They lived together harmoniously at the Phalanstery, shared expenses, and received Sunday visitors. These visitors were a mixed lot including Robert Owen, the socialist; Mrs. Milner Gibson, the wife of a Member of Parliament; and Eliza Lynn Linton, a young girl fresh from the country. Years later, Eliza Linton described her experiences with this group in *My Literary Life*, a work written in her "serene old age, when she had long since rejected the iconoclasm of her youth."[10] She recalled being

7 [James Sully], "Memorial Article: G. H. Lewes," *The New Quarterly Magazine*, XII (1879), 357; W. Minto (ed.), *Autobiographical Notes of the Life of William Bell Scott* (New York, 1892), II, 130.

8 Lewes dedicated his *Life of Robespierre* to his father-in-law. Carlyle referred to Jervis as a "disreputable Welsh member." See Sir Charles Gavan Duffy, *Conversations with Carlyle* (New York, 1892), 223.

9 Lewes identified Agnes' articles in his *Literary Receipts Book* (MS in the Berg Collection of the New York Public Library, New York). Reprinted in GE, VII, 365-83.

10 *My Literary Life* (London, 1899), 11-40. See also Linton, *The Autobiography of Christopher Kirkland* (London, 1885), I, 278; George S. Layard, *Mrs. Lynn*

disconcerted by the unconventional views of some of the people she met at the Phalanstery, but the man who shocked and embarrassed her most of all was George Henry Lewes.

He and Thornton Hunt were freethinkers on all social and moral issues, and worst of all they believed in free love. But, while Hunt discussed the issue philosophically and platonically, Lewes argued as the "frankly sensual, frankly self-indulgent . . . natural Hedonist." Furthermore, he was often guilty of indecorous behavior. "He was," she wrote, "the first of the audacious men of my acquaintance and about the most extreme. He . . . would discourse on the most delicate matters of physiology with no more perception that he was transgressing the bounds of propriety than if he had been a learned savage. I heard more startling things from Lewes, in full conclave of young and old, married and single, men and women, than I had ever dreamt of or heard hinted at before. And I know that men complained of his after-dinner talk and anecdotes as being beyond the license accorded to, or taken by, even the boldest talkers of the mess-table and the club smoking-room."[11] In view of the specific examples she gives of Lewes' transgressions, the suspicion lingers that the "boldest talkers at Victorian mess-tables" must have been rather tame by modern standards. "I myself," she wrote indignantly, "was at Mrs. Milner Gibson's when he shouted across the room: 'Arethusa, come here!' and I saw him perch himself familiarly on the arm of the chair in which she was sitting. Yet he had no cause for such a breach of good taste and good manners. . . . I remember, too, his offering to kiss a pretty young girl on her taking leave of the family one Sunday night, and his offended reproachful tone when she turned away her head and refused his kiss." One Sunday evening when the group discussed the notorious song "Sam Hall," Lewes "made it the subject of some brilliant persiflage and audacity." But even she, despite her hostility, could not avoid paying Lewes the supreme compliment: "Wherever he went there was a patch of intellectual sunshine in the room."[12]

Lewes' capacity and enthusiasm for intellectual activity were

---

Linton: Her Life, Letters & Opinions (London, 1901), 251-52; Kitchel, *op. cit.*, 15-18, 312-16.

[11] Linton, *My Literary Life*, 23-25, 18-19.

[12] *Ibid.*, 20-22, 26.

to remain his chief assets throughout his life, and, especially in this early period, they compensated for his lack of influential family and university career. His wide acquaintance with French, German, and Spanish literature resulted in the production of many articles for the *British and Foreign Review, Foreign Quarterly Review, Edinburgh Review,* and *Westminster Review.* In those early forties John Stuart Mill wrote to Lewes giving him literary advice and encouragement.[13] Moreover, Mill introduced Lewes to the doctrines of August Comte. Alexander Bain recalled that Lewes "sat at the feet of Mill, read the Logic with avidity, and took up Comte with equal avidity."[14] Lewes' first book, the *Biographical History of Philosophy* (1845), was written with the aim of ousting metaphysics from philosophical inquiry and replacing it with scientific positivism. Although it was originally a somewhat specious work, as W.R. Sorley points out, "later editions remedied many blemishes and showed the author's ability to appreciate other points of view than that from which he had started."[15] According to Frederic Harrison, the *History* influenced the thought of his generation "almost more than any single book except Mr. Mill's *Logic*. . . ."[16] Lewes also published a commentary on the Spanish drama in 1846; a novel, *Ranthorpe,* in 1847; still another novel, *Rose, Blanche and Violet,* in 1848; and the first English biography of Robespierre in 1849. He also seems at one time to have had the ambition to become an actor. He participated in the amateur performances of the Dickens' group and played professionally the roles of Shylock and Dom Gomez, the latter a character in his own play *The Noble Heart,* first produced on April 16, 1849. Even Carlyle, who in those early years was often annoyed when Lewes laughed at his "prophetics", was forced to wonder at Lewes' capacity for work.[17]

Lewes began his affiliation with the *Leader* in 1850. Managed by George Jacob Holyoake, the famous radical, and edited by Lewes and Thornton Hunt, the *Leader* was a progressive, liberal

13 Kitchel, *op. cit.*, 27-40.

14 Alexander Bain, *John Stuart Mill: A Criticism: with Personal Recollections* (London, 1882), 65.

15 W.R. Sorley, *A History of English Philosophy* (Cambridge, Eng., 1937), 273.

16 Frederic Harrison, "G. H. Lewes," *Academy,* XIV (1878), 543.

17 Kitchel, *op. cit.*, 61; Espinasse, *op. cit.*, 281-82. See Lewes' review of Carlyle's Cromwell in the *Leader,* May 23, 1857, 497.

weekly which attacked the evils of the existing economic, educational, and religious institutions and advocated secular education, free trade, and freedom of thought and religion. It was friendly to the European revolutionaries—Mazzini, Ruge, Leroux, Blanc, and Kossuth. It favored the United States and looked to socialism as the best means of achieving the ideal state of the future. It was interested in all new views in science, especially as exemplified in the fields of psychology and Darwinian theory. To the *Leader* Lewes contributed many items on a variety of subjects: articles on Comte, later published in 1853 as *Comte's Philosophy of the Sciences;* a weekly column on literature; an unfinished novel, *The Apprenticeship of Life* (1850); book reviews; and witty, dramatic criticisms written under the pseudonym of Vivian. Vivian even had occasion to review several successful comic plays that Lewes adapted from the French originals under his other pseudonym Slingsby Lawrence.

When Lewes first met Mary Ann Evans (George Eliot), assistant editor of the *Westminster Review,* in October, 1851, he was a very unhappy man. In April, 1850, Agnes gave birth to her fifth child. Although Lewes knew that Thornton Hunt was the father, he forgave Agnes and named the boy Edmund Alfred Lewes. Lewes ceased to regard Agnes as his wife when she gave birth to Rose Agnes (October 21, 1851), Thornton Hunt's second child. Shortly after the birth of Rose Agnes, Hunt's wife bore him a son, Brian Courthope Leigh Hunt (January 6, 1852). Still another two of Hunt's children were born within weeks of each other, Ethel Isabella Lewes (October 9, 1853), and Beatrice Mary Leigh Hunt (November 16, 1853). Mildred Jane Lewes (May 21, 1857) was also fathered by Hunt. This was the man Mrs. Linton described as having "a strain of asceticism" and defended as having played the most honorable role in the triangle. No doubt she was unaware of quite another type of "strain" in him. Hunt's charms and the radical views of the circle may have proved irresistible to Agnes. Lewes himself may have recognized that his youthful, unconventional views influenced his wife's actions. Unfortunately, he could not obtain a divorce because he had once pardoned his wife's adultery, and furthermore, divorce was financially impossible for him in those days. Throughout his life he maintained friendly relations with Agnes and paid her an allowance. George Eliot wrote in Lewes' *Literary Receipts Book* that "his whole earnings were absorbed in his expenses for his family," that is, in payments to Agnes and caring for his children.[18] George Eliot and Lewes' son continued the payments to Agnes after Lewes died and up until the time Agnes died.

When Lewes and Mary Ann Evans left for Germany together on July 20, 1854, they entered into a relationship which their life together completely justified. As G.J. Holyoake wrote: "For myself, I never could see what conventional opinion had to do with a personal union founded in affection by which nobody was wronged, nobody distressed, and in which protection was accorded and generous provision made for the present and future interest of everyone concerned. Conventional opinion, not even in its ethical aspects, could establish higher relations than existed in their case."[19]

In 1855, after Lewes and George Eliot returned to England, he published a work which had preoccupied him for many years, his famous *Life of Goethe*. It received immediate critical acclaim and is to this day evaluated as an important biography. According to Jacques Barzun, the best way to begin the study of Goethe is to read Lewes' biography.[20] In 1856 Lewes encouraged Mary Ann Evans to begin the writing which was to transform her into a celebrated novelist. The year 1856 was also memorable to Lewes "as the year in which I learned to employ the *Microscope*, and inaugurated by *Seaside Stories* the entrance into the vast field of marine zoology."[21] In 1854 Lewes had noted: "It is eighteen years since I first began to occupy myself—practically and theoretically—with Biology."[22] Scientific research absorbed his time as a dominant interest throughout his life. He wrote a series of articles for *Blackwood's Magazine* which were later published in 1858 as *Sea-side Studies at Ilfracombe, Tenby, the Scilly Isles, and Jersey.*

18 In Lewes' *Literary Receipts Book*, GE, VII, 382-83, George Eliot listed his income from 1855 to 1877 as being 9363 pounds; she further noted that he had only 3213 pounds left for himself and he used the rest of the money to care for his family and Agnes.

19 G.J. Holyoake, *Bygones Worth Remembering* (New York, 1905), I, 64-65.

20 Jacques Barzun, *Goethe's Faust* (New York, 1955), xxviii; Edith Batho and Bonamy Dobrée, *The Victorians and After: 1830-1914* (London, 1938), 204; Richard Friedenthal, *Goethe: His Life and Times* (Cleveland and N.Y., 1965), 534.

21 Lewes' *Diary*, January 7, 1857.

22 *Leader*, January 14, 1854, 40.

Another visit to Germany in 1858, where Lewes met several important scientists, stimulated him to complete his work on the physiology of the nervous system. In September, 1859 he read several of his papers on the sensory and motor nerves to the British Association for the Advancement of Science, and his views were defended by Thomas Henry Huxley.[23] In that same year Lewes published his *Physiology of Common Life.* This seemingly modest work found its way into Russia where it was read by Dostoevski who mentioned it in *Crime and Punishment.* When the young Pavlov visited the physiological laboratory of McGill University in 1929, he took the first volume of Lewes' work from a shelf in the library, opened it at page 230 and commented on the gastrointestinal tract there displayed: "When in my very young days I read this book . . . I was greatly intrigued by this picture. I asked myself: How does such a complicated system work? My interest in the digestive system originated at this epoch."[24] In his obituary of Pavlov, J.F. Fulton wrote: "Lewes's book contains several remarkable chapters entitled, 'Feeling and Thinking,' 'The Mind and the Brain,' 'Our Senses and Sensations,' and 'Sleep and Dreams'; these chapters form a highly important landmark in the history of physiological psychology, not only because they stimulated the young Pavlov (and incidentally also William James), but because they represent one of the earliest objective treaties on the functions of the cerebral hemispheres. Under the stimulus of this book, a copy of which he kept always beside him as a *comes viae vitaeque,* Pavlov left theology and determined to follow biological science as his career.[25]

Lewes' *Studies in Animal Life* appeared in 1862. His *Aristotle: A Chapter in the History of Science* (1864) revealed his strong

[23] Lewes' "The Necessity of a Reform in Nerve-Physiology," "A Demonstration of the Muscular Sense," and "On the Supposed Distinction between Sensory and Motor Nerves," are abstracted in the *Report of the Twenty-Ninth Meeting of the British Association for the Advancement of Science Held at Aberdeen in September in 1859* (1860), 166-170. For the story of Lewes' relationship to Huxley, see GE, II, 132, 133; III, 189; IV, 119, 214 n. 6; VII, 177 n. 3.

[24] B.P. Babkin, *Pavlov: A Biography* (Univ. of Chicago Press, 1949), 214; *The Physiology of Common Life* (Leipzig, 1860), I, 158. In Dostoevski's *Crime and Punishment,* trans. Constance Garnett (New York, 1927), 18, Marmeladov tells Raskolnikov that Sonia has read "with great interest" Lewes' *Physiology of Common Life.*

[25] "The Progress of Science: Ivan Petrovitch Pavlov," *Scientific Monthly,* XLII (1936), 375-76.

grasp of nineteenth century science; it remains today one of the very few analyses of Aristotle's physical science. On the basis of such scientific investigation, he earned the respect of other scientists. Charles Eliot Norton reported: "I have heard both Darwin and Sir Charles Lyell speak very highly of the thoroughness of his knowledge in their departments."[26] With good reason, J.T. Merz referred to him as one who had "a vastly superior knowledge of the natural, especially the biological sciences, than Mill possessed."[27]

From 1865 to 1866, despite ill health, Lewes, at the request of Anthony Trollope, undertook the editorship of the *Fortnightly Review.* Originally conceived to be a politically independent journal, under Lewes' guidance it generally attracted liberal contributors. Not only did Lewes make considerable scientific and literary contributions to the *Fortnightly,* but he also conducted a column called Public Affairs in which he surveyed the news of the day. He supported the Liberal party of Russell and Gladstone, arguing constantly for reform of the Franchise. Although he disapproved of Fenianism, he pleaded for the settlement of Irish grievances. He blamed the church for the part it played in hampering educational reform. He attacked Governor Eyre for the "murder" of George Gordon. Siding with the North, he praised Lincoln and deplored his assassination. Opposed to Bismarck, and Napoleon III, he was sympathetic to the cause of unification of Germany and Italy.[28]

The remaining years of Lewes' life were saddened by the early deaths of two of his sons and by recurring periods of ill health. He devoted his time almost exclusively to science and philosophy. The final outcome of those years of work was *Problems of Life and Mind* (1874–1879). Not only is one of the volumes, *The Physical Basis of Mind,* as a modern writer has declared, one of the

[26] S. Norton and M. A. De Wolfe Howe (eds.), *Letters of Charles Eliot Norton,* (Boston and New York, 1913) I, 317.

[27] J.T. Merz, *A History of European Thought in the Nineteenth Century* (London, 1914), III, 314.

[28] FR, I, 117-22, 242-45, 377-79, 757-64; II, 374-77, 504-5, 630-32, 756-61; III, 112-16, 240-45, 362-64, 760-61, 764-65; IV, 369-71, 499-502, 623-25, 754-57; V, 106-10, 497-500, 626; VI, 105, 358-61, 747, 879-80. From 1865 to 1866 Lewes also wrote the "Varia" and "Causeries" in the FR. See Edwin M. Everett, *The Party of Humanity: The Fortnightly Review and Its Contributors* (Chapel Hill, 1939), 28-73.

"early monuments" of psychology,[29] but also expressed in the five volumes are the detailed observations of a highly trained thinker on epistemology, metaphysics, and scientific method. Lewes never lived to revise the last two volumes of the series; this task was undertaken by George Eliot who after his death prepared the remaining portion of his manuscript for publication. On November 30, 1878 Lewes died of enteritis.

The picture of Lewes that emerges from a study of the various descriptions of him in the recollections of his contemporaries is one of a dynamic personality who was admired and loved by those who knew him well.

An unidentified author made the following comments on Lewes in 1852, in an unpublished letter to Sir Robert Vaughan: "I am glad to find that you like Lewes: he is, indeed, a most kindly, genial, guileless person & with versatility & accomplishment that make him a miracle. All who really know him, like him, and appreciate him highly."[30] However, some were alienated by his physical appearance. He was not a handsome person. According to John Hollingshead, Thornton Hunt and Henry Chorley ran George Henry Lewes a hard race for the title of ugliest man in London.[31] Charles Eliot Norton described Lewes as very odd looking: "He is very slightly built, his hands full of nervous expression as well as his face, and constantly used in gesticulation. His face is very plain, pitted with small-pox—dark, handsome, feeling eyes, but worn, and with a sadness and waywardness of expression that at times take the place of the more than common sentiment. His nose and mouth are exceedingly irregular, and straggly, thin moustaches and beard, combined with long ragged hair, quite serve to de-Anglicize his appearance."[32] However, as Justin McCarthy noted, Lewes evidently had the kind of charm which compensated for his physical inadequacies: "But when the face lighted up with earnest thought, or the eyes flashed with wit and humour and fancy, then one forgot all about the appearance,

29 A.W. Brown, *The Metaphysical Society* (New York, 1947), 49.

30 May 18, 1852, in the Beinecke Library, Yale University. See also Joan Bennett's "Unpublished George Eliot Letters," *The Times Literary Supplement,* May 16, 1968, 507. She reprints two of Lewes' heretofore unpublished letters which reveal "his characteristic warmth and kindness."

31 John Hollingshead, *My Lifetime* (2nd ed.; London, 1895), I, 65.

32 Norton and De Wolfe Howe, *op. cit.*, 308.

and yielded to the magic of intellect and vivacity and imagination, of odd conceits, of illustrations quickly succeeding each other, of unexpected citation and of startling paradox."[33] Anthony Trollope remembered "a vivacity in the man, an irrepressible ebullition of sarcasm mixed with drollery, of comic earnestness and purpose-laden fun, which we who knew him never missed in his conversation even when his health was at the lowest and his physical sufferings were almost unbearable."[34] Herbert Spencer wrote that "as a companion Lewes was extremely attractive. Interested in, and well informed upon, a variety of subjects; full of various anecdotes; and an admirable mimic; it was impossible to be dull in his company."[35]

Lewes' wit enlivens many pages of his writings. Among his humorous articles is a hilarious parody on the excesses of German scholarship, "Professor Bibundtucker's Remains," in which Lewes pretended that he had translated *Nachgelassene Schriften* von Prof. Papspoon Bibundtucker, Herausgegeben von G.H. Wesel, Narrland: Bei Herrn Noodle, Koddlebrainz and Co., 1841.[36] With great seriousness and painstaking detail, the Professor analyzes the little poem "The Milkmaid's Courtship" to reveal its political, economic, social, and philosophical significance. Espinasse noted that the following *jeu d'esprit* is not generally known to be by Lewes, although it has been reprinted in many books and articles.[37] The *jeu d'esprit* appears in his *Life of Goethe.*

> A Frenchman, an Englishman, and a German were commissioned, it is said, to give the world the benefit of their views on that interesting animal the Camel. Away went the Frenchman to the *Jardin des Plantes,* spent an hour there in rapid investigation, returned and wrote a *feuilleton,* in which there was no phrase the Academy could blame, but also no phrase which added to the general knowledge. . . . The Englishman packed up his tea-caddy and a magazine of com-

33 Justin McCarthy, *Reminiscences* (New York and London, 1899), I, 306-7.

34 Anthony Trollope, "George Henry Lewes," FR, XXXI (1879), 17.

35 Herbert Spencer, *Autobiography* (New York, 1904), I, 437. See also James Sully, *My Life and Friends* (London, 1918), 261; GE, VI, 394, 412-13.

36 *Monthly Magazine,* VII (1842), 148-52. For examples of his humor, cf. "People I Have Never Met," *Blackwood's,* LXXXIII (1858), 183-92; *Leader,* March 20, 1852, 282; February 26, 1853, 214; June 18, 1853, 597.

37 Espinasse, *op. cit.,* 286.

forts; pitched his tent in the East; remained there two years studying the Camel in its habits; and returned with a thick volume of facts, arranged without order, expounded without philosophy, but serving as valuable materials for all who came after him. The German, despising the frivolity of the Frenchman, and the unphilosophic matter-of-factness of the Englishman, retired to his study, there *to construct the Idea of a Camel from out of the depths of his Moral Consciousness.* And he is still at it.[38]

Lewes possessed certain rare qualities as a writer and thinker. John Stuart Mill, who knew Lewes as a young man, described the "buoyancy of spirit which . . . [makes him] so prompt & apparently presumptuous in undertaking anything for which he feels the slightest vocation, (however much it may be really beyond his strength) only because he does not care at all for failure, knowing & habitually feeling that he gets up stronger after every fall & believing as I do that the best way of improving one's faculties is to be continually trying what is above one's present strength."[39] After Lewes died, Bulwer Lytton wrote: "I have known and loved him since childhood. He had the most omnivorous intellectual appetite and digestion of any man I ever knew; a rare freedom from prejudice; soundness of judgment in criticism, and a singularly wide and quick sympathy in all departments of science and literature."[40] Both Herbert Spencer and George Eliot praised Lewes for being exceptionally open-minded in controversy. George Eliot wrote: "In this respect I know *no* man so great as he—that difference of opinion rouses no egoistic irritation in him, and that he is ready to admit that another's argument is the stronger, the moment his intellect recognizes it. . . . He is one of the few human beings I have known who will often, in the heat of an argument, see and straightway confess that he is in the wrong, instead of trying to shift his ground or use any other device of vanity."[41]

[38] *The Life of Goethe* (4th ed., London, 1890), 397.

[39] John Stuart Mill in a letter to Macvey Napier, February 18, 1842, British Museum, London, England, Add. Mss., 34, 622.

[40] Robert, First Earl of Lytton, *Personal and Literary Letters,* ed. Lady Betty Balfour (London, 1906), II, 137.

[41] GE, III, 359; V, 30; VI, 89, 109; Spencer, *op. cit.*, II, 375.

But Lewes received the greatest compliment from G.J. Holyoake: (Holyoake never forgot that Lewes had included him in the public list of contributors to the *Leader* at a time when he was regarded as an outcast in the fields of law and literature.)

> Lewes was intellectually the bravest man I have known. It was not that he was without the wisdom which looks around to see what the consequences of any act would be; but where a thing seemed right in itself he ignored the consequences of doing it. . . . They were to him as though they were not. When he accepted a principle, he accepted all that belonged to it. Courage means facing a danger by force of will . . . . Men of natural intrepidity never take danger into account or, if they are conscious of it, it only influences them as an inspiration of action. Mr. Lewes had intellectual intrepidity of this kind.[42]

Lewes did so many things that, as Hugh Walker observed, "nothing he attempted could astonish those who knew him; and Thackeray expressed a general feeling when he declared that he would not be surprised to see Lewes riding down Piccadilly on a white elephant. But the suggestion of mere meaningless eccentricity has to be corrected. The versatility of Lewes was the outcome of an exceedingly active intellect, continually on the watch for new ideas, and seeking new openings for its energy. . . ."[43] Lewes himself deplored the fact that versatile writers were generally regarded with suspicion. He wrote: "It is thought to be no answer to say that the man is versatile, has many faculties, and employs them: the public likes a man to confine himself to one special topic. Division of labor is the grand thing: if you have made pins' heads, content yourself with that, and do not venture upon points. Accordingly we see men always working the mine where they once discovered gold, and afraid to dig elsewhere. They repeat themselves."[44] In this modern age of specialization Lewes serves

42 G.J. Holyoake, *Sixty Years of an Agitator's Life* (London, 1892), I, 243; Bygones, *op. cit.*, 64. Holyoake bought a vacant grave near Eliot and Lewes so that he would be near them in death. For a study of the *Leader*'s role as a radical journal see Allen R. Brick, "*The Leader:* Organ of Radicalism" (Dissertation, Yale University, 1957).

43 Hugh Walker, *Literature of the Victorian Era* (Cambridge, Eng., 1921), 179.

44 "Memoir of Sir. E. Bulwer Lytton, Bart.," *Bentley's Miscellany,* XXIV (1848), 9.

as a refreshing example of the littérateur of the past who dared to reach out beyond the narrow confines of one small area of inquiry. He was aptly described as one "for whom the ordinary span of human life seems almost ridiculously inadequate. . . . He was like a man who should never find time and opportunity for the employment of all his senses; and had to forget the endowment of some, in order to profit thoroughly by the others. Such men are few."[45] Such critics are fewer.

[45] Unsigned obituary of Lewes in *Pall Mall Budget,* December 7, 1878, 15.

2

Lewes' Theory of Criticism

Since Lewes was a philosopher, we would expect his literary criticism to be philosophically oriented. It is relevant, therefore, to summarize his philosophical position in order to reveal the extent to which it influenced his criticism. Like many of his distinguished contemporaries, Lewes was preoccupied with the problem of discovering a valid method for unravelling the mysteries of the universe. Along with John Stuart Mill, Herbert Spencer, Alexander Bain, and others, he was interested in the positivism of Auguste Comte. Lewes began his study of Comte when he was twenty-three, and ten years later he helped to popularize the ideas of Comte in England by writing *Comte's Philosophy of the Sciences.* However, he could not play the role of mere disciple, and eventually he lost Comte's friendship because he criticized certain doctrines. Like Mill, Lewes disapproved of Comte's unscientific approach in the *Politique positive.* He disapproved of Comte's mania for synthesis which led him to accept questionable hypotheses. For many years Lewes considered Comte's social doctrines and his religion of humanity to be unfortunate errors of a great mind, but he later came to think more tolerantly of them as representing a Utopian dream. He also objected to Comte's acceptance of Gall's cerebral theory and to his rejection of introspection.[1]

1 "Auguste Comte," FR, III (1865-66), 409; "Comte and Mill," FR, VI (1866), 402; HP, 4th ed., II, 735-40; HP, 3rd ed., II, 585-86; SP, 54-55; CPS, 210. For Lewes' criticism of other views of Comte see A, 98; FC, I, 75-76, 108 n., 321, 357; FC, II, 249, CPS, 87, 92, 342; SP, 179.

However, Lewes was initially impressed by Comte's early doctrines because of their advocacy of naturalism. Rejecting transcendental explanations, Lewes held that the positive method of science was the only valid means for studying man as a natural being in a natural world. The positive method of science utilizes "the only Method adapted to human capacity, the only one on which truth can be found."[2] The nucleus of his exposition of scientific method was correctly described by C.S. Peirce[3] as involving an emphasis on verification. Recognizing that most schools of thought claim to derive their tenets from some type of verification, Lewes noted, however, that their notions of verification were usually fallacious because they were based upon an erroneous view of the kind of experience to be investigated. In his view, the experiential manifold consists of an inextricable combination of sensation and inference. Sensation alone cannot give knowledge. To see an apple does not mean that the apple actually exists unless other sensations normally associated with the presence of an apple are recalled, such as the sensation of taste when the apple is eaten. If we wish to know whether some given sense datum is really what we think it is, we must reinstate the sensations that accompanied the occurrence of the given sense datum in the past. Verification is a process of testing these inferred sensations to determine whether they are reducible to those directly given.[4]

Lewes distinguished between the roles of laws and of hypotheses in scientific inquiry.[5] A hypothesis is the first stage in the process of noting similarities among various phenomena and expressing them in a generalized formula. A real hypothesis explains a phenomenon by an agent or agency known to be present in it. An *auxiliary* hypothesis is a fictitious theory, used to facilitate research, that surmises the effect of an agent not known to be

[2] HP (1885), 784. Parts of the discussion of Lewes' philosophy have been reprinted from Alice R. Kaminsky's article on George Henry Lewes in *The Encyclopedia of Philosophy,* 1967, IV, 451-54.

[3] C.S. Peirce, *Collected Papers,* ed. Hartshorne and Weiss (Cambridge, 1931), I, 14.

[4] FC, I, 257, 260, 263. In the columns of the *Leader,* Lewes often derided unscientific theory and practice. In the *Leader,* June 15, 1850, 284-85, he humorously described his adventures as a scientific spy when he exposed some "clairvoyantes" at "Two Magnetic Seances."

[5] CPS, 55; FC, I, 307-41; "Imaginary Geometry and the Truth of Axioms," FR, XXII (1874), 197; FC, II, 113, 516-17; A, 32, 37, 50, CPS, 62, 98.

present in phenomena and is scrupulously accounted for in the final tabulation of the data. An *illusory* hypothesis, such as the theory of creation, substitutes ambiguous phraseology for explanation and is of no value to research.

The possession of more certain knowledge elevates a hypothesis to the rank of law. A real law—for example, Joule's law—gives a mathematical formulation of the reactions of similar phenomena when the inferences made about them are actualized; an ideal law, such as the law of inertia, is an extrapolation from a real law, expressing what the case would be if the conditions implied in the real law were changed. Since the symbols used in ideal laws have been abstracted from the real laws, ideal laws are valid to the degree in which their symbols are derived from empirical data. Thus, one of the most important functions of science is the study of the actual and possible conditions under which a phenomenon can occur, and there is no limit to the store of conditions to be scientifically investigated. "It is through successive approximations that science advances; but even when the final stage is reached a mystery remains. We may know that certain elements combine in certain proportions to produce certain substances; but why they produce these, and not different substances, is no clearer than why muscles contract or organisms die. This Why is, however, an idle question. That alone which truly concerns us is the How, and not the Why."[6] The possibilities for greater and greater certainty are inexhaustible since science deliberately creates new situations and new sources of knowledge.

At twenty Lewes had written, "We arrive then at the conclusion that we can never know but *relative* truth, our only medium of knowledge being the senses, and this medium, with regard *to all without us,* being forever a false one; but being *true to us,* we may put confidence in it *relatively.*"[7] His belief in the relativity of knowledge was to remain a life-long conviction, and in one of his last volumes he wrote: "Those who, affecting to despise the certainty attainable through Science, because it can never transcend the relative sphere, yearn for a knowledge which is not relative, [and] cheat themselves with phrases."[8]

6 PBM, 24.

7 "Hints towards an Essay on the sufferings of Truth," *Monthly Repository,* XI (1837), 314.

8 FC, I, 201.

Lewes was such a thoroughgoing empiricist that he considered even so-called self-evident truths to be experientially derived; he defined axioms as ideas generalized in the mind from uniform experiences.[9] He believed so strongly in the efficacy of scientific method that he foresaw the possibility of its application in all fields, even in religion. In 1878, the year of his death, he wrote: "We are slowly beginning to recognize that there may be a science of History, a science of Language, a science of Religion, and, in fact, that all knowledge may be systematized in a common method."[10]

He interpreted religion as man's search for the ideal. Since each man's ideal varies, it is useless for formal religion to require uniformity. Lewes' rejection of Christian theology and philosophy was unequivocal: "A Christian may be also a Philosopher; but to talk of Christian Philosophy is an abuse of language. Christian Philosophy means Christian Metaphysics; and that means the solution of metaphysical problems upon Christian principles . . . revealed and accepted by Faith, because Reason is utterly incompetent."[11] Concerning the supposed revelation offered by the intellectual intuition or ecstasy of the mystic, he wrote: "Once admit that the human mind . . . can extend its excursions into the supersensual and supernatural regions . . . and then admit reason is no competent guide into these illimitable spheres . . . what can be more natural than that . . . you should conclude the only method must be by an exaltation of the mind from out of its accustomed sphere? You conclude that you will rise above humanity by casting off your imperfections, by fasting, by subjugation of the passions, by purging your heart from all mundane desires. . . . Unhappily when men endeavor to raise themselves above humanity, they always grovel below it."[12]

Writing to a friend in 1874 about Matthew Arnold's views on religion, Lewes stated: "I, myself cannot see how the Bible 'makes for righteousness' though I profoundly agree with him that righteousness is salvation—and is not to be sought in metaphysi-

[9] SP, 168-69; HP (1885), 663.

[10] "On the Dread and Dislike of Science," FR, XXIX (1878), 809.

[11] HP (1885), 338.

[12] "Causeries," FR, V (1866), 241-42; VI (1866), 370; "How the World Treats Discoveries," *Blackwood's*, XC (1861), 546; "Algazālli's Confessions—Arabian Philosophy," *Edinburgh Review*, LXXXV (1847), 351.

cal refinements about a 'personal God' but is to be found in our idealization of human relations and human needs."[13] However, unlike other scientists in the nineteenth century who believed that religion would become extinct because it had outlived its usefulness, Lewes looked forward to a religion founded on science. Such a religion would reject the dogmas of any formalized creed which were originally the childish guesses of barbarians. "In a word, this transformed Religion must cease to accept for its tests and sanctions such tests as would be foolishness in Science, and such sanctions as would be selfishness in Life. Instead of proclaiming the nothingness of this life, the worthlessness of human love, and the imbecility of the human mind, it will proclaim the supreme importance of this life, the supreme value of human love, and the grandeur of human intellect."[14] Obviously the development of a scientific religion would involve the elimination of whatever has been known traditionally as religion, metaphysics, and theology.

Similarly, the study of morality would have to be disengaged from its usual association with religion and theology. In 1866 Lewes observed that science had freed itself of theology, and he asked, "How long will it be before Morality is rendered independent of Theology, studied by itself for itself, bearing in itself its own criterion and its own methods?"[15] Lewes never concerned himself with formulating a system of ethics, but the few observations he made on the subject illustrates again how consistently he emphasized the experiential approach: "We have intuitions of Right and Wrong in so far as we have intuitions of certain consequences; but these must have been learned in our own experience or transmitted from the experience of others. Some writers who are disposed to exaggerate the action of Heredity believe that certain specific experiences of social utility in the race become organised in descendants, and are thus transmitted as instincts . . . but the evidence in this direction is obscured by the indubitable transmission through language and other social institutions."[16]

But Lewes did believe in the existence of genuine metaphysical

13 GE, VI, 87. See also GE, IV, 72. George Eliot noted that Lewes "is not fond of reading the Bible himself, but sees no harm 'in my reading it.' "

14 FC, I, 3. See also the *Leader,* December 7, 1850, 878.

15 FR, V (1866), 243.

16 SP, 151-52; FC, I, 166-67.

problems. Through the elaboration of what he called an empirical metaphysics, he tried to indicate how metaphysical problems could be dealt with scientifically. He equated metaphysical issues with the problems of abstract science, which deals with the sensible and logical facts inherent in such general scientific principles as cause, force, life, and mind. Reaffirming Aristotle's view of metaphysics as the "science of the most general principles," Lewes designated the object of empirical metaphysics to be the determination of these general principles. Its role is to help science integrate the data of the sciences in order to achieve the maximum understanding of man and his universe. To accomplish this goal, the traditional concepts of substance, matter, causation, and the dualistic views of reality must be revised.[17]

Mind and body dualisms have enlarged the split among the various sciences and have prevented metaphysics from becoming an integrating science. Lewes maintained that no dichotomy exists between the mental and the physical. Every experience presents a "double aspect": real and ideal, particular and general. Regarded in one way, experience is subjective; regarded in another, it is objective. For different purposes it is viewed differently. Material and mental operations are merely different aspects of the same process. Body is merely the objective aspect of the subjective process known as mind.[18] Therefore, metaphysics does not have to solve the mystery of how a material phenomenon becomes a mental phenomenon, nor must it search for answers in a Platonic Form or a Kantian thing-in-itself.

The qualities of matter are our sensations; the properties of matter are the qualities viewed in reference to their effect on other objects rather than their effect on us as feelings. But these properties do not inhere in some thing-in-itself.[19] Since every phenomenal manifold contains a subjective-objective construction, every context is relational; that is, a thing *is* its relationships. To Lewes substance was no more than a name for some cluster of characteristics normally found together. Similarly, the agent or

[17] Jack Kaminsky, "The Empirical Metaphysics of George Henry Lewes," *Journal of the History of Ideas,* XIII (1952), 314-32; FC, I, 55 ff., 65.

[18] FC, II, 16 ff.; PBM, 335-38; "Spiritualism and Materialism," FR, XXV (1876), 480; A, 122; PBM, 343-44; SP, 49.

[19] FC, II, 262, 263; SP, 53-54.

power that science seeks to understand in causation is not suprasensible; it is the relationship of the elements involved.[20] Lewes was one of the first, if not the first, to distinguish between the resultant, the antecedently predictable change, and the emergent, the antecedently unpredictable transformation. "Thus, although each effect is the resultant of its components, the product of its factors, we cannot always trace the steps of the process, so as to see in the product the mode of operation of each factor. In this latter case, I propose to call the effect an emergent. It arises out of the combined agencies, but in a form which does not display the agents in action."[21] He believed that some day enough would be known about the unseen process that produces emergents to make possible the expression of its action in a mathematical formula.

More fully than Darwin or Spencer, Lewes analyzed the significant implications of biological evolution in the field of psychology.[22] He insisted that man, like the animal, must be studied in relation to the natural world. However, since man is also part of a social organism, he can no more be isolated from society than he can be from nature. All psychical activity is therefore the result of the interaction of the organism and a physical and social environment. In Lewes' view, mind and body are interdependent; every mental change has a corresponding physical change, and these changes are isolated only as convenient abstractions. Every mental act is carried on by the entire organism; it is not the brain that thinks but the entire man.[23]

Personality is a "total." Organs have no importance "except in relation to a whole, their actions however seemingly independent, having an *overruling unity and consensus*."[24] Sensibility is energy manifested as a function of various conditions existent in a neuromuscular mechanism. The "Triple Process" by means of which

20 GE, VI, 39; FC, II, 437-38; FC, I, 361; "Substance," *Penny Cyclopedia*, XXIII (1842), 197-98.

21 FC, II, 412.

22 SP, 47-81; FR, VI (1866), 389-94.

23 SP, 5, 38, 41, 118-44, 122, 159-70; MFO, 16; PBM, 31; CPS, 161; FC, I, 109; "The Modern Metaphysics and Moral Philosophy of France," BFR, XV (1843), 355. The best analysis of Lewes' psychology is to be found in H.C. Warren's *A History of the Association Psychology* (New York, 1921), 137-52.

24 MFO, 197, 149.

sensibility is achieved is actually one process involving three kinds of reactions—stimulation, coordination, and discharge, described further as sensation, thought, and will.

Using the terminology of association psychologists, Lewes referred to the sense datum, or neural tremor, as the basic element of experience. Thus, a sensation is a primary grouping of neural tremors; an image (an intermediary grouping) is formed when a sensation is reproduced; an idea is formed when an image loses its original value and becomes a symbol of a different sensation. Sensations represent the objective side of mental phenomena, since they have their origin in objective stimuli external to the organism; images represent the subjective side, for they arise out of excitations within the organism. Through words, ideas that substitute for sensations have the power of recalling an absent object or action without the intervention of any sensible qualities. Feelings are products of groupings of images that have become signs or symbols—that is, of ideas. Since ideas are translatable into language, thoughts are primarily social instruments dependent upon the social environment. Both feeling and thought are products of the same kind of operation, differing in the particular combination of elements involved.[25]

Lewes realized that his explanation could be stigmatized as materialism since it employed a material pattern to account for mental phenomena. He used the double-aspect theory to refute this charge. If sensation were viewed as a physiological phenomenon and thought were considered a mental condition, it would be absurd to relate them in any way. But feeling and thought are both functions of the sentient organism under different aspects. Viewed objectively, feeling and thought are physical states; viewed subjectively, they are mental states. No sensation can exist without involving the functions of thought, nor can any thought exist without involving the functions of sensation.[26]

Lewes further noted that a human organism is a mechanism of a very special kind. Its behavior differs in important ways from that of a machine. First, the human organism is comparable to an emergent in that the properties characteristic of its later devel-

[25] MFO, 40, 111, 123, 149, 159, 197, 246-47, 258-60, 385, 402-3, 445-53, 464-78, 483.

[26] SP, 53-54; MFO, 197.

opment cannot be reduced to or predicted from the properties characteristic of its early development. Hence its behavior patterns cannot be predicted on the basis of prior knowledge of physical and physiological conditions. But a machine is not comparable to an emergent, and its behavior patterns are always predictable. Secondly, the emergent nature of organisms makes it possible for them to react in novel ways to different stimuli. But a machine, lacking this quality, cannot react to unexpected situations by devising new plans to meet new problems.[27]

Therefore, Lewes could not accept the strict materialist position. But neither was he an indeterminist. Even though the organism has the potential for new and unpredictable action, it cannot violate any of the physical laws of nature. Human choice is always conditioned by both internal and external stimuli. Free will must be explained in terms of the functioning of the entire organism and its relationship to the environment. Thus, in reality, only choices that are compatible with physical laws and behavior patterns of the organism are possible. Lewes used the following analogy to clarify his view: "Every sailor knows that he moves with the vessel, but [he] knows also that he is free to move to and fro on deck."[28]

In the nineteenth century the cause of science had no more devoted champion than Lewes, and the main principles of his philosophy are taken for granted by contemporary empiricists. However, much of his speculation is dated. He failed, as did John Stuart Mill, to distinguish between logical and empirical validity. At times his empirical metaphysics seems to do no more than confuse metaphysics with physics. His reasoned realism suffers from the same kind of tautological oversimplification that plagues any monistic system. These failings notwithstanding, Lewes elaborated theories that are still of consequence.

As a relativist, Lewes focused attention on the nature of conditions and the type of certainty that is supposed to occur under particular conditions. He anticipated the modern pragmatic theory of truth in his notion of verification. His belief that the intelligibility of an experiential context rests upon certain implicit inferences of future experience has been reaffirmed by John

27 PBM, 353 ff.; SP, 102, 109.
28 SP, 103.

Dewey and C.I. Lewis. Although Lewes did not analyze fictions in experimentation as thoroughly as did Hans Vaihinger, his concept of auxiliary hypotheses was an interesting contribution to scientific theory. His distinction between resultants and emergents was to influence the ideas of later emergent evolutionists. Variations of his double-aspect theory have reappeared in the work of Paul Natorp, Durant Drake, C. Lloyd Morgan, Hans Driesch, Herbert Feigl, and J.J.C. Smart. Much of Lewes' psychological terminology is outmoded, but certain emphases of his system contain significant contributions to psychology. Lewes fought constantly against metaphysical views that would isolate mental phenomena as independent entities. Because his work includes the most reliable conclusions of the evolutionary hypothesis, Lewes is of special interest to the genetic psychologist. He recognized the need to study man as a complex being, an approach requiring the integrating of psychology, biology, and sociology. Finally, his demand that philosophers become scientists has been met in the work of C.D. Broad, Bertrand Russell, and A.N. Whitehead, just as his urgent insistence on the need for unification of the sciences has been confirmed by the efforts of John Dewey, Rudolf Carnap, Ernest Nagel, Charles W. Morris, and Philipp Frank.

Although Lewes' philosophy of art is not integrally related to his general philosophical position in the way that, for example, Hegel or Kant's aesthetic theories are dependent upon their metaphysics, there is a definite relationship between his philosophy and his literary principles, and it will be the aim of this work to reveal the sense in which he can be labeled a philosophic critic.

Since Lewes was preoccupied for the major part of his life with the study of scientific method, it is not surprising that he should have requested a "recognition of the legitimacy of the attempt to apply the rational procedure of Science to every question which may rationally be asked."[29] In 1843 he referred to his preference for the science rather than the metaphysics of criticism. He castigated A.W. Schlegel as a synthetic critic who spewed forth a torrent of mystical verbiage and *Schwärmerei* whereas he extolled Lessing as a great analytic critic who avoided

[29] FC, I, 13.

mysticism and displayed a clear, precise, and strong intellect. Lewes went so far as to state: "If criticism is to become a province of conjecture and imagination, not a science, the sooner it be abolished the better."[30] He noted that just as in the sciences the first principle of classification is to discover uniformity in variety, similarly, scientific method as applied to the arts would involve the classification of the real generic resemblances among the different languages, customs, and tastes revealed in the art products of different nations. But in 1851 Lewes rejected his earlier view: "Criticism," he wrote, "is an Art, not a Science. It rests upon delicacy of perception, not upon ascertained rule."[31] In 1866 Lewes decided against the conception of a science of criticism because it might prove to be tyrannically oppressive.[32] He noted that the laws of art are not reducible to a system in the same way as the laws of science. A science of criticism could only list the rules artists had followed, but it could not make such rules mandatory for future artists and it could not foresee the form of new evolutions of art under changed conditions. Since a rule of the past might be unsatisfactory for the future, critics might make serious errors by judging art in relation to certain presuppositions rather than in relation to its effect upon the emotions of an intelligent public. Scientists who might want to ignore facts they are unable to explain are forced to modify their doctrines as their knowledge increases, but critics have the power to suppress originality. As a result, Lewes preferred the state of anarchy to the state of dogmatic authority, for while criticism suffers under such conditions, art is freer. In 1872 he expressed his abhorrence of the absolute verdict in criticism which would result from the codification of rules of art into a single uniformity, and he stressed the need for preserving the individual nature of criticism. As critics, "we may fairly state how this [work of art] affects us, whether it accords with our experience, whether it moves or instructs us; but we should be very chary of absolute judgments, and be quite sure of our ground before venturing to assume that the public will feel, or ought to feel, as we feel."[33]

30 "Augustus William Schlegel," *Foreign Quarterly Review*, XXXII (1843), 181.
31 *Leader*, Sept. 13, 1851, 879.
32 "Causeries," FR, VI (1866), 759-61.
33 "Dickens in Relation to Criticism," FR, XVII (1872), 141-42.

Thus with the optimism of a scientist, Lewes predicted that knowledge would eventually be systematized in a common method, but he clearly did not include the "art" of criticism in that process. One of Lewes' most admirable qualities as a critic stemmed from his recognition that critical judgments are not final or absolute, but subject, like all of knowledge, to the modifications of enlarged experience. In replying to a writer who attacked him for his views on natural acting and called them "nonsense" Lewes remarked: "As to the nonsense I may have written, everyone knows how easily a man may set down nonsense, and believe it to be sense."[34] His criticism of Wagner's music illustrates his lack of dogmatism. Confessing that Wagner's operas seemed to him to be noisy, monotonous, and lacking in form and melody, he observed: "If the music does not flatter my ear, I can keep out of its way, unless—which perhaps would be the prudent course—I cultivated a little self-suspicion, and withheld all peremptory judgment, finding firstly, that other and more educated ears detect form and grace where mine detect none; secondly, that I myself occasionally recognise very delightful passages, and may therefore expect that on a longer acquaintance I may learn to admire what is now not admirable."[35] Aware of the dangerous tendency of critics to stultify artistic creativity by opposing innovation, Lewes tried to avoid working with fixed standards which would discourage innovation and originality.

He anticipated Arnold in his attempts to raise the status of criticism. As early as 1842 Lewes insisted that it should be recognized as a special and valuable profession.[36] Since the major outlet for criticism was the journal, the role of periodical literature was very significant to him. Aware that many regarded the periodical as a corrupting influence, he wrote in its defense: "Periodical literature is a great thing. It is a potent instrument for the education of a people. It is the only decisive means of rescuing authorship from the badge of servility. . . . A brilliant essay,

34 *On Actors and the Art of Acting* (New York, 1878), 106.

35 *Ibid.*, 198; see "Niebuhr and the Classical Museum," WR, XLI (1844), 181, where Lewes frankly admitted that he had made an error in a previous article, "Charges against Niebuhr," WR, XL (1843), 335-49. These Niebuhr essays reveal how Lewes tried to avoid dogmatism. In this connection see also "Vivisection," *Nature*, IX (1873), 145.

36 "Errors and Abuses of English Criticism," WR, XXXVIII (1842), 466-86.

or a thoughtful fragment, is not the less brilliant, is not the less thoughtful, because it is brief, because it does not exhaust the subject."[37]

Lewes never regarded writing for the journals with the attitude of the "bread scholar." In a letter to J.M. Kemble, he wrote: "I always consider an essay a work of art. I draw out a program of my intentions, dispose the parts, then work out a carefull *cartoon* & then finally set to work at the picture. Error there may be, & shortcomings but not carelessness."[38]

He played an important role in helping to eliminate one of the worst abuses in the journals: anonymous criticism. He did not mince words in his attack on the critics of his age who could viciously harry a Shelley, Keats, or Byron, sheltered by the cloak of anonymity. In fact, he broke off his friendship with Robert W. Buchanan because of his unsigned attack on Rossetti in "The Fleshly School of Poetry."[39] When Lewes took over the editorship of the *Fortnightly Review*, he practiced what he had preached. George Eliot noted that Lewes made the magazine a great success because "the principle of signature, never before thoroughly carried out in England, has given it an exceptional dignity, and drawn valuable writers."[40]

Lewes distinguished two types of critics: those who are only concerned with works of the past and those who have to make weekly and daily judgments with only their own tastes to guide them. To the latter type criticism must be, as Longinus defined it, the result of experience: "Only long experience and tact can give him that rapidity and certainty of judgment: and with all his experience, with all his tact, how often he will make egregious blunders!"[41] Lewes performed both roles as a critic: he dealt with works of the past and the present. He wrote appreciatively of many writers—Greek, Latin, English, American, French, German, Italian, and Spanish—with sympathy and knowledge. His extensive knowledge of aesthetic and critical theory was revealed

37 "The Condition of Authors in England," *Fraser's Magazine*, XXXV (1847), 289.

38 Letter to J.M. Kemble, March 23, [1844], Beinecke Library, Yale University.

39 Lewes was denounced for his views on anonymous criticism in the *Times* (London), December 7, 1842, 5. See GE, VII, 89.

40 GE, IV, 211.

41 *Leader*, August 2, 1851, 734; William Archer and Robert W. Lowe (eds.), *Dramatic Essays, John Forster, George Henry Lewes* (London, 1896), XV.

even in a very early essay on Hegel's aesthetics, where he mentioned or quoted from the writings of Plato, Aristotle, Horace, Longinus, Burke, Cousin, Jouffroy, Quatremère de Quincy, Schiller, Richter, the Schlegels, Baumgarten, Lessing, Winckelmann, Herder, Novalis, Tieck, Solger, Ruge, Bode, Muller, St. Beuve, Ulrici, Sidney, Carlyle, Shelley, Wordsworth, Coleridge, R.H. Horne, and J.S. Mill. A reading of all of Lewes' criticism confirms the impression that he was thoroughly conversant with all the important critics of the past and of his own age.

Several times he quoted with approval Schlegel's statement that the best critic has the flexibility to understand the peculiarities of all ages and nations. Surveying the state of contemporary criticism in France, Lewes castigated the French critics for their rigidity: "[Their criticism] is the most confined: excellent when treating of subjects within its proper sphere, it is absurd when endeavouring to reduce all varieties to one standard."[42] Similarly he criticized Leigh Hunt for his inflexibility: "He judges works absolutely; the effect they produce on him is taken as a test of their excellence."[43] Lewes noted that Hunt disliked Dante for his superstition and fanaticism instead of understanding his views as representative expressions of the spirit of the age. Lewes, despite his very obvious antipathy for Catholicism, considered Dante to be a great poet.

On the other hand, judging German criticism, Lewes observed that its "radical virtue . . . is precisely that desired flexibility which, so far from reducing all works to one standard, endeavors to appreciate them from their own central point."[44] German critics were superior critics because they were philosophically oriented: "Criticism, being philosophy rather than feeling, flourishes best in a land where the people can best analyze their feelings, and as it were, catch enjoyment in the act."[45] However, the Germans were often *too* philosophic. They tended to read more into a work than the content justified. To the German critic "the more remote the meaning . . . the better pleased is he with the discovery; and he sturdily rejects every simple explanation

[42] "State of Criticism in France," BFR, XVI (1844), 345.
[43] "Leigh Hunt on the Italian Poets," *Foreign Quarterly Review,* XXXVI (1846), 338.
[44] "Crit. in France," BFR, XVI (1844), 345.
[45] *Ibid.,* 349.

in favor of this exegetical Idea . . . . It is true the Idea said to underlie the work was never conceived by anyone before, least of all by the artist. . . ."[46] It is clear then that Lewes is not to be regarded as a philosophic critic because he believed that works of art should be judged in terms of a *Weltanschauung* philosophy.

His philosophy of art has been characterized as being classical, romantic, Hegelian, realistic, sociological, psychoanalytic, impressionistic, and scientific. R.A. Brett in one article described Lewes as a romantic, an empiricist, and a classicist.[47] Basil Wiley concluded on the basis of one essay that Lewes worked with a psychoanalytic theory of art. His writings on the poets seem to ally him with the romantic-idealistic tradition, while his criticism of novels seems to place him in the realist camp, and his dramatic criticism reflects a strong classical influence.[48] He wrote so many articles that it is easy to misrepresent his views by concentrating on a few essays. But a thorough reading of all he has written reveals why he can legitimately be labeled a philosophic critic. There is a direct correlation between his philosophic and critical outlook, and that correlation is to be found first in the concept of relativism.

The critic, according to Lewes, performs his highest function "by pointing out the latent meaning of a passage of 'imagination all compact,' and placing it in the clear light of the understanding. This is the highest office of criticism—the translation of the poet's emotions into their fundamental or correspondent ideas."[49] Note that Lewes here emphasizes the need to translate the poet's, not the critic's, emotions. He believed that in studying a work of art "we should proceed as in studying a work of nature; after delighting in the effect, we should try to ascertain what are the means by which the effect is produced, and not at all what

46 *Life of Goethe,* 398.

47 R.L. Brett, "George Henry Lewes: Dramatist, Novelist, and Critic," *Essays and Studies,* XI (1958), 106-14.

48 B. Willey, *Nineteenth Century Studies* (New York, 1949), 245. See also M. Greenhut, "George Henry Lewes and the Classical Tradition in English Criticism," *Review of English Studies,* XXIV (1948), 126-37; H.A. Needham, *Le Développement de l'esthetique sociologique en France et en Angleterre au XIXe siècle* (Paris, 1926), 282; *The Principles of Success in Literature,* ed. Fred N. Scott (3rd ed.; Boston, 1894), 15; (References to this edition are incorporated into the text and appear within parentheses.) R. Wellek, *A History of Modern Criticism* (New Haven, 1965), IV, 149-52.

49 "Dickens," FR, XVII (1872), 141-42.

is the *Idea* lying behind the means. . . . It is only organic analysis which can truly seize the meaning of organic elements; so long as we judge an organism *ab extra,* according to the idea, or according to our ideas, and not according to its nature, we shall never rightly understand structure and function. . . ."[50] If it is the critic's function to examine works of art through organic analysis, not through his own preconceived theories, then he would have to have the flexibility to judge disparate kinds of creative effort. Since infallible scientific rules could not be formulated, the only logical alternative to a science of criticism would have to be critical relativism.

This relativism is based upon certain principles: (1) Art is the result of an individual's personal experience in a particular society. (2) Since people and societies differ, art will reflect these differences, thereby invalidating the feasibility of prescribing absolute standards. (3) An empirical approach is the only valid approach in a world devoid of eternal truths. (4) Both the scientist and the artist attempt to convey views of the nature of reality. They use the same mental faculties, common to all men, but they use them in different ways and for different purposes.

So pervasive an influence was Lewes' scientific orientation that when he attempted to explain the relationship between criticism and aesthetics, he employed scientific analogy. "Criticism is to aesthetics what the practice of medicine is to physiology—the application to particular cases of the fundamental knowledge of the constitution and organization of man, aided by a mass of particular observations. Aesthetics is the *physiology of Art,* and as all Art has a philosophical foundation, so it necessarily demands a philosophical elucidation."[51] All philosophical elucidation in art should proceed, Lewes noted, on the basis of a law of *temporalities* which denies the existence of eternal truths. "That art is the mirror of eternal truths is one of the pompous imbecilities into which ignorance has led the critics."[52] Each age accumulates its own share of wisdom which is in turn modified by the new insights of the succeeding age. In art new interpreta-

50 "Causeries," FR, VI (1866), 759-61.
51 "Hegel's Aesthetics: Philosophy of Art," BFR, XIII (1842), 5.
52 "The Roman Empire and Its Poets," WR, XXXVIII (1842), 33.

tions of truth and beauty are influenced by the complex and ever-changing relationship between art and society. Indeed for Lewes, as for Comte, art seems to have been primarily a social product, originating out of social needs and modifying social life. He defined literature as "the *expression* of society, which it in turn *reacts upon*, you cannot separate the two. . . ."[53] Literature is the cause and effect of social progress: "It stores up the accumulated experience of the race, connecting Past and Present into a conscious unity; and with this store it feeds successive generations, to be fed in turn by them."[54]

Art has the special purpose of enlarging human sympathy and understanding so that knowledge can be accumulated without prejudicial restrictions. All of literature is "the expression of experiences and emotions; and these expressions are the avenues through which we reach the sacred adytum of Humanity, and learn better to understand our fellows and ourselves."[55] Critics have erred in not recognizing the significance of this social influence in art. "Not recognizing the social influence, men seldom appreciate the true point of view in discussions respecting ancient and modern Literature. It is undeniable that Sophocles, Plato, Aristotle, Hipparchus, and Galen were not less splendidly endowed than Shakespeare, Bacon, Newton, Comte, or Helmholtz—their intellectual lineaments may have been as grandly drawn, but it is absurd to pretend that the products of the ancient and the products of the modern mind are of anything like equal value."[56] Since Lewes expressed this view in 1874 in the first volume of *Foundations of a Creed*, it clearly represented a mature judgment. He expressed this same view in earlier works. In the *Principles of Success in Literature,* he referred to that "older superstition which believed the Ancients to have discovered all wisdom, so that if we could only surprise the secret of Aristotle's thoughts and clearly comprehend the drift of Plato's theories (which unhappily was not clear) we should compass all knowledge. How long this superstition lasted cannot accurately be settled; perhaps it is not quite extinct even yet; but we know how

53 *The Life of Maximilien Robespierre* (London, 1849), 21.
54 *Principles,* 19-20.
55 "The Lady Novelists," WR, LVIII (1852), 130.
56 FC, I, 174-75.

little the most earnest students succeeded in surprising the secrets of the universe by reading Greek treatises, and how much by studying the universe itself. Advancing Science daily discredits the superstition; yet the advance of Criticism has not yet wholly discredited the parallel superstition in Art. The earliest thinkers are no longer considered the wisest, but the earlier artists are still proclaimed the finest. Even those who do not believe in this superiority are, for the most part, overawed by tradition and dare not openly question the supremacy of works which in their private convictions hold a very subordinate rank."[57] In 1853 in the *Leader*, Lewes discussed Professor Aytoun's theory of criticism and deplored his refusal to recognize progressive development in art. Aytoun was wrong to accept Macaulay's view that the old poets are the best: "Dante, Shakespeare, Milton, and Goethe surpass . . . [Homer] on all points."[58]

In this connection Lewes' attack on the classicists of his age is particularly significant. He deplored the spirit of aristocratic exclusiveness fostered by the classical tradition and the conservatism "which clings to whatever has been established, long after its significance has passed away and left it a mere tomb of the once living."[59] He argued that Greek and Latin should not be made the basis of education, that French and German were equally effective tools for mental discipline, and that science was actually the best discipline of all. After visiting Oxford he wrote sarcastically: "When Greek and Latin, the Organon and Euclid, formed the culture of Europe, when the educated class was almost exclusively an ecclesiastical class, then, indeed, Oxford had its *raison d'être*. . . . But to suppose that such a training is the one best fitted for youth in the nineteenth century is profoundly to misunderstand the needs of our age. . . . The boasted benefits of 'intellectual training' which are claimed for the classic languages would be far more efficiently secured by Science. But Science is not dead; if it were Oxford would teach it."[60]

Furthermore, he objected strongly to the use of classical models. Too often appreciation of ancient writers may merely involve feelings of satisfaction derived from learning about older so-

[57] *Principles*, 117.
[58] *Leader*, May 14, 1853, 473.
[59] *Leader*, December 18, 1852, 1211.
[60] *Leader*, December 24, 1853, 1240.

cieties, cultures, and beliefs. Thus historical significance is mistaken for aesthetic significance. Admitting that a gifted writer, like a good scientist, could learn much from the works of the past, he denied that servile imitation of the classics could lead to truly creative and original effort. "The artist," he wrote, "is like Ulysses who learns from what he has experienced."[61] He cannot learn from servile imitation: he should use the classics for purposes of enlightenment, not as authoritative models. Rules of art are never absolute but "they are rather the conclusions which from time to time experience appears to have warranted with respect to the best methods of attaining the artist's aim."[62]

Lewes clearly did not share the classicist's reverence for the past. Reviewing Ernest Renan's *Essais de morale et de critique* in 1859, he scoffed at Renan's view that mankind deteriorates as a result of material comfort or that superiority in industrial skill necessarily results in a lowering of the level of intelligence and morality, and a decreased appreciation of liberty and the noble life.[63] While he recognized that industrialism incurs certain evils, he did not, like Arnold or Carlyle, fear that the Luddites and Philistines would rule the world. His belief in science and progress placed him in the camp of the progressionist. However, he did not believe that all of modern literature was necessarily superior and he never hesitated to derogate inferior modern works. In fact, his condemnation of modern drama was unequivocal.

Another example of the correlation between Lewes' philosophy and his critical theory is to be found in his analysis of the nature of artistic cognition and imagination in the *Principles of Success in Literature*. Originally published in *The Fortnightly Review* in 1865, it was the result of a plan which Lewes formulated in 1856.

This is a curiously uneven study which reads like the proverbial handbook for young writers. It has been handicapped by a most infelicitous title which has probably alienated many others besides George Saintsbury.[64] The word *success* has a pejorative

61 "Shakespeare's Critics, English and Foreign," *Edinburgh Review*, XC (1849), 40.

62 "A Word about Tom Jones," *Blackwood's*, LXXXVII (1860), 337; see also *Principles*, 38, 42.

63 "Another Pleasant French Book," *Blackwood's*, LXXXVI (1859), 669-80. See also "The Art of History—Macaulay," BQR, XXIII (1856), 301-6.

64 Kitchel, *op. cit.*, 171; George Saintsbury, *A History of Criticism and Literary Taste* (3rd ed., London, 1917), III, 540-42.

connotation, but Lewes used it to designate, not the financial rewards of authorship, but the real reward which is to be found in "the sympathy of congenial minds . . . the elevation of those minds, and the gravity with which such sympathy moves. . . ." (p. 31) He made explicit the aim of his book: "It is something in the nature of the Method of Literature that I propose to expound." (p. 22) He referred to scientific practice to justify his emphasis on method, for just as a knowledge of scientific method will not guarantee achievement but is indispensible if a scientist wishes to become a discoverer, so also artistic creativity is dependent upon the use of correct method. For the artist correct method involves working with principles which satisfy the aesthetic, moral and intellectual needs of man.

Concerning the aesthetic principle, Lewes takes the position we would expect him to take. Beauty is not for him a manifestation of the divine or eternal in nature; it is not a separate, hypostatized entity. Richards, Ogden, and Wood have classified for us sixteen definitions of beauty and divided them into three categories; formal, revelatory, and psychological.[65] Lewes' definition of beauty is psychological. Beauty is "only another name for Styles, which is an art, incommunicable as are all other arts, but like them subordinated to laws founded on psychological conditions." (p. 110) Unfortunately, criticism has been "formal instead of being psychological: it has drawn its maxims from the works of successful artists, instead of ascertaining the psychological principles involved in the effects of those works." (p. 112) Although great dramatists wrote five act tragedies, the only justification for writing such plays should come from the demonstration of "psychological demand" on the part of the audience for five acts. Thus the rules of style which Lewes analyzed are not formally prescribed by precedent but are validated by psychological principles. However, "genuine style," Lewes wrote, " is the living body of thought, not a costume that can be put on and off; it is the expression of the writer's mind. . . ." (p. 115) Therefore when reference is made to the laws of style, these refer only to what Lewes called the "mechanism of style," not the total effect of style that reflects the individuality, the life, and the charm of a

[65] C.K. Ogden, I.A. Richards, and J. Wood, *The Foundations of Aesthetics* (2nd ed., London, 1925), 20-21.

writer. Although no absolute rules exist, certain principles can help a writer to express the truth more adequately. A knowledge of certain "laws" of style "helps to direct the blind gropings of feeling, and to correct the occasional mistakes of instinct." (p. 147) Lewes discussed five laws of style: economy, simplicity, sequence, climax, and variety.

The law of economy can be understood best if it is compared to a law in mechanics. In mechanics every means is employed to reduce the friction of a machine and to economize its force. Every superfluous detail in its construction, no matter how beautiful, must be eliminated if it retards its effectiveness. Analogously, since the first aim of style is communication of thought and emotion, every effort must be employed to overcome the friction which results from a reader's ignorance, misconception of verbal symbols, and wandering attention. In both the machine and style "the object is to secure the maximum of disposable force, by diminishing the amount absorbed in the working." (p. 129) The law of economy requires that meaning be presented in a form which calls the least attention to itself as form, unless form is more important to the writer than the thought expressed. But economy involves rejection only of the superfluous; economy is not miserliness.

Style should not be stripped completely of ornament and redundancy. If the artist wishes to sketch the head of a man, he uses simple means to convey general characteristics, but if he wishes to convey the head in all the complexity of its form, light, shade, and texture, he must obviously use complex means. This fact has been overlooked by critics who demand simple, plain diction; they mistake meagerness for simplicity. The law of simplicity stresses the need for organic unity in a literary work. "Simplicity of structure means organic unity, whether the organism be simple or complex . . . ." (p. 138) The novel, the drama, all forms of art should have organic relations, that is, they should be constructed according to a definite plan or order in which the beginning has a specific relation to the end. In this way the law of simplicity is obeyed.

Often the laws of economy and simplicity must submit to the demands of the laws of sequence, variety, and climax which require a more liberal expenditure of language. Literature, like music, requires the condition of symmetry in which sounds and pauses play a vital role in producing the proper effect. The law of sequence helps to achieve this effect. Based on the psychological demand for balance and harmony, it stipulates that sentences have to be arranged logically and rhythmically. Only the requirements of the laws of climax and variety can take precedence over the principle of sequence. Climax and variety are based on the psychological fact that stimulation of sensibility must be progressive in intensity and varied in kind. While it may be correct to follow the sequential pattern of induction in the exposition of a thought, it may be necessary to disrupt the sequence for the purpose of achieving greater climactic effect or varied expression. Actually all the laws of style must give precedence to the law of variety, for without variety art suffers from the paralyzing effect of monotony. While this discussion of style has valid insights to offer the writer, particularly in relation to the principle of organic unity, the modern reader will probably regard the analysis as platitudinous. Lewes himself admitted that he was not offering novelty but systematization.

Nor is there anything unusual about Lewes' view of the principle of sincerity. "No talent," he wrote, "can be supremely effective unless it act in close alliance with certain moral qualities." (p. 23) These moral qualities are expressed by sincerity which "comprises all those qualities of courage, patience, honesty and simplicity which give momentum to talent. . . ." (pp. 87-89) He agreed with Hegel that art is not to be equated with morality. In the Preface to *Rose, Blanche and Violet,* he said that what is most significant about a work of art is its *truth,* not its morality.[66] In the *Principles* (p. 94) the discussion of sincerity as a moral principle takes the form primarily of an exordium to the writer to value truth above all:

> Whatever you believe to be true and false, that proclaim to be true and false; whatever you think admirable and beautiful that should be your model, even if all your friends and all the critics storm at you as a crochet-monger and an eccentric. Whether the public will feel its truth and beauty

[66] *Rose, Blanche, and Violet* (London, 1848), III; "Hegel's Aesthetics," BFR, XIII (1842), 1-49.

at once, or after long years, or never cease to regard it as paradox and ugliness, no man can foresee; enough for you to know that you have done your best, have been true to yourself, and that the utmost power inherent in your work has been displayed.

Anyone even superficially acquainted with the critical terminology of the nineteenth century will readily recognize the term *sincerity* as one of the favorite critical clichés of the age. P. Bull who has traced the fate of this concept has shown that our age has relegated it to the ash heap where it belongs.[67] We have come to recognize that "insincere or bad" men do write good books and that bad books are often written by "sincere good men."

Unquestionably the best portion of the *Principles* deals with an analysis of the nature of artistic cognition. Earlier in the *Biographical History of Philosophy,* Lewes had presented what he called a "novel explanation of the intellectual operations."[68] It served as the basis for his discussion of the psychology of artistic cognition in the *Principles,* and received further elaboration in his later *Study of Psychology* and *Mind as a Function of the Organism.*

It is important at this point to recall that Lewes was an association psychologist who analyzed mind as a function of the organism in which the basic sense data are organized under three main groupings: sensations, images, and ideas. Cognition for him included the following intellectual operations: perception, inference, reasoning, and imagination. Sensation is that which is immediately experienced, but "Perception, as distinguished from Sensation, is the presentation before Consciousness of the details which once were present in conjunction with the object at this moment affecting Sense." (p. 43) Perception is the process by which former sensations are reinstated as ideas which represent the objects sensation disclosed. Lewes used the following example to illustrate the difference between sensation and perception: ". . . When an apple is perceived by me, who merely see it, all that Sense reports is of a certain coloured surface: the roundness, the firmness, the fragrance, and the taste of the apple are not present

67 Patricia Bull, "The Rise and Fall of a Critical Term," *Modern Language Review,* LIX (1954), 1-11.

68 HP (1868), xxvii.

to Sense, but are made present to Consciousness by the act of Perception." (p. 43) Perception is a kind of immediate inference. We immediately see a certain colored surface; we do *not* see the roundness, the firmness, the fragrance, or the taste, even though these characteristics seem to be part of our sensations. Actually we *infer* the existence of such characteristics because in the past they had been sensations found in conjunction with the sensations experienced in the present. Perception is an elementary type of inference. All inference is of the same kind but of different degrees of complexity. To assume that rain has fallen because of wet streets, the inference connects wet streets and swollen gutters with causes which have been associated in experience with such results; to interpret geological facts, the inference involves immeasurable spaces of time, connecting apparent with unapparent facts.

Reasoning involves the most complex types of inference; it employs a chain of inferences which are ideal presentations of objects and relations. If the links in the chain were actualized in their real order as a visible series then reasoning would be a succession of perceptions. But since it is not usually possible to have the objects actualized, they are inferred from apparent facts. Correct reasoning "is the ideal assemblage of objects in their actual order of co-existence and succession." (p. 44) False reasoning "is owing to some misplacement of the order of objects, or to the omission of some links in the chain, or to the introduction of objects not properly belonging to the series." (p. 44)

Lewes described imagination as the power of the mind which has the specific ability to form images. The image is a secondary grouping or reproduced sensation; it is any feeling—a sight, a sound, a touch, a taste, a pain, a terror—which is recalled. When images are correctly linked and then checked by immediate sensation, knowledge is being accumulated. Sometimes words are used as *signs* of objects and help to produce inferences with few or no images of the objects under consideration. A great deal of defective reasoning is caused by the substitution of signs for images. For example, when a person speaks of taking a cab to go to the railway by the shortest possible route, he will most likely form no image of either the cab or the railroad or the streets through which the cab will pass. Whereas certain complex mathematical, astronomical, and physical problems require the use of signs for their successful solution because the signs accurately represent the abstract relations involved, the use of signs in the realm of concrete things can become a source of weakness. The ordinary mind sees only the sign and is more prone to become the victim of a verbal fallacy. But the sensitive, superior mind always sees the concrete image, and this is especially true of poets and great writers who create most effectively because they see the image most vividly. Their keener mental vision enables them to deal with images rather than abstractions, and the significant detail, which to most people is vague, is to them as vivid as the original object.

Imagination as the image-making faculty can supply an indefinite number of images to any sensory reaction. Some minds may be aptly described as unimaginative because they can form very few images in connection with sensory impressions. But in truly imaginative minds the sensory impression is only the first step in the observation of an object. The most important step is the forming of images which make the obscure elements surrounding an object or idea distinct, when they are not actually present to sense. This does not mean that imagination is to be equated with memory. Memory merely recalls past experiences passively, and unlike imagination, it has reference only to the past, not to the present or future. We *imagine* a lion standing before us now, or tomorrow, but we remember the lion we saw yesterday. The specific characteristic of imagination is its active tendency to select, abstract, and recombine. It selects elements to symbolize an object or emotion, and either by a process of abstraction makes them represent the whole object or emotion, or else by a process of recombination, which is commonly known as invention, creates new objects and new relations out of the selected elements. The resulting vivid image has no corresponding external reality.

In spontaneous imagination, images that were formerly sensations spontaneously combine in dreams, reveries, and thoughts. In plastic imagination, images are combined as the result of controlled, conscious effort. This latter type of imagination has resulted in the creativity of art. So remarkable and important have been the products of plastic imagination that "we can well understand how Imagination has been not only personified, and transformed into an independent agent, but has taxed the rhetorical ingenuity of writers in describing it."[69] Lewes made it clear that he did not consider imagination to be an inexplicable, divine power of the mind which owes its origin and inspiration to preternatural forces. Imagination, he observed, "is usually spoken of in vague rhapsodical language, with intimations of its being something peculiarly mysterious." (p. 57) But it is no more mysterious or divinely inspired a process than the other three powers of the mind, perception, inference, and reasoning, which combine with imagination to produce the mental vision of all creators, whether they be scientists, philosophers, or artists. Lewes did not agree with those who feel that the power of imagination belongs exclusively to poets and artists. "The artist is called a creator, which in one sense he is; and his creations are said to be produced by processes wholly unallied to the creations of Philosophy, which they are not. Hence it is a paradox to speak of the 'Principia' as a creation demanding severe and continuous exercise of the imagination. . . ." (p. 57) For the creation of the *Principia* Newton utilized as intense and sustained imagination as Shakespeare did for the creation of *Othello.*

While science and art differ in that science appeals primarily to the intellect for the purpose of instruction, and art appeals primarily to the emotions for the purpose of pleasure, they are similar in that they both make use of logic and imagination. But imagination is used by science and art in different ways and for different ends. Strong imagination was required for the creation of both the *Principia* and *Othello.* However, since Newton and Shakespeare had different kinds of minds, they employed imagination in different ways. Newton's mind was essentially ratiocinative, concerned with the abstract relation of things, whereas Shakespeare's mind was emotionally oriented, concerned with the concrete relation of things.

To discover the secrets of nature, the scientist must employ his imagination continuously and vigorously, for the relations of sequence among the hidden phenomena of nature can only be seen mentally, that is, can only be imagined. It is just as difficult to imagine a good experiment as to invent a good story, for in

[69] MFO, 122, 454.

both instances the known qualities and relations of all the objects as well as the effect of introducing a new qualifying agent must be visualized mentally with great distinctness. To elicit the unapparent fact from the apparent fact, the scientist forms an image of the unapparent fact, and then he attempts to prove that the image has a corresponding reality. In other words, he forms a hypothesis and then subjects it to verification. Contrary to what is commonly believed, a hypothesis is not more imaginative when it is unrelated to experience. In order to imagine or to form an image, the multiform relations of things must be seen by the mind in what is considered to be their actual order, and in this goal the scientist is aided by the mass of organized experience which enables him to make a consistent guess that event *x* is caused by event *y* or that object *z* will react in a given way. The scientist abstracts and isolates a particular quality of the object under investigation, mass or density or refracting power, and then tries by the use of imagination and experiment to determine how such a quality reacts under specified conditions.

On the other hand, the poet uses an abstraction in order to present the object in its relation to men. While the scientist permits only one quality to preoccupy his field of vision, ignoring the object and its distracting elements, the poet utilizes an abstraction to reveal the object itself and its selected qualities more vividly. "In other words, the one aims at abstract symbols, the other at picturesque effects. The one can carry on his deductions by the aid of colourless signs, *x* or *y*. The other appeals to the emotions through the symbols which will most vividly express the real objects in their relations to our sensibilities." (p. 61) The scientist seeks the relation between property *a* and property *b*; the artist seeks the relation between an object and an emotional response.

Another distinction to be noted is the fact that the poet has greater freedom in the use of images than the scientist, for the poet is at liberty to preoccupy himself with the unknown and the unproven. The poet is permitted the image of a hippogriff because his vision includes the world of the future and the non-existent world. The license of working with such worlds is granted him so long as he offers pleasure to others by making them see what he sees. But although he is not under the obligation of the scientist to present the truths of the existing world of nature, the poet is not free to write irresponsibly about anything. Although his images do not have to conform to objective realities, they do have to satisfy the peculiar demand of consistency in a particular context. No matter how fantastic the image the poet uses, it has its origin in experience: ". . . Imagination can only recall what sense has previously impressed." (p. 64) The poet can combine the half of a woman with the half of a fish and he can legitimately write about a mermaid, so long as he does not confuse a mermaid with a human being. Such combinations of sense data are not very different from the combinations produced by the scientist. But the poet seeks those combinations which produce emotional effects while the scientist wants only those which have pragmatic effects. As a result, the poet uses metaphors and similes and anthropomorphism, for these cause emotional reactions. Since the scientist wishes to show how objects react with one another, he uses laws, hypotheses, and theories. But, "obviously the imagination has been as active in the one case as in the other; the *differentia* lying in the purposes of the two, and in the general constitution of the two minds." (p. 65)

According to Lewes, the most effective image affects the emotions through the evocation of experiences common to all of mankind. "[It is a . . .] psychological fact," he wrote, "that fairies and demons, remote as they are from experience, are not created by a more vigorous effort of imagination than milkmaids and poachers." (p. 69) The sole test of imaginative power in the artist is intensity and clarity of vision. This is why the true image in art must be the distinct image. Images which appear in different ways either as a succession of sudden illuminations or as a series of slowly emerging details must be detained long enough in the artist's mind to achieve the condition of distinctness.

Lewes called attention to the passage in Burke's *A Philosophical Inquiry into the Origin of Our Ideas of the Sublime and Beautiful* in which Burke denied that distinct imagery is required for the description of passion.[70] According to Burke, if a poet wishes to depict an obscure or indefinite idea such as eternity or

[70] *The Works of the Right Honorable Edmund Burke* (3rd ed., Boston, 1869), I, 132-38.

death, he will employ an indefinite image. Any attempt to obtain visual distinctness would be false. Milton's famous description of Satan in *Paradise Lost* (Book I, Lines 589-99) is effective because it consists of crowded, confused images. Lewes argued that Milton's poem consists of crowded but not confused images. If Milton achieves his effect merely through crowded, confused images, then any set of crowded, confused images would prove equally satisfactory. Obviously this is false. Milton achieves his effect because his images give a *clear* picture of the confusion that reigned in Hell. "And so far from the impressive clearness of the picture vanishing in the crowd of images, it is by these images that the clearness is produced. . . . The poet indicates only that amount of concreteness which is necessary for the clearness of the picture. . . . More concreteness would disturb the clearness by calling attention to irrelevant details." (p. 77)

The Romantic theory of imagination, formulated by Coleridge, Wordsworth, and Hunt, conceived of imagination as a faculty that enables the artist to see the infinite in the finite. This view has been very influential and persists strongly to this day. To observe that someone is imaginative is to imply that he has a faculty which ordinary men lack. Saintsbury was under the influence of the Romantic attitude when he wrote that Lewes' "view of Imagination is confessedly low and almost returns to the Addisonian standpoint of 'ideas furnished by sight.' "[71] Alba H. Warren more recently observed that Lewes "reduced the imagination to the mere image-making faculty."[72] Lewes did not have a "low" view of imagination, nor did he use the word *image* naively, in a restricted sense, to signify only what the eye can see. Both Saintsbury and Warren ignored the psychological implications of Lewes' analysis. When he defined imagination as the power of forming images, he did not mean to derogate it as a low, mechanical function of the mind any more than he would have derogated such processes as inference, perception, and reasoning by analyzing them respectively as intellectual powers of the mind. His explanation of the imaginative process was presented in the language of the physiological psychologist, and far

71 Saintsbury, *op. cit.*, 541.
72 Alba H. Warren, *English Poetic Theory 1825-1865* (Princeton, 1950), 19.

from minimizing the potency of imagination, Lewes extended its functioning to include powers which *all* thinking, creative minds must employ.

His classification of artists further reveals how much he was influenced by the philosopher's high valuation of intellect. Although, as we shall see later, he objected to *excessive* intellectualism in art, he gave the highest rating to the keenest minds. He distinguished three types of artists: geniuses possess a superiority of mind which enables them to assimilate more rapidly and effectively the general and special relationships of experience; merely talented men have somewhat less superior minds but they can learn by observing the minds of originators; the third and largest class consist of mere emulators in art and compilers in philosophy whose intellects are clearly inferior.

But the most direct relationship between Lewes' philosophy and his critical thought is to be found in his theory of realism, which is essentially a reformulation in critical terms of the philosophical position which he called Reasoned Realism. It will be recalled that Reasoned Realism maintains that every experience contains a "double aspect," real and ideal. Not only did Lewes apply the double aspect theory to explain the nature of substance, matter, causality, and mind, but he also applied it to his critical theory. He was aware that various terms had been used to describe the double aspect of reality, such as Platonist-Aristotelian, classic-romantic, subjective-objective, personal-impersonal. He preferred not to use the terms *classic-romantic* except for purposes of classification in a historical context because they had been overworked and misused. In his early writings he often used the subjective-objective distinction which he admitted was ambiguous, and he once mentioned that he thought the personal-impersonal dichotomy was preferable.[73] But in his more mature writings he dropped this terminology and developed a theory of realism which made use of the realism-idealism distinction. Lewes discussed the theory not only in the *Principles* but in various articles.

Just as he had denied the antithesis between realism and idealism in his philosophy, so he denied this antithesis in art. Since literature is "essentially the expression of experience and emotion

[73] "Shelley and the Letters of Poets," WR, LVII (1852), 506.

—of what we have seen, felt, and thought . . . only *that* literature is effective . . . which has *reality for its basis* . . . and effective in proportion to the depth and breadth of that basis."[74] But art at best can only be a representation of reality, "a Representation which inasmuch as it is not the thing itself, but only represents it, must necessarily be limited by the nature of its medium. . . ."[75] The artist's creation is a copy, and it can never duplicate the characteristics of what it is copying. But there are many ways of copying nature. "The greater the fidelity, the greater will be the merit of each representation; for if a man pretends to represent an object, he pretends to represent it accurately; the only difference is what the poetical or prosaic mind sees in the object." (p. 83) The poetical mind will give us a vision of realities in their highest and most affecting forms, in the significant complexities of emotional and reflective existence. "And the true meaning of Idealism is precisely this vision of realities in their highest and most affecting forms, not in the vision of something removed from or opposed to realities." (pp. 82-83) Lewes used Titian's "Peter the Martyr" to illustrate the distinction between realism and idealism: ". . . In it we have a marvelous presentation of reality as seen by a poetic mind. The figure of the flying monk might have been equally real if it had been an ignoble presentation of terror—the superb tree, which may almost be called an actor in the drama, might have been painted with even greater minuteness, though not perhaps with equal effect upon us, if it had arrested our attention by its details—the dying martyr and the noble assassin might have been made equally real in more vulgar types—but the triumph achieved by Titian is that the mind is filled with a vision of poetic beauty which is felt to be real. An equivalent reality, without the ennobling beauty, would have made the picture a fine piece of realistic art." (p. 83)

Lewes did not accept the traditional dichotomy between realism and idealism. For him idealism is simply a special kind of realism: "Realism is thus the basis of all Art, and its antithesis is not Idealism but *Falsism*."[76] Realism is supposed to be charac-

74 "Lady Novelists," WR, LVIII (1852), 130; see also FR, IV (1866), 637.

75 "Realism in Art: Recent German Fiction," WR, LXX (1858), 493; *Leader*, August 6, 1853, 762.

76 "Realism," WR, LXX (1858), 493.

terized by the artist's unswerving devotion to nature. But, Lewes asked, what does it mean to be true to nature? He answered that it can only mean "truth of kind," that is, congruity in the representation of the varied and complex kinds of nature. The angels of Fra Angelico, the cows of Cuyp, and the vacillations of Hamlet are equally natural. While the natures of angels, cows and Hamlets differ in kind, the artist is being just as truthful when he depicts the qualities attributed to an angel as when he describes with detailed accuracy the process of milking a cow or the frenzied state of Hamlet. Realism requires that "there be no *incongruous* mixture of reality with fiction," whereas falsism is incongruity or misrepresentation.[77] Realism is therefore a concept defined broadly enough to apply to different kinds of reality.

We can now understand the sense in which Lewes is to be described as a philosophic critic. The most important emphases of his philosophy are basic to his critical theory: empiricism, intellectualism, relativism, reasoned realism, and a psychological approach to cognition and imagination. But Lewes was never a mere theoretical critic. He spent a lifetime reviewing and analyzing all kinds of writing. In the following pages we will examine the practical application of his theories as he criticized poets, novelists, and dramatists. First we will turn to his discussion of poetry which is represented to a considerable extent by early criticisms written in the forties.

[77] "Shakespeare," *Edinburgh Review,* XC (1849), 55.

3

Lewes on Poetry

In 1842 Lewes reviewed Hegel's *Vorlesungen über die Aesthetik.*[1] He devoted fewer pages to an exposition of Hegel's aesthetic theory than he did to the presentation of his own ideas on poetic theory. This early article is not one of his best; structurally it is a potpourri of quotations from many sources, and it suffers as well from the confusion resulting from his use of Hegelian terminology in a positivistic sense. However, it is interesting for a number of reasons: it expresses certain ideas which formed the theoretical basis for Lewes' criticism of various poets in the forties; it resulted in a correspondence between Lewes and John Stuart Mill; and it reveals how widely read Lewes was in the fields of aesthetics and criticism.

Lewes evidently sent Mill a draft of his paper, and Mill criticized his views of form in poetry and his definition of poetry. Lewes had relatively little to say about the form of poetry. "Verse," he wrote, "is the form of poetry; not the form as a thing *arbitrary,* but as a thing vital, and essential; it is the incarnation of poetry."[2] Mill was not convinced that meter distinguishes poetry from prose, and he preferred his own distinction between poetry and eloquence, or the artistic expression of feeling for feeling's sake and the artistic expression of feeling for the sake of attaining a goal. Lewes must have replied to make his position

1 "Hegel's Aesthetics: Philosophy of Art," BFR, XIII (1842), 1-49. Lewes contributed several mediocre poems to the *Leader*: "The Remorse of Pontius Pilate," November 30, 1850, 860; "Thoughts in Despondency," May 11, 1850, 165; "A Picture in Music," May 18, 1850, 189.

2 "Hegel," BFR, XIII (1842), 13.

clearer, for Mill wrote again admitting the difference between them to be primarily one of classification. He admitted that Lewes had the right to use poetry to mean "art by the instrument of words," and in this sense "metre is of the essence of it or at least necessary to the higher kinds of it."[3] Mill had even stronger reservations about Lewes' conception of poetry, and his criticism led Lewe to revise or clarify his definition.

First Lewes rejected various famous views of poetry: Aristotle's conception of imitative art, Schlegel's "mirror of ideas eternally true," Schiller's "representation of the sensuous," Hegel's "absolute incarnate in the beautiful," and that "mysterious something which English critics derive from Creation.' Lewes' own definition reads as follows:

> 1. Its *abstract* nature, *i.e.* Art as Art—the "spirit which informs" architecture, sculpture, painting, music and poetry, considered in its abstract existence.
> 2. Its *concrete* nature, *i.e.* poetry as an individual art, and as such distinguished from the others and from all forms of thought whatever. These definitions we offer as 1. *Poetry is the beautiful phasis of a religious Idea,* 2. *Poetry is the metrical utterance of emotion.* [This either expressive of emotion in itself, or calculated to raise emotion in the minds of others.] These two definitions, united into one general definition may therefore stand thus:—the metrical utterance of emotion, having beauty for its result, and pervaded by a religious Idea which it thereby symbolizes.[4]

Without doubt Mill must have approved of the part of the statement which describes poetry as the "utterance of an emotion," for in "What is Poetry" he had also characterized feeling as the primary element of poetry. In this connection both Lewes and Mill were affirming the emotional-expressionist theory of art which Wordsworth, Coleridge, Shelley, Keats, Keble, Hazlitt and others espoused in the nineteenth century. In a letter he wrote to Lewes on the Hegel paper (April 24, 1941) Mill commented: "As one hint among many towards a definition of poetry that has

[3] Kitchel, *op. cit.*, 32.
[4] "Hegel," BFR, XIII (1842), 8-9.

occurred to me, what do you think of this—'feeling expressing itself in the forms of thought?'" But Mill's objection was that Lewes had not clarified the meaning of the term *religious.* "Your notion of the essentially religious nature of poetry seems to me to need a world of explanation. I think it will give entirely false ideas to English readers, & is only true in any degree if we, *more Germanico,* call every idea a religious idea which either grows out of or leads to feelings of infinity & mysteriousness. If we do this, then religious ideas are the most poetical of all, an inmost circle; but surely not the only poetical, especially if your other definition of poetry be right."[5] Lewes then must have revised the article and sent it to Mill in the form in which it was to be published. Mill wrote him reassuringly: "I like it better and better." What Lewes probably added was the clarification that he used the term *religion* in its broadest sense, to signify the synthetical expression of each significant characteristic of the spirit of an age. The religious idea "is the formula of any truth leading to new contemplations of the infinite or to new forms in our social relations."[6] He explained that he meant *religious* to refer to such concepts as liberty, equality, humanity and morality. These are not doctrinal concepts in all formalized religions, "but inasmuch as they express (in the final analysis) the object and faith of the crusade in which all Europe is now sensibly or insensibly engaged, and as they have to complete a great social end, so may they be considered as eminently religious."[7]

The references to the religious character of poetry, to the infinite, to the spirit of the age, to synthesis, might at first glance lead one to believe that Lewes was a Hegelian. But his equation of poetry with religion did not involve Hegel's infinite cosmic mind or universal spirit. Poetry "is in its essence one with religion; and its deviation from its sacred office, as civilization progresses, is only *apparent,* for the end of both must ever be one and the same. The end of religion, universally considered, is not its *speculative belief,* but its *practical result;* the translation of that hieroglyphic alphabet of *faith* into its corresponding symbols of *action;* thus leading mankind to a higher, purer state of being than the uneducated instincts and unrestrained passions ever could attain. Such

[5] Kitchel, *op. cit.,* 32.
[6] "Hegel," BFR, XIII (1842), 19–20.
[7] *Ibid.,* 20.

is also the end of poetry, pursuing that end however through the Beautiful."[8] For Lewes, poetry is religion in the sense that it represents an attempt to reform and improve the universe. He assigned extraordinary vatic powers to the poet, and described him as a very special being: "[The poet] is something different from what other men are. He has indeed no faculties he does not share with them, but he has them in such different degrees of intensity, and so differently *combined,* that he becomes thereby distinguished from them. . . . The poet is a Seer and a Singer."[9] In expressing this viewpoint, Lewes echoed the faith of others in his century, Shelley, Mill, Hunt, Carlyle, Arnold, Dallas, Ruskin, that the poet is the prophet, the seer, the "unacknowledged legislator, the original mind" in love with truth. The poet "stands at the head of his age at once its child and prophet, and [his] psalm . . . retains the one burthen—*elevation of the race he addresses into a higher sphere of thought.*"[10] Thus he exercises a moral influence by symbolizing a religious idea through emotive images rather than facts, prayers, or sermons.

However, since a religious idea can be only the "truth of a period," the poet is always dealing with relative truths. The fundamental law of aesthetics is the law of *temporalities* in art. In this connection Lewes suggested that a valuable essay might be written on "Variations of Aesthetic Feeling in the different Epochs of Poetry."[11] Each age has its own wisdom to transmit and the poet performs the function of conveying its dominant ideas. However, even though all dominant ideas in a period must be expressed in poetry, all ideas are not equally appropriate for poetic expression. For example, the eighteenth century was primarily an age of reason and analysis; reason served the scientists well but not the poets whose primary concern is emotion rather than intellect. Since poetry is "the metrical utterance of emotion," it must always express emotion or excite it through some method. Poetry is feeling for feeling's sake. For this reason, Wordsworth and Coleridge were correct in designating science rather than prose as the true antithesis to poetry, for science is thought for thought's sake. Lewes objected to Gongorism as exemplified in

8 *Ibid.*
9 "Shelley and the Letters of Poets," WR, LVII (1852), 510.
10 "Hegel," BFR, XIII (1842), 18.
11 *Ibid.,* 48.

the poems of Gongora in Spain, Marini in Italy, and Cowley and Donne in England; their poems did not originate in emotion but were the products of affectation and wit. In the true poet "imagination acting on the feeling, or the feeling acting on the imagination, condenses and fuses a whole series of ideas into one *nexus* of expression. . . ."[12]

Although the poet is primarily concerned with feeling, he has to be aware of the best thought of his age. In other articles written at about the same time as the Hegel paper, Lewes emphasized the poet's intellectual role. The scientist "sneers at the poet, because he knows only his own ideas, comprehends only his own purposes. . . ."[13] But this derogation of the poet is absurd. Lewes asked,

> Shall the poet's utterance get no heed because it is rolled forth in music? Such seems to be the conclusion; with a bull-headed perverseness we persist in associating the good with the immediately practical, and conceive verse to be too flimsy and tinsel-like to be serious. A serious error this. Poets have in all times and in all ages been the first reformers! The poets who blame their feebleness upon the usurpation of imagination by the "cold reason" of science deceive themselves. It was as difficult to create good poems years ago when many more original ideas were provided by the credulities and superstitions of men; it was just as difficult then to find a Homer as it is to find a Shakespeare or Goethe today.[14]

In 1858 Lewes stated quite emphatically: "The progress of science can in no way *cripple* genius, nor *aid* it, except by rendering its work more worthy of immortal honour, by giving it more of immortal truth to work upon. The exact sciences cannot themselves be poems, yet the progress of scientific knowledge will free poetry from absurd mistakes."[15] To have clearness of vision a poet needs the wisdom of experience, logical power, and scientific knowledge: "Good sense will assuredly create no poetry, but neither will poetry be created by the mind that is unable to distinguish sense from nonsense. The poet is not great by the un-

12 *Ibid.*, 11.
13 "Character and Works of Göthe," BFR, XIV (1843), 105.
14 "Shelley," WR, XXXV (1841), 308.
15 "A Pleasant French Book," *Blackwood's*, LXXXIV (1858), 679.

restricted activity of Imagination but by the plastic power which shapes realities into forms of beauty. . . . But you do not call dreams poems—you do not accept reveries as philosophy. The power of the poet and philosopher is shown not in this barren activity of unwedded thought, but in the fecundity which issues from the actual embrace of thought with reality."[16]

Thus, like Plato, Lewes insisted upon the cognitive value of poetry and demanded from the poet the wisdom which he required from the philosopher. For he believed that a poet's rank is determined "not by the grandeur and depth of his conceptions, nor by the beauty and melody of his song, but by the degree in which the two are *united*."[17] In 1841 Lewes distinguished three classes of poets. In the group of the greatest poets he placed Homer, Dante, Chaucer, and Shakespeare; in the second class he placed Virgil, Milton, Tasso, Calderon, and Wordsworth, and in the third group were the artificial poets Boileau and Pope. In 1852 he referred to Homer, Sophocles, Shakespeare, Dante, Milton, and Goethe as the greatest poets because "the depth and clearness of their vision, the exquisite melody of their song, are peculiarities which have never been so combined by others."[18]

Lewes' use of the noetic criterion for poetry is clearly revealed in his criticism of the romantic poets. He judged their poems primarily in terms of the cognitive principle. Wordsworth, Southey, and Coleridge "started back at the apparition of Liberty they had called up. . . ." Wordsworth fled from the present "to an impossible state of country life . . . hymning nature as the only healthy nurse, but stopping short whenever he came to any important point."[19] Southey, Scott, and Moore fled to foreign past scenes; Coleridge dreamed "in the slumbers of the past;" Keats, "seeing much that was wrong, but not clearly seeing where and how it could be righted," also sought refuge in the remote past. Byron reflected the disease of his age, "the disease of unbelief and self-anatomy." "Shelley alone was the poet standing completely on his truth; giving up his life to it, and

[16] "Shelley," WR, LVII (1852), 510.
[17] *Ibid.*
[18] *Ibid.* See also "The Roman Empire and Its Poets," WR, XXXVIII (1842), 35, 534-35, and the *Athenaeum*, March 10, 1849, 246-47.
[19] "Shelley," WR, XXXV (1841), 319-20.

eternally preaching it."[20] In assuming the distinctive position of reformer, Shelley expressed the highest character of the poet, the "high priest-like character." Lewes used such terms as *priest-like* and *apostle* to characterize Shelley as the poet of futurity, the genuine poet-prophet. In him Lewes found the closest approximation to the ideal of the true poet. To both Shelley and Lewes poets were "the unacknowledged legislators of the world." Shelley shared Lewes' belief in the exalted function of poetry, and Shelley performed the role of poet as a man of vision, an original mind in love with truth, a reformer, a seer, a prophet. For this reason Lewes lavished more praise upon Shelley than he did upon any other Romantic poet.

In 1838 the *National Magazine* and *Monthly Critic* included in their lists of forthcoming works "The Life of Percy Bysshe Shelley." On December 21, 1839, Lewes asked Mary Shelley to read his manuscript. But the book never appeared. Perhaps Mary Shelley asked him not to publish because of her promise to Shelley's father. Lewes later helped Rossetti prepare his biography of Shelley.[21]

In an age when most critics made a sharp bifurcation between the so-called infidelity of Shelley's thought and the beauty of his verse, Lewes did not apologize for his ideas. Writing against the mainstream of opinion which categorized Shelley as a blasphemous, immoral poet, Lewes commended him for the very qualities for which most contemporary critics berated him. Newman Ivy White has praised Lewes' article on Shelley as "one of the best of all the reviews of *The Poetical Works of Percy Bysshe Shelley* . . . enthusiastic and genuinely critical. . . ."[22] Lewes interpreted Shelley's supposed infidelity as an "earnest deep-grounded faith" which Shelley expressed as a dialectic skeptic to achieve his dream as an ethical believer. The soul of man requires a harmonious blending of the dialectic and the ethic: "There are men who dialectically are Christians, yet are nevertheless ethically infidels in the strictest sense—intellectual believers, but practical Atheists—who will write you 'evidences' in perfect faith in their logic, but cannot carry out the Christian doctrine

20 *Ibid.*
21 N.I. White, *Shelley* (New York 1940), II, 402-3.
22 *Ibid.*

owing 'to strength of the flesh.' On the other hand, there are many dialectical skeptics, but ethical believers; and as we have shown ethics to be the end of religion, so are the ethical believers more worthy, and such was Shelley!"[23] It must be remembered that Lewes did not use the term *religion* in its usual sense, but that he defined it as the moral influence of any philosophical Idea, such as Liberty or Democracy. Thus when he characterized Shelley as a religious poet, he meant that Shelley's religion was an ethical ideal based on the philosophy of perfectibility. His "ethical belief" was based on the hope that humanity could be perfected through love and hope, and he "joined the most constant sympathy and tolerance of all concrete existences . . . with all the pious vehemence of an apostle."[24]

Like Luther, Shelley deplored error and evil in the world, but, declared Lewes, "it is a mistake to say Shelley was 'always wailing'; there is more love and hope, and gladness, and delight in beauty and nature, in his poems, than in almost any other poet."[25] There is a misconception of Shelley as the poet of unsubstantiality who naively believed that his Utopian ideal could be realized effortlessly. Unlike Wordsworth, Shelley did recognize the futility of overt didacticism, and in the presentation of his vision he attempted to inspire those who might fall asleep over Godwin's *Political Justice*. For as much as Shelley desired the amelioration of mankind, he was aware of what had to be accomplished before this could be achieved. "If his hopes were dreamy—his theories ideal—yet he knew too well the world and the world's ways, to suppose that those hopes could be realized in an equally dreamy manner. . . ."[26] The lofty aspirations of his poetry were often ridiculed, but to many his work symbolized the highest mission of the poet, the mission of hope and love.

Shelley's religion, his doctrine of perfectibility, not only enriched the philosophical substance of his poetry but also served to enhance its aesthetic value, and to illustrate this idea, Lewes compared the aesthetic value of the poetry of Byron and Shelley. There are, Lewes pointed out, three stages in the development of an individual. In the first stage the individual regards the world

23 "Shelley," WR, XXXV (1841), 315.
24 *Ibid.*, 307.
25 *Ibid.*, 317.
26 *Ibid.*, 334.

as the "couleur de rose"; in the second stage he becomes aware of evil and contemplates life with a "skeptic sneer"; in the final stage of maturity, he envisions the world as really "neither black nor white." The philosophy of scorn or despair is harmful to those in the second stage because it tends to prevent them from attaining the freedom of spirit which the third stage alone brings. Since it is the very aim of poetry to help man attain freedom of spirit, the poet's art should be affirmative. Because Byron's poetry contains a "mud-waste of negation," a philosophy of scorn, it is, on aesthetic grounds, the atheism of art and engenders ugliness. On the other hand, Shelley's poetry is aesthetically superior to Byron's because in treating of the beauty of love and hope, it does not block the path to the third and most desirable phase of development which is maturity. Shelley's poetry engenders the beautiful by utilizing a doctrine of affirmation.

Lewes admitted that Shelley was sometimes not as great an artist as he was a reformer. His command of language was remarkable, his imagery was "luxuriant," and his sense of versification was "exquisite." But the descriptions in the longer poems, containing too much glare and brilliance, are difficult to identify because "they seem rather to have been broken memories of many a scene woven into one than the description of any particular scene. It has the effect of dreaminess—as one who has basked in the sun with his eyes closed in some lovely spot, and on opening them looks around and all seems unreal—a dim, dreamy haze is spread between the scene and him."[27] Lewes attributed this lack of concreteness to the fact that Shelley's mind was reflective or subjective, rather than plastic or objective. He was essentially concerned with reflections about phenomena in the light of his own feelings and preconceptions; he was not primarily intent, as would be the objective intellect, on definite, sensuous representations of phenomena.

As for the individual poems, *Queen Mab,* a remarkable composition for a boy of eighteen, has a "strange mixture of poetic beauty and crude deformity, of clear insight and heated extravagance, of deep views and chimerical absurdities." While it possesses the same awareness of the corruption of the existent world as Schiller's *Die Räuber* or Goethe's *Werthers Leiden,* it

[27] *Ibid.,* 322.

also contains their distorted views of the causes of evil. Even though Shelley actually used the word *God* as a "bugbear of conventional superstition," not as the expression of an intellectual ruler, he shocked people by pushing to an offensive extreme the idea that kings and priests are the causes of evil. Not an atheist even at this early stage, Shelley merely condemned the distorted view of God in which people believed. His mistake was that he forgot the proverb "the same words, *but* softer." His fierce attack on his own chimeras lacked the restraint of reason which could have counteracted the qualities that alienated most people. On the other hand, *Alastor* pleased many because Shelley's usual vehement and fiery tone of anguish was replaced by a more quiet mood.

In the *Revolt of Islam,* Shelley is revealed as the poet of women *par excellence.* His conception of love as a perfect sympathy and equality is an extremely modern manifestation in art. Shelley's women have depth and beauty; they are intellectual as well as physical creations, capable of participating in the spiritual regeneration of mankind. Cyntha participates in such action when she shares the task of reform with Laon. In them Shelley embodies the powers and loveliness of human affection. Laon is Shelley and Cyntha is a phase of his mind, a symbol of his poetical character. Both Laon and Cyntha are poets and philosophers, but Cyntha teaches the beauty of the truth of Laon's doctrine. In their failure, Lewes found more proof of his conviction that Shelley was aware of the obstacles to quick or easy reform; in their failure is expressed, implicitly not explicitly, the moral of the poem: the poem reveals the futility of the means employed, and emphasizes the lesson that society will be reformed only after man himself reforms.

In 1852, eleven years after he wrote the *Westminster Review* criticism, Lewes wrote another article, "Shelley and the Letters of Poets." It reveals that his admiration for Shelley was more than a youthful enthusiasm. "Of all his contemporaries Shelley seems to us to have been the nearest approach in life and works to the ideal of a poet; we do not say he was the greatest, but he was the purest poet. He reminds us of the plants called *Oscillatoriae* which continue in a state of rhythmical vibration throughout the greater part of their lives. He was not poetical by fits and starts;

his whole life was one rhythmic evolution."[28] To Lewes, Shelley most closely approximated the ideal of a poet because he regarded the writing of poetry as a consecrated dedication. Moreover, what he did preach had vital truth in it; his truth became the dominant Idea—the philosophy and faith throughout Europe—a belief in progress, humanity, civilization, democracy, perfectibility. Many may laugh at his doctrine of perfectibility, but was it merely the impractical dream of a poet? Actually what Shelley embodied in his visions all men seek, either on the subconscious or conscious level: "Why must we need daily fight the desperate but irresistible battle of improvement, but that we have all, lying down in the dim souls of the meanest of us, however obscured by errors and worldly shows, some pregnant Idea tantamount to this doctrine of perfectibility, some religious Idea, which we indefinitely seek to realize, if not for ourselves at least for our children, and exhort them to do the same? When is this to stop? . . . It will never stop; it is the restless spirit of man impelling him from within."[29] Thus Shelley's poetry speaks to "the restless spirit of man."

Since Lewes believed that poetry, like all of literature, is "*vision,* not *caprice;* the poet is a seer," he, therefore, considered the absence of thought a serious deficiency in a poem. Originally, he characterized Keats as an essentially sensuous poet: "He will always remain in our literature as a marvelous specimen of what mere sensuous imagery can create in poetry."[30] Lewes interpreted the famous lines "Oh for a life of sensations rather than of thought" to mean that Keats had a predilection for the sensuous rather than for the intellectual. The mystery of life and the human soul were not perplexing problems to him. Indeed "Keats neither seems to have understood himself, nor the world."[31] Lewes admitted that Keats was able to infuse a more poetic spirit into ancient mythology than any of his predecessors because he regarded mythologic people as living creatures rather than abstractions. But these living beings bore no resemblance either to Greeks or humans. The world of fancy was more real to Keats

28 "Shelley," WR, LVII (1852), 509.

29 "Shelley," WR, XXXV (1841), 321.

30 "A Review of R. Monckton Milne's *Life, Letters and Literary Remains of John Keats,*" BQR, VIII (1848), 329.

31 *Ibid.,* 330.

than the world of reality. However, it is "comparatively easy and comparatively worthless" to depict the world of fancy. Lewes doubted whether Keats could have dealt with the more difficult and more ambitious end of poetry which "shapes into beauty all that we have felt, thought, and suffered." Keats instinctively chose such subjects as Endymion, Hyperion, and Lamia which were the fanciful rather than the realistic subjects of antiquity. To him "the mystery of life was no burden on his soul. . . . He questioned nothing. He strove to penetrate no problems. He was content to feel and to sing."[32] Several years later Lewes recognized that he had been unjust to Keats, for in 1852, he commented on Keats' letters: "Turning over the pages the eye is arrested by many a felicitous phrase, and many a suggestive thought, implying far greater range and variety in Keats' mind than one had given him credit for."[33]

Lewes also expressed qualified admiration for Wordsworth's poetry. In the *Principles,* he used Wordsworth as an example of the poet who employs distinct images. He wrote concerning the famous lines on ice skating in Book I of the *Prelude*: "Every poetical reader will feel delight in the accuracy with which the details are painted, and the marvelous clearness with which the whole scene is imagined, both in its objective and subjective relations, i.e. both in the objects seen and the emotions they suggest."[34] In the *Leader,* he referred to Wordsworth as "the greatest descriptive poet that ever lived."[35] But in Lewes' judgment, Wordsworth's poetry is too descriptive. Like Solger, Lewes believed that poetry must be vitalized by emotion or action, and he judged Wordsworthian poetry to be deficient in both elements. Moreover, he disagreed with the two major premises of Wordsworth's poetic theory, namely, that poetry does not differ essentially from prose, and that the diction of poetry should be the simple language of men.

Because of Wordsworth's mistaken notion that prose and poetry are essentially similar, his poems contain descriptions which are often nothing more than mere catalogues of scenes and prosaic passages replete with trivialities. The language of Harry Gill and

32 *Ibid.*
33 "Shelley," WR, LVII (1852), 508.
34 *Principles,* 72.
35 August 17, 1850, 496.

Betty Foy is ludicrous. It may be true that simple words are more appropriate in sad situations to create the effect of sorrow, but the danger also exists that these simple words might produce drivel. Insensitive to this danger, Wordsworth intermingled "risibilities and puerilities" with magnificent, intense poetry. His error lay in not distinguishing between homely and vulgar expressions; "accordingly he often raised a laugh where he most wished to move sympathy."[36] Imagine, Lewes suggested, that Wordsworth had changed the lines spoken by Lear:

> I am a very foolish, fond old man,
> Fourscore and upwards; and, to deal plainly,
> I fear I am not in my perfect mind—

to read:

> I am a very *silly*, fond old man,
> More than eighty years of age; and 'pon my word,
> I fear I'm not quite in my senses.

In the Shakespearean version, the selection and collocation of simple words make for true pathos; in the hypothetical version the extreme use of the homely turn of expression might easily evoke laughter instead of tears. In the poem which begins "Spade with which Wilkinson has till'd his land!" Wordsworth does not avoid the pitfall of using ridiculous language. Wilkinson "no doubt denotes many a respectable family . . . [but] its abundant use by comic writers, coupled to its oddity as a sound, have consecrated it to fun, and not to poetry. . . ."[37] Wordsworth was justified in revolting against affectation and the misuse of poetic diction, but he was not justified in revolting against poetic diction itself. Lewes struck at the root of Wordsworth's theory when he stated: "Such ornaments as coquettes put on the bosoms of their verses are but as gauds to hide the wrinkled skin on which they glitter; still those who, in their fury of simplicity—who, in their disgust at dowager-diamonds, declare that a lovely maiden shall not place a rose in her hair, because ornament is unnecessary, commit a sad blunder, and slight the beautiful because the deformed will ape it."[38]

36 "State of Criticism in France," BFR, XVI (1844), 355-56.
37 "Hegel," BFR, XIII (1842), 17.
38 *Ibid.*, 12.

Lewes also denied Wordsworth the status of philosophical poet when he reviewed *The Prelude* in 1850, in the *Leader*.[39] Containing an uncoordinated series of rather trivial incidents, the poem is sometimes "lofty, picturesque and instinct with poetry," but more often it is "surcharged with a dense prosaism," and fails as a philosophical survey of a poet's mind. Books I and II are the most successful portions, but the other books are replete with philosophic absurdities. For example, Book VI expresses the cardinal point of Wordsworth's philosophy, "the wretched absurdity, that man to keep himself pure and pious, should shun cities and the haunts of men, to shut himself in mountain solitudes, and there . . . impregnate his mind with the solemnities and beauties of landscape nature—an ignoble, sensuous asceticism, replacing by an *artistic* enthusiasm and craving lusts of the eye that religious enthusiasm which moved the ancient recluse to tear himself from man and commune in loneliness with the Eternal." By accepting the questionable view that love of nature leads to love of man and that absence from cities is a necessary condition for attaining such love, Wordsworth ignored what the ancients had taught centuries ago. They knew that landscape was, after all, only a background for the human soul. Wordsworth forgot that "man was made to live *as man* and not as the stars or flowers," and as a result he subordinated man to nature. Human beings he loved "something better than his dog, a little less than the rocks and sounding cataracts." What was human interested him only to the extent that it was picturesque; he avoided "the great theatre whereon the tragic passions and exalted heroisms are displayed, to throw his whole poetic sympathy upon parochial woes!"

Wordsworth was a meditative, contemplative poet, but he was not ratiocinative or systematic in the true philosophic sense. There are no universal insights in his poetry, no truths a philosopher arrives at after careful investigation of the experiences of others. His truths were those revealed to him by his own personality; indeed "Wordsworth was the universe to Wordsworth." Lewes described him as "an astonishing and . . . solitary example of great genius without geniality—of creative power without wide sympathies. . . . Do we not all feel that this magnificent intellect . . .

[39] *Leader,* August 17, 1850, 496.

which can be excited to tears by a daisy, but has only cold sermons for mankind—which moves in a small circle of emotions sacrificing man to nature, is on the whole shut out from our hearts . . . ?" His letters as well as his poems reveal him to be a great egoist.[40] He excelled as a descriptive poet, as a creator of genuine imagery; he was original and did inspire a revolution in taste. But generally his poetry is marred by subjectivism and naïveté.

Lewes used the noetic criterion not only in relation to the Romantics, but again and again in his reviews of other poets. He always introduced the subject of the intellectual range of the poet's mind. He wrote the first article in England on Leopardi to introduce his art to the English public. Although Lewes' approach was primarily eulogistic, he commented on the limited range of Leopardi's poetry. His poems contain the "most exquisite choice of diction which his poet's instinct and his classic taste alike taught him." As the poet of despair he was unequalled. "He was a stoic-skeptic. In everything he wrote . . . you may see the traces of a deep sense of the nothingness of life, a poignant feeling of its unhappiness, and a stoic contempt for the suffering which bowed him to earth."[41] But his experiences were too confined and his poetry reveals only his own thoughts and sufferings without imaging more universal experiences.

Lewes criticized Victor Hugo's *Les Chanson des Rues et des Bois* for its lack of imagination, lack of philosophy, and lack of common sense. Unrestrained by common sense, and without genuine perception, Hugo employs incongruous metaphors such as those which describe April as "*ce portier de l'été*" and "*un vieil intrigant.*" Mocking such *preciosité,* Lewes asked, "Why not call April a poor law commissioner?" Hugo's imagery is kaleidoscopic rather than representative: "As in a kaleidoscope the juxtaposition of forms and colours which have no corresponding objects in nature gratifies the incurious eye, so in this kind of poetry the juxtaposition of verbal suggestions having no corresponding

40 One of Wordsworth's friends wrote to the *Leader* (August 24, 1850, 519-20) objecting to Lewes' derogation of Wordsworth and defending him as a generous, unselfish person. Lewes replied that he based his judgment of Wordsworth's personal character upon DeQuincy's *Confessions of an English Opium-Eater* and the reports of those who knew and admired him. "If that impression is erroneous," Lewes wrote, "let it be shown to be so. We have no personal feeling or interest in the matter."

41 "Life and Works of Leopardi," *Fraser's Magazine,* XXXVIII (1848), 664-65.

thoughts gratifies the indolent mind."[42] Lewes ended by advising Hugo to restrain "the diseased excitability of his organ of language," and to relinquish his unfortunate pretensions to be a profound thinker.

Lewes unleashed his critical scorn on Robert Buchanan's *Balder* because of its obscene, dull, and foolish substance.[43] Even though he overrated Elizabeth Barrett Browning and underrated Robert Browning, he compared them justly as thinkers. Although Elizabeth Barrett Browning was a "born singer," her experience was narrow, and generally she did not create the real world, but the world of fancy. On the other hand, Browning with all his deficiencies, his tiresome obscurity, and harsh versification, had a greater intellectual range than his wife. Not a particularly profound thinker, he had the prime quality of seeing for himself and writing in his own language: "Robert Browning is Robert Browning—call him sublime or call him feeble, take any view you will of his poems, you must still admit that he is one standing up to speak to mankind in his speech, not theirs—what he thinks, not what they think."[44]

We have already seen how much value Lewes placed on the artist's own vision and imagination and how he derogated the principle of imitation. In 1847 he described the age as a period of intellectual anarchy which had much faith in application but little sympathy for great ideas. According to Lewes, all the great eras in the history of literature have been disturbed periods when the poet jubilantly looks to the future or bemoans the past. In 1847 the poet created inferior works because "there was nothing for him to sing."[45] As a result he imitated Scott, Shelley, or Keats. But as Lewes never tired of reiterating: "To be able to see for yourself, and to picture to others what you have seen are the first great characteristics of genius."[46] In his analyses of Homer, the Roman poets, and Matthew Arnold, he objected to the influence of the classical tradition because it induced imitation.

While the name of Homer was retained in Lewes' second list of

42 "Victor Hugo's Latest Poems," FR, III (1865-66), 183. See also "Modern French Literature," BQR, XIII (1851), 573-76.

43 "Robert Buchanan," FR, I (1865), 457-58; *Leader*, January 28, 1854, 91.

44 "Robert Browning," BQR, VI (1847), 495.

45 *Ibid.*, 492.

46 *Ibid.*, 494.

the greatest poets, in 1846, in an article on the authorship of the Homeric Poems, Lewes challenged the belief in Homer's *unexcelled* greatness.[47] After examining the different theories of Bentley, Vico, Wolf, Heyne and Grote, Lewes had concluded that neither the historical nor the internal evidence was conclusive enough to decide the question. Unlike those who were unable to accept the possibility of multiple authorship because of aesthetic objections to the idea that the Homeric poems were originally a collection of separate ballads, Lewes found it easier to believe in the existence of many Homeric geniuses than in the existence of two Virgils, two Dantes, two Miltons, or two Shakespeares. He was inclined to believe that the Homeric poems were originally separate ballads, although most of the *Iliad* was written by one author.

He reasoned that Homer's genius was not unique in his age. As Shelley correctly observed, in the infancy of society, every author was a poet. He lived unrestrained with nature, employing vivid metaphorical language instinctively. The *Odyssey* and the *Iliad* contain the very qualities which these conditions produce: "vivid imagery, clear pictures, healthy vigour, naiveté, simple passions, and untrammelled originality."[48] What was natural and spontaneous to Homer *was* poetry. However, this does not mean he was unique. Much of the pleasure in reading these epics is primarily critical and historical rather than aesthetic; we delight in their simplicity, in their indications of barbarism, in their pictures of an old civilization. But we do not seek in them the refinements of modern poetry, and even their faults, their rudenesses, and tautologies offer delights to the reader which would be condemned in a Virgil or Milton. In Homer "artlessness has the effect of exquisite art." But any dispassionate reader of Homer must be struck "with the excessive rudeness and artlessness of his style—with the absence of any great o'ermastering individuality . . . with the absence, in short, of everything that can, properly speaking, be called art."[49] The art of the poet consists in what Goethe has described as *Gestaltung* or formation. The true and

[47] "Grote's History of Greece: The Homeric Poems," WR, XLVI (1846), 381-415. See also Lewes' review of T.A. Buckley's translation of the *Iliad* in the *Athenaeum*, April 19, 1851, 428-30.

[48] "The Homeric Poems," WR, XLVI (1846), 409.

[49] *Ibid.*, 410.

only final test of the artist is to be found in his style. Now Homer's style is unquestionably that of a real poet—it is vivid, graphic, and direct—but at the same time, it contains careless, naive, tautologous elements which, although interesting as signs of the antiquity of the poem, are poetical defects. Homer employed one of the most melodious and flexible languages known, "yet much of his verse is a mere jingle, and is stuffed out with idle epithets and particles, or with tautologies, merely thrust in to keep up the jingle."[50] His poems lack the refinements of art, the artistic excellence of the great modern poets. Moreover, his powers of characterization are greatly overrated. His "characters are *true;* but they are merely outlined. They are to the characters of Shakespeare—to which rash admiration has sometimes compared them —as the rude outline of a figure on the wall is to the perfect sculpture of a Phidias."[51]

Thus by interpreting Homer as a spontaneous rather than an artistic poet, Lewes was able to accept the theory of multiple authorship. Since Homer's genius was not unique, there were undoubtedly other poets in his age who were capable of similar achievements. In 1853 Lewes reiterated his disbelief in the "unrivalled intrinsic merit" of the Homeric poems.[52] But while he disapproved of the unqualified admiration of Homer, he never seemed to question Homer's right to a place among the greatest artists.

In his scathing denunciation of the early Roman poets, Lewes revealed even more clearly his lack of reverence for the idols of the classicists. To him, the art of Rome was only an imitative art at best, and Virgil, Ovid, Lucretius, Horace, and Catullus had exhausted all the possibilities of imitation. Their successors, Phaedrus, Persius, Juvenal, Lucan, and Martial, owed their fame merely to the fact that they were Romans. Living during a period of national corruption, their poetry reflected the moods of an uninspired present, ignorant of the traditions of the past and oblivious of the promise of the future. This explains why they had recourse to jest, satire, saturnalia, scandals; this explains "their cold and faithless mythology, hence their pedantry, hence the torturing of their language into new and unheard-of combi-

50 *Ibid.*, 411.
51 *Ibid.*, 410-11.
52 *Leader,* May 14, 1853, 473.

nations, to express old ideas, and to hide their poverty with glitter; a circumstance which has given employment to so many illustrious commentators, who thought the labour of a life well bestowed in settling these disputed readings."[53]

By now, there should be no doubt about Lewes' attitude toward the classical tradition! As we have seen, the contention that "idolatry of the past is vicious" is not casual observation, but a view which he reiterates in his philosophic and literary writings. Yet, one writer has claimed that Lewes himself represents a link in the continuity of the classical tradition in nineteenth-century England, because in the forties he anticipated Arnold's concept of culture and the function of criticism.[54] It is true that Lewes anticipated some of Arnold's ideas on the function of criticism, but these are hardly to be associated only with the classical tradition. Moreover, his conception of culture is different from Arnold's and more closely resembles that of Thomas Henry Huxley. But the most conclusive evidence of Lewes' rejection of Arnold's classicism is to be found in his review of the 1853 edition of Arnold's poems.[55]

Lewes disagreed with the basic premise of Arnold's theory of poetry as expressed in the Preface to this edition. Arnold accepted Aristotle's view that the highest problem of art is the imitation of actions. But Lewes maintained that art involves representation, not imitation. Action in this view can only be the means, not the end of art. Arnold's text was "study the classics, and beware of the syren charms which enervate the moderns." In essence he advised the conscious imitation of the ancients. But as we have seen, Lewes disapproved of conscious imitation, for "models produce no real good, though little harm, because the servile mind is one which if emancipated would not be strong. To study models with a view to *emulate* them is not the same as to study them with a view to imitate them; the one is an invigorating—the other an enervating study." Thirteen years later in the *Fortnightly Review,* Lewes continued to object to the conscious imitation of models: If there is one thing which it is supremely unnecessary for a man in this nineteenth century to do, and which it is next to impossible that he should ever do well, that impossible super-

[53] "The Roman Empire and Its Poets," WR, XXXVIII (1842), 36.
[54] Morris Greenhut, "George Henry Lewes and the Classical Tradition in English Criticism," *Review of English Studies,* XXIV (1948), 126-37.
[55] *Leader,* November 26, 1853, 1147.

fluity is the composition of Greek or Latin poetry; and by a curious misapprehension of the very purposes of Education, which will seem to posterity as deplorable as the wasted ingenuity of the Schoolmen now seems to us, the best years and freshest energies of youth are largely given to a futile pursuit of this superfluity.[56] Admitting that it is necessary to study both the classics and the moderns, Lewes warned in the *Leader's* review of Arnold's poems "Beware of the rudeness and baldness of the one, no less than of the rhetoric and glitter of the other. . . . When the classics are good, they are so by virtue of qualities in all excellent works of art; when they are bad . . . they are so by vice of qualities noticeable in every age—rudeness, incongruity, untruth, greater regard for manner than for matter, and for the mere fopperies of manner." Homer could be "rude as hemp," Aeschylus was often "fantastic, obscure, incongruous," and Virgil, like the worst specimens of modern times, was sometimes "feeble, affected, and unpictorial."

However, Lewes liked many of Arnold's poems. He predicted that "Sohrab and Rustum" would prove to be the favorite, but its Grecism would appeal to the cultured few. In copying the lengthy similes and encumbering narrative from Homer, Arnold forgot that Homer would not write like his imitators. "Empedocles on Etna" is "altogether a mistake," because it is a means by which Arnold combined stray thoughts and images. It belongs to that kind of versified meditation which Wordsworth popularized, but which ignores the lyrical quality, the "song" in poetry. Arnold evidently was not alienated by Lewes' remarks, for in a letter he wrote to his mother in 1858 he said, "I am very anxious to see what Lewes says about Merope, as I have a very high opinion of his literary judgment. . . ."[57]

Lewes believed that a good critic has to have the ability to recognize greatness in new writings with no precedent but his own taste and judgment to guide him. His review of Tennyson's *In Memoriam,* in the *Leader,* 1850, offers us an example of his ability to be a good critic in this sense. He lavished great praise upon this poem, ranking it above the elegies of Moschus, Milton, and Shelley. *In Memoriam* is not artificial like *Adonais* or *Lycidas;*

[56] "Causeries," FR, VI (1866), 370.

[57] G.W.E. Russell (ed.), *Letters of Matthew Arnold* (London, 1895), I, 58.

it contains "truthful passion." In this great work, "Tennyson sings a deeper sorrow, utters a more truthful passion, and, singing truly, gains the predominance of passion over mere sentiment."[58] Since Lewes believed that poetry is the "metrical utterance of emotion," his encomium of *In Memoriam* is consistent with his theory. He praised the music of the poem, the rhymed stanzas free from conceits yet filled with memorable imagery and diction. He predicted that the work "would become the solace and delight of every house where poetry is loved. . . ." When it was published a month later in a second edition, Lewes interpreted its success to reflect the public's love of good poetry: "Does not Tennyson's success sufficiently prove that if a poem, or volume of poems, rise above the accomplished mediocrity of verse . . . then there is as great a public awaiting it as ever awaited "Christabel," "The Revolt of Islam," or the "Eve of St. Agnes?"[59]

In 1847 Lewes had described Tennyson as a "distinguished poet . . . perhaps the only one of our day who deserves the name of poet."[60] In the above mentioned review of *In Memoriam,* he called Tennyson "the greatest living poet." Although in the *Leader,* 1852, Lewes criticized the "Ode on the Death of the Duke of Wellington" as being a very poor poem, he hastened to add that he "loved" Tennyson.[61] Obviously such adulation would not have hampered the friendship which developed between the Leweses and the Tennysons in later years. In his *Diary* for March 30, 1877, Lewes recorded that he had given a party to hear Tennyson read *Maud* and the two *Northern Farmers.*[62] Both George Eliot and Lewes admired the famous poet's plays, and Lewes encouraged him to continue with his dramatic efforts. Lewes wrote to Tennyson in 1877: "We [Lewes and George Eliot] have just read 'Harold' (for the first time) and 'Mary' (for the fourth) and greatly wished you had been here to read certain scenes, especially that masterly interview between Harold and William, or that most pathetic close of 'Mary.' It is needless for me to say how profound a pleasure both works have given us—they are great contributions! and your wretched critics who would dissuade you from enrich-

58 *Leader,* June 22, 1850, 303-4.
59 *Ibid.,* July 20, 1850, 400.
60 "Robert Browning," BQR, VI (1847), 492.
61 *Leader,* November 20, 1852, 1116.
62 GE, VI, 360.

ing literature with such dramas must be forgiven, for they know not what they say."[63] In 1878 Lewes wrote his son: "The other day Tennyson was to read to the Mutter and me his new play [Becket] (for which I am responsible in so far that he had relinquished the subject in despair until my encouragement of his dramatic power made him take it once more in hand). . . ."[64] Lewes then told Alexander MacMillan that *Becket* was "full of fine *dramatic* power."[65]

Thus far we have seen that Lewes' criticism of the poets emphasized certain key ideas stressed in the Hegel article and in the *Principles* as well: relativism, expressionism and cognition as two indispensable elements of art, and the objection to imitation, particularly of the classics. In his Goethe biography, he uses the concept of realism as a significant critical principle.

Lewes was often in the position of introducing or explicating the works of European writers such as Leopardi, Spinoza,[66] Comte, Hegel, the Spanish dramatists, and Goethe. But none of his writings on the poets grew out of the extensive research he applied to his study of Goethe. In 1843 he wrote an article on the great German, in which he analyzed the nature of Goethe's ability and urged that he be judged as a human being rather than as an infallible genius. John Stuart Mill praised it very highly in a letter he wrote to Lewes: "I think your article on Goethe decidedly your highest flight as yet. Without being the *dernier mot* on such a man, it recommends itself to my knowledge of him as *truer* than any other writing on the subject which I have met with. . . ."[67] In 1844 Lewes made a comparison of the Faust versions written by Marlowe, Calderon, and Goethe, which he later incorporated into *The Life of Goethe.*[68] He returned to Germany in 1854 in the company of George Eliot and spent three months in Weimar visiting the places where Goethe had lived and meeting the

[63] H. Tennyson, *Alfred Lord Tennyson: A Memoir by His Son* (New York, 1898), II, 192.

[64] CE, VII, 64.

[65] *Ibid.*, 65.

[66] "Spinoza's Life and Works," WR, XXXIX (1843), 372-407; "Spinoza," FR, IV (1866), 399; HP (1885), xxx; "Spinoza," *Penny Cyclopedia*, XXII (1842), 350-53. In the WR article Lewes made the first attempt in England to do justice to the philosophical system of Spinoza.

[67] Kitchel, *op. cit.*, 27.

[68] "The Three Fausts," BFR, XVIII (1844), 51-92; *Life of Goethe,* 475-83. References to this edition are incorporated into the text in parentheses.

people who had known him. When his biography finally appeared in 1855, it revealed his interest in Goethe as a personality, as an artist, and as a thinker.

Unlike many biographers who studiously avoid critical commentary, Lewes concerned himself with both the man and his writings. His biography has the value which accrues to any study that is close to its subject in time and sympathy. *The Life of Goethe* was widely read. Even the Germans accepted it as a successful biography, despite the fact that they found within its covers a disparagement of German culture and a description of the man, not the God, Goethe. Indicative of the book's success was the attempt by Dr. Gotthold Kreyenberg, who wrote an attack on *The Life of Goethe,* to demonstrate to his fellow Germans "how improper it is for Germans to be making such an ado about this foreign production."[69] But even the altruistic Kreyenberg was forced to admit that Lewes had a beautiful style and a "pleasing, smooth manner of representing facts." Havelock Ellis has explained why the biography was so successful: "Lewes was an artist and a man of science, a thinker, and a man of the world. It was an invaluable combination of qualities for approaching a personality of Goethe's immense scope: none of his successors have possessed a similar excellent qualification. . . . Lewes's position in relation to his subject gave him a freedom and independence, a sanity and balance of judgment which we can scarcely expect from the ordinary 'Goethe-investigator.' "[70]

In the nineteenth century, Goethe's tepid politics and his love affairs proved disturbing to those who found him lacking in those qualities which their ideal of greatness demanded. He was criticized for his indifference to social and political problems, and he was sometimes described as an artist who was corrupted by a servile life at court. As a result, his genius was derogated as being too limited. In *The Life of Goethe,* Lewes pointed out that this view was based upon a misunderstanding of Goethe, both as man and artist. His genius was not "of that stormy kind which produces great Reformers and great Martyrs. . . . He was a Poet,

69 Dr. Gotthold Kreyenberg, *A Concise Examination of the Value and the Merits of G. H. Lewes' Celebrated Inquiry into the Life and Works of Goethe* (Graudenz, 1866), 8. See also H. Siegfried, *An G. H. Lewes eine Epistel* (Berlin, 1858).

70 Havelock Ellis, introd. to Everyman ed. of Lewes' *Life of Goethe* (London, 1908), viii-ix.

whose religion was Beauty, whose worship was of Nature, whose aim was Culture." (pp. 222-23) Lewes considered it futile to judge Goethe in terms of what he might or should have been. Goethe shared the faults of humanity—he was not an ideal man—but his critics gave his faults undue emphasis. His supposed coldness and insensibility were the external manifestations of a self-mastery which dominated all of his actions. He was "very human, often erring; but viewing his life . . . I say that in him, more than in almost any other man of his time, naked vigour of resolution, moving in alliance with steady clearness of intellect, produced a self-mastery of the very highest kind." (pp. 9-10)

The objective tendency of Goethe's intellect helped him to attain self-mastery and influenced the direction his genius took. This objectivity displayed itself in his strong attraction for the real, the concrete, and the living, and in his strong aversion for the vague, the abstract, and the supersensuous. "His constant striving was to study Nature, so as to see her *directly*, and not through the mists of fancy, or through the distortions of prejudice —to look at men and *into* them—to apprehend things as they were . . . Nature, Nature, Nature, is everywhere the burden of his striving. . . . To overlook and undervalue the facts of Nature, and to fix attention on fleeting impersonal impressions, or purely individual fancies, was a sign of decadence at every period of history. . . . His vision was all directed outwards." (pp. 52-53) Goethe could not even separate God from Nature, and this explains his religious pantheism. He conceived of God as permeating the universe and investing all of Nature with divine life. "His worship was Nature worship, his moral system an idealisation of Humanity. The human being was the highest manifestation of the Divine on earth, and the highest manifestation of Humanity was therefore the ideal to which morality tended." (p. 527)

Unlike many poets who, indifferent to truth, enjoy combining ideas into the most fantastic patterns, Goethe insisted that art requires above all a love of truth. He used images primarily to secure realistic effects. Both Goethe and Shakespeare were realists and made use of vivid, concrete images, but, unlike Shakespeare, Goethe usually avoided extraneous imagery and the excessive use of metaphor and simile. "Shakespeare's imagery bubbles up like a perpetual spring: to say that it repeatedly *overflows,* is only to say that his mind was lured by its own sirens away from the direct path. He did not master his Pegasus at all times, but let the wild careering creature take its winged way. Goethe, on the contrary, always masters his: perhaps because his steed had less of restive life in its veins. Not only does he master it, and ride with calm assured grace, he seems so bent on reaching the goal, that he scarcely thinks of anything else." (pp. 53-54) Besides objectivity, Goethe had the indispensable quality of sincerity. His poetry was the product of real experience. "He sang what he had felt, and because he had felt it; not because others had sung before him. He was the echo of no man's joys and sorrows, he was the lyrist of his own." (p. 47) Of course, he did not reject the knowledge and experiences of others, but as a thorough artist he perceived "the insufficiency of abstract theories in the production of a work of art which should be the expression of real experience." (p. 118)

Goethe' *Faust* and his lyrics earned him a preeminence with the modern poets, a preeminence he shares only with Shakespeare. Such ballads as "The Fisherman," the "Bride of Corinth," "God and the Bajadere," and the "Erl King" are lovely minor lyrics written in a simple, direct, clear style which makes use of remarkably pictorial images. They are "instinct with life and beauty against which no prejudice can stand. They give musical form to feelings the most various and to feelings that are *true.*" (pp. 486-487) Lewes judged "Herman and Dorothea" to be the most perfect of Goethe's poems. He described it as "full of life, character and beauty, simple in its materials, astonishingly simple in its handling; written in obvious imitation of Homer, and yet preserving throughout the most modern colour and sentiment. Of all Idylls, it is the most truly idyllic." (p. 420) It contains less ornamentation and idealization than the idyllic poetry of Theocritus, Virgil, Guarini, Tasso, Florain, Gesner, or Thomson and is most truthful in describing country people. Goethe's peasants are as real as poetry can make them. His objectivity led him to utilize a clear, direct style, shorn of insignificant details. The poem can appeal to simple, popular tastes because its subject matter avoids the political and the critical, and centers on the individual, human interest of such ordinary, unromantic events as the love of two peasants. Critics who deplored the absence of conventional imagery in the poem mistook its simplicity for "baldness." But the people who loved "Herman and Dorothea" and read it on the coarsest paper at the lowest prices were truer judges than the prosaic critics who saw in the poem only an infelicitous imitation of Voss' *Luise.*

For *Faust,* Part I, Lewes had the highest praise. He called it the "greatest poem of modern times. . . ." (p. 453) *Faust* is not a drama but a poetic, legendary spectacle. Many critics who have tried to explain the meaning and construction of the poem have become lost in a "swamp of conjectural metaphysics." Even Coleridge who succeeded in discovering the organic unity of Shakespeare's art (with Schlegel's help, of course) could find no unity in *Faust* and derogated it as a flat poem. Coleridge had an *a priori* conception of the *Faust* theme and blamed Goethe for not treating the subject in the way that he, Coleridge, conceived it. According to Coleridge, the theme of *Faust* is concerned with the consequences of misology, a theme of which he disapproved since he believed that a love of knowledge could never produce misology. Faust was to Coleridge a mere conjurer who aroused his *incredulous odi.* But Lewes insisted that misology is only a part of the theme of *Faust;* the important part is the theme of the struggles of Goethe's soul. Experience had made him aware of the vanity of philosophy and the corruption of civilization. The theme of *Faust* "is the cry of despair over the nothingness of life. . . . [Faust] is restless because he seeks,—seeks the Absolute, which can never be found. This is the doom of Humanity. . . ." (p. 484)

As for its form, *Faust* has so many varied scenes, it seems to have no form at all. However, it is unified by a general plan and interdependence of scenes. In the sentence spoken by the manager in the theater prologue appears the clue to the composition of the poem, "From heaven to earth, and thence thro' earth to hell." Not only do these words refer to the mental phases of the drama, but they also reveal the plan with which the actual scenes of life are represented. Because of the two-fold nature of *Faust,* it has two prologues, one on the stage and one in heaven. The theater prologue symbolizes the world's struggles and the prologue in heaven symbolizes the individual's struggles to attain heaven. The two-fold nature of the poem explains the fascination it has over the minds of men: "In *Faust* we saw as in a mirror the eternal problem of our intellectual existence; and, beside it, varied lineaments of our social existence. It is at once a problem and a picture. . . . The problem embraces questions of vital importance; the picture represents opinions, sentiments, classes, moving on the stage of life. The great problem is stated in all its nudity; the picture is painted in all its variety." (p. 453)

Marlowe gave the *Faust* theme a literal treatment; he simply made it a tale of sorcery. Disagreeing with Charles Lamb, Lewes found *Dr. Faustus* to be "wearisome, vulgar, and ill-conceived." Like most of Marlowe's plays, it has the virtue of magnificent passages, but it also has the defects of low buffoonery and lack of dramatic evolution and characterization. Calderon's *El Magico Prodigioso* is concerned with a different version of the legend in which the Christian Cyprian of Antioch sells his soul to the devil, so that he will help him seduce the virtuous Justina. Essentially a vehicle for the religious instruction of Christians, it lacks even the virtues of Marlowe's naive treatment of the legend. When Goethe took up the Faust story, no one believed in the literal version; and in conformity with its own genuis and age, he treated the Faust story as being representative of fact. To accomplish this, he employed symbolism effectively, maintaining always in the first part of the poem a balance between its emotional and intellectual elements.

No such balance exists in the second part of *Faust*. As Lewes wrote: "In the presence of this poem, I feel more embarrassment than with any other of Goethe's works." (p. 548) He judged it to be "of mediocre interest, very far inferior to the *First Part*, and both in conception and execution an elaborate mistake." (p. 548) This second part is really a separate poem, the product of Goethe's old age. In his later years a tendency towards mysticism and reflection gained ascendancy over his normally objective nature. As a result it made this "clearest and most spontaneous of poets as fond of symbols as if he had been a priest of Isis." (p. 549)

Although Lewes, as we have seen, believed in the cognitive value of art, he was critical of the view which equates art with philosophy. Art requires intellectual substance; but when thought assumes the dominant role, it is a sign of the decay of art. Art is different from philosophy and its symbols have beauty independent of their philosophic signification. If the artist wishes to express certain philosophic ideas by means of symbols, "he must never forget that, Art being Representation, the symbols chosen must possess *in themselves* a charm independent of what they mean. The forms which are his materials, the symbols which are his language, must in themselves have a beauty, and an interest, readily appreciable by those who do not understand the occult meaning. Unless they have this they cease to be Art; they become hieroglyphs." (p. 550) Critics may disagree about the meaning of the first part of *Faust,* but they all agree that it has beauty. Enchanted by the form, even though the mystery may baffle them, they believe in the reality of its people and its scenes. If the symbolism is understood, that much more enjoyment is derived from the poem. But symbolism alone is not effective if the story is uninteresting, if the form is neglected, and if the characters are unimpressive. The second part of *Faust* fails because "there is no direct appeal to the emotions. There is no intrinsic beauty in the symbols. . . . There are many passages of exquisite beauty, some lines of profound thought, and some happy sarcasm; but there is no incident, no character, no one scene which lives in the memory like the incidents, characters and scenes of the *First Part.*" (p. 551) To those who argue that in the second part the shift from the individual to the universal necessitates symbolism of the kind Goethe utilizes, Lewes replied: ". . . To conduct Faust into a higher region it was not necessary to . . . sacrifice beauty to meaning. The defect of this poem does not lie in its occult meanings, but in the poverty of the life which those meanings are meant to animate." (p. 551)

Thus by the time Lewes wrote his *Life of Goethe,* he was using realism as an important critical term. Fortunately, it was to replace the earlier confusing Hegelian terminology. Realism was to be the standard he consistently employed in his criticism of the novel and the drama.

4

Lewes as a Critic of the Novel

Lewes' criticism of the novel is of special interest because of his relationship to George Eliot. However, his writings on the novel warrant attention for their own sake, for they reveal him at his critical peak. Although his own career as a novelist was short lived, the invaluable firsthand experience he must have gained made him aware of the special difficulties involved in writing fiction.

Ranthorpe, his first novel, was written in 1842 and published in 1847. Percy Ranthorpe, the young hero, is a clerk who wishes to gain literary glory as a poet. His betrothed, Isola Churchill, delays their marriage to enable him to achieve his aims. When his poetry is published, he becomes the "lion" of society. Overwhelmed by his success, he neglects his work and, infatuated with the coquette Florence Wilmington, begins to regret his engagement to Isola. When Isola learns of his love for Florence, she nobly renounces him and begins a lonely existence, solaced only by her efforts at painting, her means of earning a living. Meanwhile, Ranthorpe, who has been rejected by Florence, leads a dissolute life. His second book of poems is criticized severely, and he is sorely in need of money. Harry Cavendish, a medical student, befriends him; and while living with Harry, Percy writes a play which proves to be a dismal failure when it is performed. Ranthorpe is prevented from committing suicide by Richard Thornton, an old man who encourages him and employs him as his secretary. Thornton is killed by his nephew, Oliver, and Ranthorpe is accused of the crime. However, Harry Cavendish discovers that Oliver is the real murderer. While Ranthorpe is in Germany, Cavendish meets Isola and falls in love with her. She promises to marry him, although she still loves Ranthorpe. When Ranthorpe returns to England, he settles down in earnest to pursue his literary career. Realizing that Isola and Percy still love each other, Cavendish gives up Isola who marries Percy; eventually Cavendish finds happiness with another woman. Florence Wilmington retires to a convent after marrying Lord Hawbucke whom she hates.

Both Edgar Allan Poe and Charlotte Brontë praised Lewes for revealing in this novel a true feeling for the high aims and dignity of literature.[1] It contains scenes which describe effectively the trials of the poet and dramatist and the pitfalls of a literary career in London. The novel is of interest to the literary historian since it is probably the first of its kind to portray literary life in London. But the truth is that Poe and Brontë were much too charitable in their evaluation of *Ranthorpe.* It is a mediocre work; the main characters are not lifelike, and Ranthorpe never materializes into more than the shadowy type of aspiring literary figure.

The plot of *Rose, Blanche, and Violet* (1848) concerns the romances of the three Vyner sisters referred to in the title. Their father, Meredith Vyner, a stuffy pedant who is preparing an edition of Horace, marries the young and lovely Mary Hardcastle shortly after his wife's death. Mary had promised to marry Marmaduke Ashley after his return from Brazil, but instead she marries Vyner for his wealth and position. Jealous of her step-daughters, she sends them away to school, and upon their return three years later, the following complications ensue. Marmaduke returns from Brazil and becomes a house guest of the Vyners, planning revenge for Mary's rejection. Cecil Chamberlayne, another house guest, a weak but charming wastrel, aspires to be both artist and rich gentleman. At first Cecil falls in love with Violet, a dark, tall, strong-minded beauty, but their relationship is ruined when he reveals his cowardly nature. Cecil then turns to the humble and sweet Blanche who loves him. Blanche is loved by Captain Heath, an old friend of the family, who attempts to

[1] J. H. Ingram (ed.), *Edgar Allan Poe: His Life, Letters, and Opinions* (London, 1880), II, 205; C. Shorter (ed.), *The Brontës: Life and Letters* (London, 1908), I, 367-68.

dissuade her from marrying the weak Cecil. Cecil, somewhat hesitant about marrying Blanche when he learns that she is to receive no money from her parents, is finally motivated by jealousy of Captain Heath to elope with her. They live in poor but clean lodgings in a rooming house in London where Cecil begins to paint. Meanwhile, Marmaduke and Violet have fallen in love while the lively, witty, and intelligent Rose has become attached to Julius St. John, Marmaduke's friend. Julius is short and ugly, but kind and intelligent. When he finally summons up enough courage to ask her to marry him, Rose, out of sheer playfulness, makes him think she has rejected him. Before she can admit that she really loves him, Julius leaves for Italy.

Mary Vyner, by now thoroughly bored with her husband, attempts to regain Marmaduke's love. Marmaduke pretends that he loves her, but his better nature finally forces him to abandon his plan for revenge. Violet refuses to marry Marmaduke because of her scruples about his past relationship to her stepmother. Cecil gives up his painting for a dissolute life of gambling. He meets Hester Mason, an ambitious, unconventional woman, the mistress of an old lord, Sir Chetsom Chetsom. She loves Cecil but decides to become Sir Chetsom's wife when she realizes that Cecil really loves Blanche. Unfortunately, Sir Chetsom dies suddenly before the marriage, and Hester is left penniless. Unsuccessful as a writer she becomes a prostitute. Desperately in need of money Cecil forges a check, and when he loses all his money gambling, he commits suicide. Mary Vyner runs away with her cruel, egotistical lover, George Maxwell, whom she leaves after he mistreats her. She writes to Meredith, but she never receives the letter in which he offers to take her back. She is seen again once, miserably dressed and aged by suffering. In the end, Julius marries Rose, Marmaduke marries Violet, and Captain Heath gets his Blanche.

Dickens praised the novel highly, but Carlyle, with more critical acumen wrote in his wife's copy of *Rose, Blanche, and Violet*, "A book of some talent and much folly—Je suis plus fou que toi!"[2] In 1875 Lewes himself reread the novel with "unpleasant sensa-

[2] W. Dexter (ed.), *The Letters of Charles Dickens* (London, 1938), II, 90; Mrs. Carlyle's book is in the Berg Collection, New York Public Library.

tions."[3] Small wonder that he did, for it contains many silly, melodramatic scenes, replete with learned quotations in Greek, Latin, Italian, Spanish, French, and German. Lewes editorializes excessively, and as a result, as Charlotte Brontë shrewdly observed, he himself seems to be the most important character in the novel. However, as a reviewer observed in the *British Quarterly Review*, its pages are "always lively, often witty, never dull."[4]

Meredith Vyner is somewhat reminiscent of the stuffy pedant of *Middlemarch*, but he is a more humorous and kindly Casaubon. Perhaps the most interesting character is Julius St. John who seems to be a projection of Lewes' personality. Such identification is at best tenuous, but anyone familiar with the descriptions of Lewes cannot fail to note the similarity. Both are short, ugly men who charm by means of intellect, wit, and kindness. Julius loves a girl named Rose, and in the *Leader* Lewes referred to his wife as "a human Rose."[5] The satire of such types as Sir Chetsom Chetsom, Mrs. Langley Turner, Tom Wincot, Miss Harridale and Lord Boodle is mildly amusing. The novel contains clever drawing room conversations and clever observations on drama, music, philology, literature, architecture, and politics. For these reasons, it is easy to understand Leslie Stephens' preference for *Rose, Blanche, and Violet,* although it is unquestionably as mediocre a novel as *Ranthorpe.*[6]

Lewes also wrote the unfinished *Apprenticeship of Life*, and several short tales, such as "The Great Tragedian," "Metamorphoses," "Mrs. Beauchamp's Vengeance," "The Forester's Grave," "Lesurques; or the Victim of Judicial Error," "Falsely Accused," and "Murders at Deutz."[7] When, in 1878, William Blackwood wrote to Lewes requesting permission to reprint two of his stories, Lewes answered: ". . . I have the strongest objection to avowing their authorship, as I have so long seen that Fiction is not my

[3] Lewes' *Diary,* December 6, 1875.

[4] BQR, VII (1848), 332-46; Shorter, I, 409-12.

[5] *Leader,* June 15, 1850, 258.

[6] *Dictionary of National Biography,* XI (1937-38), 1044.

[7] *Leader,* March 30-June 8, 1850, 16-18, 42-44, 67-68, 114-15, 139-41, 163-65, 187-89, 211-13, 236-37, 260-61; *Blackwood's,* LXIV (1848), 345-58; LXXIX (1856), 562-78, 676, 691; LXXX (1856), 61-76; LXXXIX (1861), 537-54; LIII (1843), 24-32; LXXXV (1859), 208-22; *Fraser's Magazine,* LVIII (1858), 411-22.

Forte; and moreover the writer of heavy philosophical works ought not to appear in pubic as a writer of light tales!"[8]

When Lewes objected to the light tale, he meant the *second rate* tale. For unlike many reviewers of his time who regarded the novel condescendingly as an inferior form of literature primarily witten to entertain female readers, he was always conscious of the novel as a serious art form. In 1847 he placed good novels in the first rank of literature.[9] In 1865 he deplored the "presumptuous facility and *facundia* of indolent novelists," and urged critics to help achieve "a more serious conception of the art, and a more earnest effort to make novels . . . in all respects conformable to sense and artistic truth."[10] Not only did he criticize the view which regarded the novel as a formless, aimless type of literature to be employed merely for the gratification of individual eccentricities, but he also insisted that the novel be recognized as a distinct art, different from the other arts in function and form. He defined the art of the novelist specifically as involving the "representation of human life by means of a story. . . ."[11] In his view, the plot is only the means to an end; the end is always the representation of human life. To the artist "human life is the end and aim."[12] Moreover, the novel in its best form demands a *real* representation of human life. While certain novels have value primarily as entertainments or moral treatises, they are inferior to that type which attempts to realize the highest function of art by revealing some aspect of human experience truthfully.[13] Novelists who are accused of writing unreal works may excuse themselves with the truism "Truth is stranger than Fiction." They may insist that unbelievable experiences actually do occur. According to Lewes, such reasoning is invalid, for although truth is stranger than fiction, art by its very nature refuses to countenance such an excuse. Just as in real life a knowledge of all the details involved in a strange circumstance makes what originally seemed improbable probable, in fiction it is the author's

8 GE, VII, 43.

9 "Recent Novels: French and English," *Fraser's Magazine,* XXXVI (1847), 686.

10 "Criticism in Relation to Novels," FR, III (1866), 361.

11 "The Novels of Jane Austen," *Blackwood's,* LXXXVI (1859), 101.

12 *Life of Goethe,* 513.

13 "The Lady Novelists," WR, LVIII (1852), 130; cf. also FR, IV (1866), 637.

responsibility to create the kind of detail which will transform the improbable into the probable. Otherwise, a novelist might with impunity justify any extravagance or absurdity by contending that, since truth is stranger than fiction, fiction does not have to distinguish between the possible and the impossible.[14]

Obviously Lewes championed realism in the novel: "Only those works which are distinguished by any felicity of realism in their treatment are capable of conveying any durable pleasure to the cultivated reader, and this in exact proportion to the truthfulness of the treatment."[15] Again he wrote: "Either give us true peasants, or leave them untouched; either paint no drapery at all, or paint it with the utmost fidelity; either keep your people silent, or make them speak the idiom of their class."[16] But how much did he mean the term *realism* to signify? If the novelist is to portray life truthfully, is he free to describe *any* experience? Lewes referred contemptuously to the gross being whose sensualism is aroused by art. He said, "It is quite true that nude statues and voluptuous verses may be the suggestion of 'animalism'; but their natural effect upon all healthy minds we take to be analogous to . . . that insensible, inappreciable sexual feeling which lies at the bottom of the tenderness and reverence we feel for all women, whether we love them or not."[17] This frank observation seems to imply that Lewes considered any experience to be valid subject matter for art. But the kind of realism he sanctioned was limited by his belief that "Realism in Art has Truth as an aim, Ugliness as a pitfall."[18] He wrote, "I am not prudish, nor easily alarmed by what are called 'dangerous' subjects. . . . The *banale* excuse that 'such things are,' is no justification: every hospital has its horrible realities, which it must keep from the public eye, and which Art refuses to acknowledge as materials."[19] Thus Lewes believed in a modified realism. No doubt he would not have approved of the modern naturalistic novel which deals with certain horrible realities. He would have maintained that

14 *Leader,* November 27, 1852, 1141-42.
15 "Realism in Art: Recent German Fiction," WR, LXX (1858), 518.
16 *Ibid.,* 493.
17 *Leader,* January 17, 1852, 60.
18 *Ibid.,* April 27, 1850, 111.
19 *Ibid.,* April 2, 1853, 333.

through emphasizing the sordid and the ugly, such a novel fails to engage the sympathies of man.

One other element of Lewes' theory of realism deserves special notice, namely, his insistence on psychological characterization. Since the aim of the novelist is the truthful depiction of human life, he must understand the nature of character to be "of a mingled woof, good and evil, virtue and weakness, truth and falsehood, woven inextricably together."[20] Character, dependent upon both heredity and environment, "is to outward Circumstance what the Organism is to the outward world: living *in* it, but not especially determined *by* it. A wondrous variety of vegetable and animal organisms live and flourish under circumstances which furnish the means of living, but do not determine the *specific forms* of each organism. In the same way various characters live under identical circumstances nourished by them, not formed by them. . . . Every biologist knows that circumstance has a modifying influence; but he also knows that modifications are only possible within certain limits."[21] The true artist, who understands the roles of heredity and environment in the shaping of character, recognizes that character is not formed but modified by circumstance. The story he writes describes the relationship between character and circumstance; "A story is the result of character acting upon circumstance, and of circumstance acting upon character."[22] Since a novel depicts the interaction of subject and object, the novelist should combine the faculty of objective representation with a "strong power of subjective representation . . . We do not simply mean the power over the passions—the psychological intuition of the artist, but the power also of connecting external appearances with internal effects—of representing the psychological interpretation of material phenomena."[23] This ability to correlate the external manifestation of character with its internal equivalent achieves "true psychology in a novel [which] consists in the presentation of the actual emotions, mo-

20 *Life of Goethe,* 513.
21 *Ibid.,* 20.
22 "The Rise and Fall of the European Drama," *Foreign Quarterly Review,* XXXV (1845), 328.
23 "Recent Novels," *Fraser's Magazine,* XXXXVI (1847), 693.

tives, and thoughts at work in the action of the drama."[24] The novelist usually finds it easiest to describe these "actual emotions, motives, and thoughts," but the more difficult and the more effective method is dramatic representation of character or, as Lewes termed it, "dramatic ventriloquism," the means by which the writer makes the character reveal himself through his own actions and words.

However, novels that fulfill the requirements of psychological realism do not necessarily have equal value in Lewes' judgment. He assigned the highest value to those works which contain the most profound experiences and wisdom. In 1847 he designated the necessary requirements of a novelist as "perception of character, and power of delineating it; picturesqueness, passion; and knowledge of life."[25] According to Lewes, the novel in its ideal form must also reflect the author's poetic (picturesqueness), emotional (passion), and intellectual (knowledge of life) sensibilities. Now intellectual or poetic substance will not necessarily make a novel better, but it may give it higher value. A novel perfect in execution of plot and delineation of character with a limited range might be an excellent work, but it would not be the highest art because it would not appeal to the highest faculties. The more difficult the nature of the art, the more genius it requires. Thus novels containing complex themes demanding culture and knowledge are more difficult to write than simple stories devoid of intellectual content. However, perfection in any form, whether it be simple or complex, is not easy to attain; certainly more genius is needed to create a simple, beautiful lyric than a complex, mediocre tragedy. Analogously, it is harder to write a simple but perfect novel of character than a pretentious novel filled with bad philosophy and imperfect knowledge.[26]

Lewes also commented on the form of the novel. Since one of the general principles which works of art must follow is the rule of organic unity, the parts of a novel should have organic relations. To achieve organic unity, the novel must obey the law of economy which requires the "rejection of whatever is superfluous." By superfluity Lewes meant those elements which detract

[24] "Realism in Art," WR, LXX (1858), 499.
[25] "Recent Novels," *Fraser's Magazine*, XXXVI (1847), 691.
[26] "Jane Austen," *Blackwood's*, LXXXVI (1859), 109.

from the end that the novel seeks to fulfill; for example, the use of symbols which mislead or confuse the reader. But, while the general rule demands organic unity, the technical principles of a particular art form may permit modifications of that rule. Unlike the dramatist, the novelist is not hampered by time and the public's impatience: he can, therefore, prudently introduce digressive descriptions, dialogues, and events, without seriously endangering the effective development of his story. However, he does not enjoy unlimited freedom, for the peculiar requirements of the novel impose certain restraints upon him. If he combines an unrelated group of chapters, no one will consider his potpourri a novel, and the more unorganized it is, the less effect it will have on the emotions of the reader. Lewes wrote of Goethe's indifference to form in the novel, "I must frankly say, that either from want of constructive instinct, or from an indolent and haughty indifference towards the public, [Goethe's] novels are quite unworthy of a great artist in point of *composition.* He seems to have regarded them as vehicles for the expression of certain views, rather than as organic wholes."[27]

It is important to note that Lewes was not rigidly committed to a theory of realism. He was aware that the novel legitimately assumes many different forms. It is to his credit that he wrote appreciatively of *Wuthering Heights* and *Moby Dick.* Allen R. Brick has praised Lewes for being "the first eminent critic to grant the strange novel, [*Wuthering Heights*], which revolted many, its due regard." In the *Leader*, in 1850, Lewes wrote the following lines about this novel:

> And yet, although there is a want of air and light in the picture we cannot deny its truth; sombre, rude, brutal, yet true. The fierce ungoverned instincts of powerful organizations, bred up amidst violence, revolt, and moral apathy, are here seen in operation: such brutes we should all be, or the most of us, were our lives as insubordinate to law; were our affections and sympathies as little cultivated, our imaginations as undirected. And herein lies the moral of the book. . . .
>
> Heathcliff, devil though he be, is drawn with a sort of dusky splendour which fascinates, and we feel the truth of

[27] *Ibid.*, 101-2; *Principles,* 138; *Life of Goethe,* 516.

> his burning and impassioned love for Catherine, and of her inextinguishable love for him. Edgar is the husband she has chosen . . . but although she is ashamed of her early playmate, she loves him with a passionate abandonment which sets culture, education, the world at defiance. It is in the treatment of this subject that Ellis Bell shows real mastery, and it shows more genius, in the highest sense of the word, than you will find in a thousand novels.[28]

An even more striking example of Lewes' critical flexibility and discernment is to be found in his laudation of *Moby Dick* in a review in the 1851 *Leader*. Referring to the "thrilling" pages of this book, he wrote: "[Moby Dick] is not a romance, nor a treatise on Etology. It is something of both: a strange, wild work with the tangled overgrowth and luxuriant vegetation of American forests, not the trim orderliness of an English park. Criticism may pick many holes in this work; but no criticism will thwart its fascination."[29]

However, it is true that Lewes generally reserved his highest praise for the kind of novel which fulfills the requirements of psychological realism. Among his favorite continental novelists were Goethe, George Sand, Balzac, and Turgenev. But Lewes took Balzac to task for employing an extreme type of realism. Although he was infinitely superior to Dumas and Hugo, Balzac was guilty of distorting reality when he repetitiously permitted the cunning and the wicked to defeat the virtuous. As for the English novelists, Lewes' admiration for Fielding, Charlotte Brontë, and Dickens was mitigated by what he considered their deficiency in realistic characterization. Fielding satirized manners, not people; Charlotte Brontë, who had the power to be realistic when she described her own experiences, was too often melodramatic and affected; Dickens with his remarkably vivid imagination created unforgettable types, but they were essentially caricatures rather than real, complex human beings. Thackeray was primarily the satirist rather than the novelist, but in Becky Sharp and other characters, he revealed his ability to portray real personalities. Lewes' criticism of Jane Austen was

[28] *Leader*, December 28, 1850, 953; see also Allen R. Brick, "Lewes's Review of *Wuthering Heights*," *Nineteenth Century Fiction*, XIV (1960), 355.

[29] *Leader*, November 8, 1851, 1068; Kitchel, 106.

the most laudatory in tone: "As an artist, Miss Austen surpasses all the male novelists that ever lived. . . ."[30] But her emotional and intellectual range was too limited. What seems to be Lewes' only published comment on the art of George Eliot is to be found in his 1859 essay on Jane Austen: "Mr. George Eliot [is] a writer who seems to us inferior to Miss Austen in the art of telling a story, and generally in what we have called the 'economy of art'; but equal in truthfulness, dramatic ventriloquism, and humour, and greatly superior in culture, reach of mind, and depth of emotional sensibility."[31]

Lewes' personal involvement with George Eliot provided him with the golden opportunity to play the role of critical pygmalion. It is generally known that he helped her to develop as an artist by offering her sympathy and affection. But the real nature of his influence has not been determined. In 1883 George W. Cooke based Chapter VII of his biography of George Eliot on the premise that she had written the 1852 article on "The Lady Novelists," in the *Westminster Review*. He quoted extensively from this work to illustrate her theory of the novel. When he subsequently discovered that Lewes was its author, he did not revise Chapter VII in the second edition of his biography because he noted that Lewes' theories in the 1852 paper were substantially those of George Eliot.[32] Ignoring Lewes' 1852 essay, Mathilde Blind reasoned that since the opinions Lewes expressed in 1858 in his "Realism in Art: Recent German Fiction" were identical with George Eliot's ideas, Lewes' views on the novel were influenced by George Eliot's powerful intellect.[33] P. Bourl'honne was the first critic to suggest the contrary. He observed that the ideas in Lewes' 1852 and 1858 articles were similar, and

30 "The Lady Novelists," WR, LVIII (1852), 133. According to Oscar Browning, *Life of George Eliot* (London, 1890), 126, Lewes considered Turgenev "the greatest living novelist." Lewes praised George Meredith as a writer of genius when he reviewed *The Shaving of Shagpat,* in the *Saturday Review,* January 19, 1856, 216.

31 "Jane Austen," *Blackwood's,* LXXXVI (1859), 104. The discussion on pages 96 to 112 is reprinted by permission of the Modern Language Association from A.R. Kaminsky's "George Eliot, George Henry Lewes, and the Novel," *PMLA,* LXX (1955), 907-1013.

32 *George Eliot, A Critical Study of Her Life, Writings and Philosophy* (2nd ed.; Boston, 1883), Pref. and Chap. VII; "Lady Novelists," WR, LVIII (1852), 129-41.

33 *George Eliot* (Boston, 1904), 89 ff.; "Realism in Art," WR, LXX (1858), 488-518.

he therefore argued that George Eliot was indebted to Lewes for her discussion of the novel in 1856 in "The Natural History of German Life: Riehl."[34] Furthermore, he found in Lewes' two essays the essentials of George Eliot's aesthetic doctrine and he concluded: "On peut donc penser que Lewes a joué un grand rôle dans l'élaboration de cette doctrine, bien que nous n'ayons rencontré nulle part une confirmation formelle de cette conjecture."[35]

George Eliot knew Lewes as an influential critic before she made his personal acquaintance. In 1851 she wrote to her friends: "Herbert Spencer . . . has just brought out a large work on 'Social Statics' which Lewes pronounces the best book he has seen on the subject."[36] At that time Lewes had already gained a wide reputation through his *Biographical History of Philosophy* and his novels. At her request he wrote "The Lady Novelists" for the *Westminster Review*; in 1852 she told Sara Hennell: "Lewes has written us an agreeable article on Lady Novelists." (I, 230) In it Lewes analyzed woman's contribution to literature as an aesthetic representation of specifically feminine forms of suffering. He advised lady novelists to avoid imitating the writings of men and to draw upon the truths of their own experiences. He also distinguished between the legitimate and illegitimate employment of experience: "The author is bound to use actual experience as his material, or else to keep silent; but he is equally bound by all moral and social considerations not to use that experience in such forms that the public will recognise it. . . ."[37] George Eliot similarly pleaded for better and more truth-

[34] *George Eliot: essai de biographie intellectuelle et morale 1819-1854* (Paris, 1933), 156 ff; George Eliot, "The Natural History of German Life: Riehl," WR, LXVI (1856), 51-79. Much of Bourl'honne's study is vitiated by his rather unfortunate penchant for amateur psychoanalysis which leads him to make questionable assertions about the relationship between Lewes and George Eliot.

[35] P. Bourl'honne, 157-58. Morris Greenhut in "George Henry Lewes as a Critic of the Novel," SP, XLV (1948), 491-511, made the first noteworthy attempt to appraise Lewes' theory of fiction, but he was not concerned with correlating Lewes' and George Eliot's ideas on the novel.

[36] J.W. Cross (ed.), *George Eliot's Life as Related in Her Letters and Journals* (3 vols., Cabinet Ed., Edinburgh and London [1855], I, 210). All references to this edition are incorporated into the text and appear within parentheses. Lewes reviewed *Social Statics* in the *Leader* in 1851, March 15, 248-50, March 22, 274-75, and April 12, 347-48.

[37] "The Lady Novelists," WR, LVIII (1852), 139. Basil Willey, *Nineteenth Century Studies* (New York, 1949), 245, credits Lewes with propounding in

ful lady novelists in an essay, "Silly Novels by Lady Novelists" (1856), in the *Westminster Review*.[38] In *Fraser's Magazine* (1847) Lewes had counseled Charlotte Brontë, upon whom he exerted a significant influence: "Has the author seen much more and felt much more than what is . . . communicated? Then let new works continue to draw from that rich storehouse. Has the author led a quiet, secluded life; uninvolved in the great vortex of the world . . . ? Then let new works be planned and executed with excessive circumspection; for unless a novel be built out of real experience, it can have no real success. To have vitality, it must spring from vitality."[39] The truth of such observations must have struck George Eliot with singular force, for when she began her career as a novelist she wrote about the world she knew.

In her letters and journals she gave clear evidence of how highly she valued his critical ability. Perhaps the obviousness of her remarks about Lewes' influence has led critics to ignore their implications. When she explained how Lewes first urged her to write fiction, she revealed her desire to attain his standards. "His prevalent impression was, that though I could hardly write a *poor* novel, my effort would want the highest quality of fiction —dramatic presentation. He used to say, 'You have wit, description, and philosophy—these go a good way towards the production of a novel.'" (I, 336-337) After Lewes read the first part of *Amos Barton*, he was convinced of her ability to write dialogue. Then she acted on his suggestion that she use a story told her by her Aunt Elizabeth Evans as a plot for a novel. She recalled that she never mentioned this tale "till something prompted me to tell it to George in December, 1856. . . . He remarked that

advance of his time, in "The Lady Novelists," "a psychoanalytic theory of artistic creation, that it is a resolution of, and compensation for, the artist's inward conflicts and dissatisfactions." Willey is here repeating Bourl'honne's view, but they both seem to read more into Lewes' remarks than is warranted. Whether Lewes conceived of all of literature as a cathartic release from suffering is not made explicit in his criticism. He discussed the influence of sorrow in relation to certain subjective writers such as George Sand and Charlotte Brontë, but not with regard to an objective artist like Jane Austen. After all, Lewes said only that "almost all literature has some remote connexion with suffering" (WR, LVIII [1852], 133 and 105).

38 George Eliot, "Silly Novels," WR, LXVI (1856), 442-61. George Eliot was as merciless in her satire of several ridiculous novels as was Lewes in his criticism of worthless books. In the *Leader*, September 27, 1851, 925, he noted that Lady Dormer in her novel, *Lady Selina Crawford*, "has nothing to say—and says it."

39 "Recent Novels," *Fraser's Magazine*, XXXVI (1847), 691.

the scene in the prison would make a fine element in a story; and I afterwards began to think of blending this and some other recollections of my aunt in one story, with some points in my father's early life and character." (II, 53-54) Several changes in *Adam Bede* were the direct result of his recommendations: "Dinah's ultimate relation to Adam was suggested by George, when I had read to him the first part of the first volume; he was so delighted with the presentation of Dinah, and so convinced that the readers' interest would centre in her, that he wanted her to be the principal figure at the last. I accepted the idea at once, and from the end of the third chapter worked with it constantly in view." (II, 55) After Lewes expressed his fear that Adam's part was too passive and suggested that he be brought into more direct collision with Arthur, George Eliot introduced the fight scene between Adam and Arthur.

Lewes' interest in *Silas Marner* gave her confidence of its value and she wrote: "I should not have believed that any one would have been interested in it but myself (since Wordsworth is dead) if Mr. Lewes had not been strongly arrested by it." (II, 246-247) In 1861 Lewes approved her decision to write *Romola*, a different kind of novel: "Mr. Lewes has encouraged me to persevere in the project, saying that I should probably do something in historical romance rather different in character from what has been done before." (II, 229) She published her "slight tale" *Brother Jacob*, "which G. thinks worth printing." (II, 231) Moreover, she actually stopped work on *The Spanish Gypsy* in 1865 "at Mr. Lewes's request, after writing four acts, precisely because it was in that state of creation—or *Werden*—in which the idea of the characters predominates over the incarnation." (II, 376) Work on the drama was resumed when Lewes advised her to "take it up again with a view to recasting it. He thinks hopefully of it." (III, 13) He suggested that she write a shorter poem: "Mr. Lewes has prevailed on me to return to my original conception, and give up the additional development, which I determined on subsequently." (III, 33) After she finished each novel, she invariably mentioned how delighted Lewes was with her effort, and she inscribed the manuscripts of her books to him in language that became more endearing with each successive dedication. In such remarks as "Walked with G. We talked of my Italian novel"

(II, 265), and "I read aloud what I had written of Part IX to George, and he, to my surprise, entirely approved of it," (II, 294) she revealed her need for his critical discernment and sympathy. When she sent the manuscript of *Felix Holt* to Frederic Harrison to obtain verification of its legal aspects, she told him, "Hitherto I have read my MS. (I mean of my previous books) to Mr. Lewes, by forty or fifty pages at a time, and he has told me if he felt an objection to anything. No one else has had any knowledge of my writings before their publication. (I except, of course, the publishers)." (II, 359) In 1871 she confided in Alexander Main: "If I had not had a husband who is not only sympathetic, but so sagacious in criticism that I can rely on his pleasure in my writing as a satisfactory test, it would be difficult for me to bring myself into print." (III, 122) Finally, in 1875 she made a similar comment in a letter to Charles Ritter: "If it were not for his [Lewes'] firmness of opinion as to the worth of what is already written, I could not carry out my intention. In this way he has always supported me—by his unreserved sympathy and the independence of his judgment."[40] Thus she herself made it quite clear that she got more than emotional support from Lewes.

It is apparent that George Eliot respected and utilized Lewes' criticism. What has been overlooked is the important fact that she could have done so only if she agreed with the fundamentals of his theory of the novel. She shared Lewes' belief in the social and moral value of literature. In 1856, she described the function of art in terms that closely resemble those used by Lewes in 1852, in "The Lady Novelists": "Art . . . is a mode of amplifying experience and extending our contact with our fellow men beyond the bounds of our personal lot. . . . The greatest benefit we owe to the artist, whether painter, poet, or novelist, is the extension of our sympathies."[41] This view of literature as the means by which the sympathies of humanity are broadened serves as the *raison d'être* of all her novels. As Bourl'honne observed: "Lewes pose en principe que la plus haute fonction de la littérature est d'amener les individus à pénétrer plus profondément dans leur commune humanité et à se mieux comprendre les uns les autres; c'est à la lettre près, la théorie de l'art, source de sympathie uni-

40 GE, VI, 109.
41 "Riehl," WR, LXVI (1856), 56, 54.

verselle et d'unité morale entre les hommes que G. Eliot a reprise et illustrée avec tout d'éclat."[42] Admittedly, in selecting the social and psychological realities which best illustrated her point of view, George Eliot did not always escape the pitfall of didacticism. But at least in theory she agreed with Lewes that the writer must avoid sacrificing reality in order to prove a moral thesis. If teaching in art, she wrote, "ceases to be purely aesthetic—if it lapses anywhere from the picture to the diagram—it becomes the most offensive of all teaching." (II, 375).

After Lewes persuaded her to employ the medium of the novel for the realization of her aims, she clearly was concerned with the requirements he stipulated. He had demanded, "Either give us true peasants or leave them untouched." And she gave us true peasants in her first novel. In Chapter XVII of *Adam Bede,* she told her reader, "I am content to tell my simple story, without trying to make things seem better than they were; dreading nothing, indeed, but falsity." Ben Euwema conjectured that her interest in German scientists and her knowledge of new art movements caused her to include the highly self-conscious discussion of realism in Chapter XVII.[43] But its presence is more likely due to the influence of Lewes who constantly emphasized the need for realism and the need for the avoidance of falsism. In the *Athenaeum* in 1848, Lewes praised George Sand for making a strong effort in *François le Champi* "to recal [sic] novelists to a right sense of their office, and bring back their vagabond imaginations to the proper starting-point—Nature. . . . Persuaded that the nearer artists approach to Nature the more perfect will be their Art, she undertakes in 'François le Champi' to interest the public by a narrative of the simplest every-day events, told in the simple language of the people."[44] Lewes might have used these words to describe the achievement of George Eliot in her early novels.

She interpreted realism in the same modified sense as Lewes. She avoided the depiction of certain truths which she considered to be unsuitable for artistic treatment. But the aim and end of all

[42] Bourl'honne, *op. cit.,* 156.

[43] *The Development of George Eliot's Ethical and Social Theories* (Dissertation, University of Chicago, 1934), 51.

[44] *Athenaeum,* May 20, 1848, 502.

her novels is a realistic representation of human life which she achieved by utilizing the psychological realism that Lewes favored. Moreover, her novels illustrate his distinction between realism and idealism. In *Adam Bede, The Mill on the Floss,* and *Silas Marner* she aimed to portray human actions sympathetically in relation to a comparatively simple environment with which she was personally familiar. But her aims became more ambitious as her artistic and intellectual faculties were stimulated and challenged by success. She became concerned with depicting human behavior in relation to a complex environment with which she was not personally familiar, as in the case of *Romola* and *Daniel Deronda.* Because the "Dutch realism" she used in her first three novels could not convey adequately the deeper truths of the higher mental life that she wished to describe, she felt the need for a special kind of realism which would expose more satisfactorily spiritual realities and their relationship to social, political, and religious conditions. In this connection, Lewes' conception of idealism helps to clarify her method in the later novels in a way that has not been explained before. She used idealism in his sense as a special form of realism. Adam Bede and Daniel Deronda are both unusually good human beings. For the creation of Adam, a simple personality, the realistic strokes of homely realism were sufficient. But for the creation of Deronda, a complex figure whose fate is interwoven wtih the destiny of the Jewish people, idealism was a more adequate technique. George Eliot idealized Deronda by assigning to his character the quality of "exquisite goodness," because she wished the reader to believe in the beauty of his mental life. He represents the aspiration of the human soul to achieve the highest good, and thus illustrates what was to George Eliot a deeply felt, spiritual reality. Those who criticize Deronda, Romola, Savonarola, and other characters in the later novels as inferior products of George Eliot's realism must take into consideration an important distinction. The difference between the early and later novels is not merely one of *quality* but of *kind* of realism. If there is aesthetic justification for her idealism, it is to be found in Lewes' interpretation of realism and idealism.

George Eliot also placed as much value upon psychological characterization as Lewes did. Leaving behind her the flat kind of character portrayal which vitiated the novels of most of her contemporaries, she presented her people "in mingled woof," to use Lewes' terminology, showing the effect of outward events on inward life. She said specifically, "My artistic bent is directed not at all to the presentation of eminently irreproachable characters, but to the presentation of mixed human beings in such a way as to call forth tolerant judgement, pity, and sympathy." (I, 349) Hence she rendered the feelings and thoughts of even the most reprehensible characters with the utmost compassion. Bulstrode is a hypocrite; but never before Bulstrode had a hypocrite been described in like fashion, so that the reader could dislike his deceptive nature, yet sympathize with and even pity the human weakness which produces the peculiar combination of greed and piety in him. To compare Pecksniff and Bulstrode is to compare caricature with character. Casaubon personifies the pedantic scholar, but while his aridity and narrowness of soul are psychologically analyzed with clinical precision, the pathos and tragedy inherent in his situation are at the same time profoundly and sympathetically revealed. Even though George Eliot obviously disapproved of the vanity of Hetty Sorrel, she recorded Hetty's suffering compassionately, communicating the universal, human feelings inherent in her tragedy. George Eliot's all-embracing sympathy imbued events with a significance that has been derogated as overly moral. But far from being the school teacher like Richardson, who offered his readers a standard of conventional morality, she was the teacher of a morality profoundly and philosophically complex in its awareness of the subtleties in the relationship between character and environment. Like Lewes, she was conscious of the role of heredity and environment in the molding of character; she was aware that environment can have only a modifying influence upon inherited organic structure. Therefore, she never permitted her people to undergo radical transformations; instead she demonstrated how the modifying effects of environment develop and actualize the basic tendencies in personality. Even in *Silas Marner,* which is essentially a fairy tale despite its realistic details, she prepared the reader for the appearance and disappearance of Silas' miserliness by showing how external events impinge upon his consciousness to develop latent tendencies in his nature.

Ironically enough, in the few instances when Lewes' influence on George Eliot's theory of the novel was noticed, he was usually blamed for fostering the defective elements in her art. Bourl'-honne, who deplored what he considered her subjective obsession with moral problems, held Lewes responsible for encouraging this obsession by his emphasis on personal experience. On the other hand, Mathilde Parlett, who approved of George Eliot's use of personal experience, thought it strange that Lewes "did not use his unbounded influence to enforce George Eliot's adherence to this principle when she wished to try the experiment of making philosophical abstractions incarnate."[45] Both Parlett and Henry James disliked the preponderance of reflection in the later novels. But James, who blamed Lewes for the excessive reflection, wrote: "The truth is perception and reflection at the outset divided George Eliot's great talent between them; but as time went on circumstances led the latter to develop itself at the expense of the former—one of these circumstances being apparently the influence of George Henry Lewes."[46] Thus Lewes was used as a means of explaining the undesirable elements in her work, and depending upon the aesthetic presuppositions of the critic, he was reproved for advocating either the subjectivity of the early novels or the intellectuality of the later ones.

Undoubtedly, Lewes encouraged George Eliot to utilize to the fullest extent her perceptive and reflective faculties. Starting with his premise that a novelist should deal with real experience, she developed as an artist to the point where she realized his ideal of a superior novelist, by supplementing her realistic studies with the ideas of a mind that had thought deeply and wisely. It will be recalled that when Lewes expressed his belief in her ability to write novels, he told her, "You have wit, description, and philosophy." He believed the greatest novelist to be one who combined the fundamental powers of observation with the insights of a cultured and philosophic intellect. Now no one can read George Eliot's writings without being aware of what V.S. Pritchett described as "the clarifying force of a powerful mind."[47]

[45] "The Influence of Contemporary Criticism on George Eliot," *Studies in Philology*, XXX (1933), 107.

[46] Henry James, *Partial Portraits* (London, 1911), 52.

[47] V.S. Pritchett, *The Living Novel* (New York, 1947), 98.

Unquestionably, one of the most widely read women of her age, she exhibited less of her learning in her early work, but she revealed more directly her extraordinary grasp of history, politics, religion, science, philosophy, and literature in the later novels, *Romola, Middlemarch,* and *Daniel Deronda.* Lewes' strong philosophic and scientific interests certainly served to intensify her preoccupation with philosophy and science. For example, he taught her the physiology of the brain in Prague to familiarize her with some form of medical investigation needed in connection with her characterization of Lydgate.[48] He was also responsible for arousing her interest in Comte's philosophy. It was Lewes' chapter on Comte in the *Biographical History of Philosophy* which first led her to read Comte for herself. In 1853 she read the proofs of Lewes' *Comte's Philosophy of the Sciences,* and in a letter to John Chapman, she defended this work against Huxley's criticism.[49] In the following years she and Lewes studied and discussed Comte's ideas; they both admired certain Comtean doctrines.

Perhaps Lewes was aware that her perceptive and reflective insights were sometimes improperly fused. He obviously recognized that an overabundance of intellectualism could have a devitalizing effect upon art when he stated: "Modern Art, as representative of the complexity of Modern Life, demands a large admixture of Reflection; but the predominance of the reflective tendency is a sign of decay."[50] While he considered reflection to be a necessary condition for the creation of a novel, he did not regard it as the most important condition. He criticized Goethe for misusing philosophic speculation in the elaborate and mystifying symbolism of the second part of *Faust* and in *Wilhelm Meister.*

He always insisted on the supreme value of the dramatic quality in fiction. In her first stories George Eliot tried to achieve what he considered the highest power of the novelist's art, dramatic representation of character. But, although Lewes praised her highly in the Jane Austen article, he admitted that she was "inferior to Miss Austen in the art of telling a story, and generally

48 B.C. Williams, *George Eliot: A Biography* (New York, 1936), 99.

49 GE, II, 132-33. For Huxley's article see "Science," WR, LXI (1854), 254-70.

50 *Life of Goethe,* 549. See also the *Leader,* August 31, 1850, 544.

in what we have called the 'economy of art.'" Moreover, to assert that Lewes influenced George Eliot's theory of the novel is not to give him credit for its application, or to deny that she had similar ideas of her own before she met him. There is no *post hoc* reasoning involved here; obviously Lewes could not *cause* Eliot to be a great writer. For the creative act of fusing the varied components of imagination and intellect in her writings, no one was responsible but George Eliot. On the whole, Lewes' principles would tend to have a salutary effect on the writer who was guided by them; in fact, *Middlemarch* is the best example of what a novelist can accomplish who accepts Lewes' theory of fiction. George Eliot's works have been described as "more or less successful approximations to an ideal unwritten novel that haunts her imagination and constitutes her personal vision of human life."[51] This "ideal unwritten novel" was of the same kind that Lewes envisaged in his critical discussions, and with *Middlemarch* she came closest to fulfilling his ideal. *Middlemarch* was her masterpiece because it contained a truly organic fusion of perceptive and reflective elements. This was exactly the kind of fusion Lewes required of the greatest works of fiction.[52]

Lewes also had an interesting critical relationship with another woman novelist, Charlotte Brontë. They began to correspond after Lewes read *Jane Eyre*. He told Mrs. Gaskell: "When *Jane Eyre* first appeared, the publishers courteously sent me a copy. The enthusiasm with which I read it made me go down to Mr. Parker, and propose to write a review of it for *Fraser's Magazine*. He would not consent to an unknown novel—for the papers had not yet declared themselves—receiving such importance, but thought it might make one on 'Recent Novels: English and French,' which appeared in Fraser, December, 1847. Meanwhile I had written to Miss Brontë to tell her the delight with which

51 G. Bullett, *George Eliot: Her Life and Books* (New Haven, 1948), 205.

52 Besides Bourl'honne, Lawrence and Elisabeth Hanson, *Marian Evans & George Eliot: A Biography* (London, 1952), 192; Basil Willey, 245; Weldon Casey, "George Eliot's Theory of Fiction," *Philological Papers West Virginia Univ. Bulletin*, IX (1953), 20-32; William J. Hyde, "George Eliot and the Climate of Realism," *PMLA*, LXXII (1957), 147 n. 4 accept the view that Lewes influenced George Eliot's theory of fiction. For a dissenting view see Gordon S. Haight's review of A. Kaminsky's "George Eliot, George Henry Lewes, and the Novel," *The Victorian Newsletter*, X (1956), 2-3. See also Lionel Stevenson (ed.), *Victorian Fiction: A Guide to Research* (Cambridge, Mass., 1964), 305.

her book filled me; and seem to have 'sermonized' her to judge from her reply."[53] Lewes had warned Charlotte Brontë to beware of melodrama and to rely upon real experience. In her friendly reply she questioned the wisdom of his advice. She believed the real experience of most writers to be very limited, and she insisted upon the potency of the imaginative faculty. Then she wrote to her publisher's reader, W.S. Williams, to inquire about Lewes. Williams' high regard for Lewes, and her reading of *Ranthorpe* made her confident that Lewes was a "just, discriminating man."[54]

Lewes guessed that the author of *Jane Eyre* was a woman, and he praised the novel highly in the review in *Fraser's*. Not only did he find the plot unusually interesting, "naturally evolved, unflagging to the last, but it fastens itself upon your attention, and will not leave you. . . . Reality—deep, significant reality—is the characteristic of the book. . . . The machinery may have been borrowed, but by means of this machinery the authoress is unquestionably setting forth her own experience. This gives her book its charm; it is soul speaking to soul; it is an utterance from the depths of a struggling, suffering, much-enduring spirit. . . ."[55] He praised her psychological insight and her peculiar style, free from artificiality, reflecting her individuality. She handled Jane's childhood at Lowood and much of the strange love story with "remarkable beauty and truth." But Rochester "is the portrait of a man drawn by a woman. . . ." Also too much melodrama and improbability are apparent in the mad wife scenes and during those portions in which Jane wanders after she leaves Thornfield. Lewes ended his review by wondering whether the experience exhibited in *Jane Eyre* reflected artistic mastery over a limited source of materials, and by recommending that future novels be planned with "excessive circumspection."

On January 12, 1848 Charlotte wrote to thank Lewes for the review which pleased her. Impressed by his advice she informed him that she would use "excessive circumspection" in her future novels because she had limited experience and acquirements. However, she was troubled by his admiration for Jane Austen. She

[53] Shorter, *op. cit.*, I, 364-65.
[54] *Ibid.*, 365-66, 368.
[55] "Recent Novels," *Fraser's Magazine*, XXXVI (1847), 691.

felt that *Pride and Prejudice* dealt with a limited world lacking in passion and imagination. She told Lewes that she could respect George Sand but not Miss Austen who was "only shrewd and observant." She was uncertain about whether she wanted to follow Jane Austen's example and become a more finished and subdued artist, for she believed in the potency of inspiration which rejects regulation. In another letter (January 18, 1848) she quoted Lewes as saying: "Miss Austen is not a poetess, has no 'sentiment,' . . . no eloquence, none of the ravishing enthusiasm of poetry, . . . but she is, nevertheless, '*one of the greatest artists,* [one] *of the greatest painters of human character,* and one of the writers with the nicest sense of means to an end that ever lived.' "[56] Charlotte admitted the truth of the last point concerning means and end, but she asked Lewes to forgive her for questioning "the perfection of his darling." Jane Austen had no poetic sensibility and this a great artist had to have. Charlotte closed her letter by promising to read more of Jane Austen's novels. The Hansons have explained why Lewes' opinion of Jane Austen affected Charlotte adversely: "Because Jane Austen contented herself with a limited world, Charlotte assumed her to be without imagination and passion. . . . The possibility that greatness could assume many forms did not apparently occur to her . . . Lewes . . . had touched his correspondent where she was most sensitive. Jane Austen, he said, lacked poetry, lacked sentiment, yet must be reverenced as one of the greatest artists. The implication to Charlotte was plain, if mistaken; Lewes had said in effect that neither poetry nor sentiment was essential to greatness. Yet these qualities were precisely those in which *Jane Eyre* excelled."[57]

After Charlotte published *Shirley* she wrote Lewes that reviewers would be more just if they did not measure her work by what they considered appropriate to the charm and elegance of femininity. In 1850 Lewes reviewed *Shirley* for the *Edinburgh Review.* He began the article with a discussion of the mental equality of the sexes—in other words, with a discussion of the very subject that Charlotte had asked him to avoid. While Lewes admitted that he did not believe in the organic inferiority of women, he did believe in an organic difference. Woman's high

[56] Shorter, *op. cit.*, I, 386-88.
[57] Lawrence and Elisabeth Hanson, *The Four Brontës* (London, 1949), 251-52.

function, he noted, has to be maternity and it prevents her from applying the intense application which science and other fields require. He asked: "What should we do with a leader of opposition in the seventh month of her pregnancy? or a general in chief who at the opening of a campaign was doing as well as could be 'expected'? or a chief justice with twins?"[58] Lewes even disqualified virgins and widows because they usually discovered too late that they were not to be mothers and therefore did not begin training soon enough as artists, scholars or politicians. Even the women who distinguished themselves in literature erred in trying to write like men instead of women. Generally without a sense of humor, they were most successful as writers of fiction when they did not try to imitate men.

Although Lewes praised Currer Bell for being a remarkable female writer, he devoted a good deal of his analysis to pointing out the deficiencies of *Shirley*: *Shirley* lacks artistic fusion, and is nothing more than a "portfolio of random sketches for one or more pictures." The novel moves slowly leaving no distinct impression because the author never decided whether she wanted to write a study of Yorkshire habits and manners, to describe character, or tell a love story. The heroes Robert and Louis Moore have sordid minds and repulsive natures. Shy Caroline sounds like Harriet Martineau when she orates on women's rights. The eloquent tirade against Milton's Eve offered by Shirley is hardly credible as forming the substance of quiet conversation between two young ladies. Mrs. Pryor's motivation for abandoning her daughter is hardly credible. She assumes her daughter will be bad because she is born pretty and therefore she deserts her for eighteen years! The style is also crude and affected because of the frequent and inappropriate intrusion of French phrases. Finally, the reviewer concluded by assuring the author that he took the trouble to indicate her faults only because he believed her to have great talent. He warned her to beware of stepping out of her sex without elevating herself above it.

Although Charlotte had urged Lewes to be frank: "I earnestly conjure you to say honestly what you think . . . ," she did not expect his kind of frankness. She wrote angrily to Lewes: "I can

[58] "Currer Bell's 'Shirley'," *Edinburgh Review*, XCI (1850), 155.

be on my guard against my enemies, but God deliver me from my friends!"[59] When Lewes asked her why she was angry, she answered that his review was objectionable "not because its criticism was keen or its blame sometimes severe; not because its praise was stinted (for, indeed, I think you give me quite as much praise as I deserve), but because after I had said earnestly that I wished critics would judge me as an *author*, not as a woman, you so roughly—I even thought so cruelly—handled the question of sex."[60] She assured him that she bore him no malice for she knew that he was basically a kind, good-natured person. However, in a letter to W.S. Williams (September 5, 1850), she expressed her real feelings about Lewes' critique when she wrote that in the review "forced praise, given by jerks, and obviously without real and cordial liking, and censure, crude, conceited, and ignorant, were mixed in random lumps—forming a very loose and inconsistent whole."[61]

Although Franklin Gary has praised Lewes' criticism of *Shirley* very highly, claiming that "a good part of it is, in my estimation, the most acute criticism of *Shirley* that has yet appeared,"[62] there is no question but that Charlotte Brontë's reaction to the review was justified. Perhaps if she had had a sense of humour she would have been entertained by the ridiculous remarks on the second sex. What she did not know was that Lewes' review had been changed by Lord Jeffrey. In a letter to Elizabeth Gaskell (April 15, 1857), Lewes wrote: "Lord Jeffrey tampered with the article, as usual, and inserted some to me offensive sentences, but the main argument as far as I recollect it—is complementary to women not disrespectful."[63] It seems fair to assume, then, that Lewes who was to devote a good deal of his life to encouraging a "female writer" was not responsible for the inane remarks on the subject of women.

Gary has attempted to explain why Charlotte reacted so bitterly to Lewes' comments: "[Lewes] made her more acutely aware of the necessity of self-criticism in her writings, opened

59 Shorter, *op. cit.*, II, 80, 106.
60 *Ibid.*, 106.
61 *Ibid.*, 126.
62 F. Gary, "Charlotte Brontë and George Henry Lewes," *PMLA*, LI (1936), 540.
63 GE, II, 316.

her eyes to genuine artistic problems, made her artistically more self-conscious in a way that no other criticism did."[64] His admiration for Jane Austen disturbed and puzzled her. Although she protested that she could find little to admire in the art of Jane Austen, she was actually impressed by Lewes' emphasis on realism. Gary claims that the following second paragraph of page one, Chapter I, "Levitical," of *Shirley* reveals that Charlotte tried to follow Lewes' advice:

> If you think, from this prelude, that anything like a romance is preparing for, reader, you never were more mistaken. Do you anticipate sentiment, and poetry, and reverie? Do you expect passion, and stimulus, and melodrama? Calm your expectations; reduce them to a lowly standard. Something real, cool, and solid, lies before you; something unromantic as Monday morning. . . . It is not positively affirmed that you shall not have a taste of the exciting, perhaps toward the middle and close of the meal, but it is resolved that the first dish set upon the table shall be one that a Catholic—ay, even an Anglo-Catholic—might eat on Good Friday in Passion Week: it shall be cold lentils and vinegar without oil; it shall be unleavened bread with bitter herbs, and no roast lamb.

According to Gary, in this passage Charlotte seems to be saying to Lewes, "I am following your advice." No wonder then that she was hurt by his criticism. However, it is also possible to interpret this passage in a different way. She may have been ridiculing the realism that Lewes and Jane Austen favored as being nothing more than "cold lentils and vinegar without oil." After all, she promises something more exciting in the middle and close of the meal; the "lowly standard" appears only in the beginning. In effect she may have been saying to Lewes, "I'll try it your way in the beginning; but see how devoid of poetry, passion, and excitement such realism is."

Gary uses *Villette* as an example of how much Charlotte had learned from Lewes. In this masterpiece, she succeeded in fusing her personal experiences into an artistic whole and disciplining her energies by developing a sense of the proper relation of means

[64] Gary, "Charlotte Brontë," *PMLA*, LI (1936), 540.

to end. Gary does not refer to Lewes' review of *Villette* in the *Westminster Review* (1853), in which Lewes also described it as a novel of astonishing power and passion. He found defects in it: the unreal, melodramatic characterization of Madam Beck, the over-aged feelings of the young Polly, the indistinctness of John Bretton, and the exaggerated fondness for allegorical expressions of emotion. But he considered *Villette* a remarkable work in which we "read the actual thoughts and feelings of a strong, struggling soul; we hear the cry of pain from one who has loved passionately, and who has sorrowed sorely. Indeed, no more distinct characteristic of Currer Bell's genius can be named, than the depth of her capacity for all passionate emotions. Comparing 'Villette' and 'Ruth' in this respect, we are comparing sunlight with moonlight, passion with affection."[65]

When Charlotte and Lewes finally met, she immediately recognized him, but he was not able to single her out in the crowded room. He later described her to George Eliot as "a little, plain, provincial, sickly looking old maid."[66] Charlotte felt drawn to him when she met him: "I could not feel otherwise to him than half sadly, half tenderly,—a queer word that last, but I use it because the aspect of Lewes's face almost moves me to tears; it is so wonderfully like Emily, her eyes, her features, the very nose, the somewhat prominent mouth, the forehead, even, at moments, the expression. . . ."[67]

In 1859 in a study of the novels of Jane Austen, he wrote that the test of rereading old favorites had resulted in a reaffirmation of his admiration for Jane Austen but that it had proved damaging to *Jane Eyre* and *Tom Jones*. The process of reading *Jane Eyre* aloud again "very considerably modified our opinion of that remarkable work; and to confess the truth, modified it so far that we feel as if we should never open the book again."[68] He quoted from one of the letters in which Charlotte expressed disapproval of Jane Austen, and he referred to her as one who, "utterly with-

65 "Ruth and Villette," WR, LIX (1853), 490. See also the *Leader*, February 13, 1853, 162-63. Lewes praised *Mary Barton* in WR, LVIII (1852), 138-39, and *Cranford* in the *Leader*, July 2, 1853, 644.

66 GE, II, 91. Lewes also reviewed *The Professor* in the *Leader*, July 4, 1857, 641.

67 Shorter, *op. cit.*, II, 143.

68 "Jane Austen," *Blackwood's*, LXXXVI (1859), 100.

out a sense of humor . . . by nature fervid and impetuous," was incapable of appreciating Jane Austen. He also blamed her inability to appreciate the merits of Jane Austen upon her contemptuous indifference to characterization. Even her most successful people, Jane Eyre, Rochester, Paul Emmanuel, were no more than "vigorous sketches." But the act of reading Jane Austen for the fourth time led Lewes to make the following judgment of her genius: ". . . If the *truest* representation, effected by the *least expenditure* of means, constitutes the highest claim of art, then we say that Miss Austen has carried the art to a point of excellence surpassing that reached by any of her rivals."[69] She excelled in the art of plot construction and dramatic representation of character. Often the novelist who chooses everyday life finds it difficult to create real human beings who will also be interesting; consequently he gives ordinary people extraordinary characteristics. In this way he sins against the rule of economy by employing means that are not appropriate to the end. Jane Austen never made this mistake. Although her stories are rather commonplace, they contain nothing unreal or superfluous. Only Sophocles and Molière excelled her in the use of economy in art. Essentially a dramatic genius she relied completely on action and conversation to achieve effects which were "exquisitely and inexhaustibly" humorous. Lewes judged *Pride and Prejudice* to be the best story with the greatest variety of characters. While he did not care much for Fanny Price, he singled out *Mansfield Park* for special praise and even in *Persuasion,* which he considered the weakest of the novels, he found lovely touches and remarkable characterizations.

However, Lewes was well aware of her limited appeal. The general mass of people who read fiction do not require truth or probability, but ask only that their emotions be aroused. They are impressed by caricatured or exaggerated passion or adventure. But "the nicer art which mingles goodness with villainy, and weakness with virtue, as in life they are always mingled, causes positive distress to young and uncultivated minds."[70] In the greatest works of art, breadth and massiveness of effect are so combined with this "nicer" art that even the majority are impressed, but a novelist who has only the "nicer" art to her credit

[69] *Ibid.,* 101.
[70] *Ibid.,* 106.

will never become popular. Jane Austen's subjects are not intrinsically interesting but become so through treatment which only critical and refined tastes can appreciate. "Every reader will be amused by her pictures, because their very truth carries them home to ordinary experience and sympathy; but this amusement is of a tepid nature, and the effect is quickly forgotten."[71] Moreover, even some of the cultivated minority do not like her novels, for example, those with passionate and emotional natures are unimpressed with her art. Lewes observed that Charlotte Brontë could not appreciate Jane Austen because Jane Austen's temperament was very different from her own.

Other novelists are more passionate, more imaginative, with greater inventive powers, deeper insight, and broader range. Jane Austen's novels have no sudden philosophic illuminations, no epigrams, no eloquent descriptions. In fact, the absence of physical detail in her novels led Lewes to remark: "It is not stated whether she was shortsighted, but the absence of all sense of the outward world—either scenery or personal appearance—is more remarkable in her than in any writer we remember. . . . As far as any direct information can be derived from the authoress, we might imagine that this was a purblind world, wherein nobody ever saw anybody, except in a dim vagueness which obscured all peculiarities."[72] Balzac and Dickens would have made us *see* Mr. Collins, but Jane Austen merely describes him as a "tall, heavy looking young man of five and twenty." Thus aware of her limitations, Lewes predicted the following rank for her among the classics: "Her fame, we think, must endure. Such art as hers can never grow old, never be superseded. But after all, miniatures are not frescoes, and her works are miniatures. Her place is among the Immortals; but the pedestal is erected in a quiet niche of the great temple."[73] The persistence of Lewes' admiration for Jane Austen is attested to by his comment in 1875: "Miss Austen's novels are marvels of art, because they are exquisitely true, and interesting in their truth."[74]

In 1847 Lewes stated that he would rather have written *Pride*

[71] *Ibid.*, 107.
[72] *Ibid.*, 106.
[73] *Ibid.*, 113.
[74] *On Actors,* 104.

and Prejudice and *Tom Jones* than any of the Waverly novels, and he attempted to refute the notion that Fielding was inferior to Scott.[75] In 1926, in his study of Fielding, F.T. Blanchard praised Lewes as one of the critics "who defended Fielding most valiantly in the magazines . . . ," and Morris Greenhut, in 1948, also noted that Lewes considered Fielding one of the greatest English novelists.[76] Blanchard was aware of what he called a "root and branch denunciation" of the art of *Tom Jones* in *Blackwood's* (1860).[77] What he did not know was that Lewes was the author of this denunciation. In the 1859 study of Jane Austen, Lewes admitted that he was no longer very enthusiastic about *Tom Jones,* a very much overrated work. In comparison to Jane Austen, Fielding "has greater vigour of mind, greater experience, greater attainments, and a more effective *mise-en-scène* than Miss Austen; but he is not only immeasurably inferior to her in the highest department of art—the representation of character—he is also inferior to her, we think, in real humour; and in spite of his 'construction,' of which the critics justly speak in praise, he is inferior to her in the construction and conduct of his story, being more commonplace and less artistic. He has more invention of situation and more vigour, but less truth and subtlety."[78] In the 1860 article Lewes completely reversed his original opinion and attacked the art of Fielding and the construction of *Tom Jones.*

Lewes admitted that Fielding had a sense of humor, a talent for storytelling, an eye for characteristics of manner and speech, and an easy, energetic, idiomatic style. His pictures of eighteenth century life are of amusing value to the historian. But he is inferior to both Scott and Austen and his supposed "great comic masterpiece" is not a masterpiece at all. Including superfluity and improbability, the plot of *Tom Jones* lacks economy of construction. The effect of variety Fielding aimed for, through the

[75] "Recent Novels," *Fraser's Magazine,* XXXVI (1847), 687; "Lady Novelists," WR, LVIII (1852), 134-35; however, cf. Lewes' statement in "Historical Romance: *The Foster Brother,* and *Whitehall,*" WR, XLV (1846), 37: Scott "divined important historical truths which have escaped the sagacity of all historians."

[76] F.T. Blanchard, *Fielding the Novelist: A Study in Historical Criticism* (New Haven, 1926), 390; Morris Greenhut, "George Henry Lewes as a Critic of the Novel," *Studies in Philology,* XLV (1948), 507.

[77] "A Word about Tom Jones," *Blackwood's,* LXXXVII (1860), 331-41.

[78] "Jane Austen," *Blackwood's,* LXXXVI (1859), 101.

use of the episodical plot, is achieved at the sacrifice of the unity so necessary to every work of art. While the story does contain a great variety of interesting characters and adventures, they are produced by a very vulgar kind of art: "It is no great feat to achieve variety, when the hero is sent forth on his adventures; and in passing from place to place, and inn to inn, every person he meets on the road is made to sit for his portrait, and vanish, or to be used up afterwards, at any point of the story where his introduction may be convenient." Such construction requires no real skill: "To crowd coincidences of the most improbable kinds; to bring to every spot the *very* persons needed at the very time; to make every adventure link itself on to the story by the simple method of making the persons, hitherto unmentioned, related to the actors in the story;—to do this may give variety and animation, and with uncritical readers may look like skillful storytelling; but it is the vulgar art of inferior writers. . . ."[79] As for the matter of Fielding's supposed cleverness in keeping the secret of Jones's parentage, since the reader is never led to suspect the existence of Tom's father, since he is not even mentioned till near the end, the author hardly exhibits great cleverness in hiding the secret.

Nor is the humor of *Tom Jones* equal in quality to the humor of Uncle Toby or Walter Shandy. It depends on physical rather than mental incongruities and practical joking. "Without the discovery of two persons breaking the seventh commandment, and the cheap humour of a bloody nose . . . [Fielding] would often be put to it to raise a laugh."[80] Fielding's vivacity and irony had none of that quiet humor which delights the mind without actually eliciting positive laughter. Lewes also depreciated Fielding's supposed knowledge of human nature. Expressing amazement at Hazlitt's comparison of Fielding to Shakespeare, Lewes observed: "We cannot ascribe a profound knowledge of human nature to one so utterly without seriousness, so ludicrously incompetent to portray any of the deeper, emotional and intellectual forms of life."[81] Although Fielding had strong powers of observation, he was without the profound and extensive sympathy

79 "Tom Jones," *Blackwood's*, LXXXVII (1860), 335.
80 *Ibid.*, 336.
81 *Ibid.*, 337.

of Shakespeare. His range was narrow: he knew country squires, pettifoggers, waiting-women, and ignorant parsons. His most completely drawn character is Squire Western, but most of his people are caricatures. They usually reveal themselves "antithetically and transparently" when in real life they do so "incidentally and involuntarily." In actuality people are more complex than Fielding's characters; their reactions are often uncontrolled and unpredictable.

Lewes doubted that Thackeray could have been serious when he ascribed philosophic and poetic genius to Fielding. The absence of poetic genius is particularly apparent in Fielding's "deadness to nature," a deadness typical of eighteenth century writers. He hid his incompetence by burlesquing nature. Perhaps this burlesque may have been part of his intention; if so, it makes for rather dreary comedy. Worst of all, when Fielding is seriously poetical, he becomes maudlin, as in Tom's apostrophe to Sophia on a June evening. Lewes then concluded on a humbler note. No one, he said, was greater than Fielding as a painter of manners, and his skill in this direction and as an amusing storyteller makes him a valuable possession for literature. But Lewes claimed only to have proved the inferiority of the construction of *Tom Jones.*

Thackeray, probably unaware that Lewes was the author of this curious depreciation of *Tom Jones,* angrily retorted in one of his *Roundabout Papers*: "Why did not a wiseacre in Blackwood's Magazine lately fall foul of *Tom Jones*? Oh hypercritic! So, to be sure, did good old Mr. Richardson, who could write novels himself—but you, and I, and Mr. Gibbon, my dear Sir, agree in giving our respect, and wonder, and admiration, to the brave old master."[82]

In 1847 Charlotte Brontë asked W.S. Williams whether a certain criticism of *Vanity Fair* was written by Lewes: "Mr. Lewes with his penetrating sagacity and fine acumen, ought to be able to do the author of *Vanity Fair* justice."[83] The review she referred to was not by Lewes but he did do Thackeray "justice" when he reviewed his four books: *Book of Snobs, Vanity Fair, Pendennis,* and *Henry Esmond.*

[82] "Thorns in the Cushion," Roundabout Paper No. 5, *Cornhill,* II (1860), 124.
[83] Shorter, *op. cit.,* I, 377.

When Lewes reviewed Thackeray's *Book of Snobs* in 1848, he criticized Thackeray for showing "*everywhere* corruption under the mask. His skepticism is pushed too far. While tramping on cant, while exposing whatever is base and mean and despicable, he is not attentive to honour, and to paint what is high, and generous, and noble in human nature."[84] Thackeray wrote a letter to Lewes about this criticism and noted that he appreciated the "kindness of the reproof. . . . I am quite aware of the dismal roguery wh [sic] goes all through the Vanity Fair story—and God forbid that the world should be like it altogether: though I fear it is more like it than we like to own. But my object is to make everybody engaged, engaged in the pursuit of Vanity and I must carry my story through in this dreary minor key, with only occasional hints here and there of better things. . . ."[85] In judging Thackeray's other novels, Lewes showed more understanding of his aims as a satirist.

In the *Athenaeum* Lewes praised *Vanity Fair* very highly: "Knowledge of life, good humoured satire, penetration into motive, power of characterization, and great truthfulness are qualities in fiction as rare as they are admirable; and no work that has been published for many years past can claim these qualities so largely as *Vanity Fair*."[86] Lewes was quick to appreciate the special skill revealed in Becky Sharp's characterization.

> The character of Becky is amongst the finest creations of modern fiction. . . . With great art, she is made rather selfish than wicked—though the excess of the selfishness rises to the surface and has the effect of wickedness. Profound immorality is made to seem consistent with unfailing good humour. Becky has neither affections, nor passions, nor principles. . . . It is very strange that the reader has a sort of liking for her in spite of his better knowledge. The fact is, the author has contrived in a surprising way to represent not only Becky's *mind,* but her *manner.* We are in some sort under her spell,—as Rawdon was. To us she is almost as

84 *London Chronicle,* March 6, 1848, 3.
85 Gordon N. Ray (ed.), *The Letters and Private Papers of William Makepeace Thackeray* (Cambridge, Mass., 1946), II, 353-54.
86 *Athenaeum,* August 12, 1848, 797.

> lively, entertaining and good humoured as she was to those amongst whom she lived. . . . Her equability of temper is a nice touch:—it belongs to the physiology of such a character. They who have no affections and no principles can be wounded only in their self-love, and may obtain the character of being good-tempered at the cheapest possible cost.[87]

According to Lewes, Thackeray was primarily a satirist; therefore he had no basic need to concentrate upon passion or feeling. From this stem the deficiencies of his novels in relation to characterization. Feelings are not revealed in the process of growth and incidents are not dramatically conceived. They are presented, described as a *fait accompli.* Lewes considered *Pendennis* to be superior to *Vanity Fair* because *Pendennis* reveals more understanding and tolerance of humanity as a mixture of both good and evil. While it is true that *Vanity Fair* has Becky Sharp and a superior story, *Pendennis* is a masterly work written in an incomparable style, caustic, subtle, pathetic with unrivalled descriptions of human life and character. Lewes considered *Henry Esmond* to be a new phase in Thackeray's artistic growth because it attempts more than the merely satirical or comical with its simple touching story of two devotions, its quiet reserve, and its characters.

Comparing Disraeli and Thackeray, he wrote: "Disraeli [saw] society—not very clearly, but he [saw] it; Thackeray saw it, and [saw] through it, [saw] all the human feelings, all the motives high and low, simple and complicated, which make it what it is."[88] A perfect Janus Bifrons, Thackeray viewed society as a world dominated by antitheses. The same view which enabled him to perceive that a hero has gout made him perceive that a scamp is not completely evil. Had he portrayed Caesar he would have exposed the baldness beneath his laurel wreath. In *Pendennis,* Warrington consumes endless amounts of beer, like a coal beaver, but he acts like a gentleman; Faker has vulgar tastes, but the feeling of a gentleman; Miss Fotheringay is a good actress, but she is as "ignorant as a horse." Like Goethe, Thackeray understood

[87] *Ibid.,* 796.

[88] *Leader,* December 21, 1850, 929-30. Lewes was hostile to Disraeli's political and literary efforts; cf. "Benjamin D'Israeli," BQR, X (1849), 118-39.

that nature is not one-sided. But his antitheses, unlike those of Eugene Sue and Victor Hugo, were based upon the actual truths of nature, not upon a Hegelian desire to demonstrate the law of opposites.[89]

Just as Lewes gained the friendship of Charlotte Brontë and Thackeray because his reviews pleased them, so he made the acquaintance of Dickens, after Dickens read what he had written about *Pickwick Papers.* In 1838, at the age of twenty, Lewes was invited to the great man's house in Doughty Street and thus began their friendship which was sustained throughout Dickens' life.[90] When the first two volumes of Forster's *Life of Dickens* were published, Chapman and Hall asked Lewes to discuss the biography in the *Fortnightly Review.* Although Lewes had devoted himself primarily to philosophical and psychological inquiry after 1868, he accepted their offer, and in 1872, he wrote for them "Dickens in Relation to Criticism." The article had very little to do with Forster's biography, and except for several casual references to it, Lewes used it merely as an excuse to launch his own criticism of Dickens.

Lewes began by attempting to explain the paradoxical phenomenon of critical contempt and public approval of Dickens' novels. He believed that Dickens had serious shortcomings which were offset by a remarkable source of power. He was a greater humorist than Fielding or Smollett, and his humor was undoubtedly a primary cause of his success. However, the art of providing amusement would not have assured him fame as a great novelist. What endeared him to readers was "an imagination of marvellous vividness, and an emotional, sympathetic nature capable of furnishing that imagination with elements of universal power." (p. 144) There is nothing startling or original about this observation; certainly others before Lewes had been impressed by the vividness of Dickens' imagination. However, when Lewes ana-

89 *Leader,* November 6, 1852, 1071-72.

90 "Dickens in Relation to Criticism," FR, XVII (1872), 141-54. See especially 152. References to this article are incorporated into the text and appear within parentheses. See also Lewes' *Diary,* November 10, 1859, "Dined with Dickens. 23 years ago went to see him at Twickenham." In his *Journal* entry for June 17, 1857, Lewes noted that he wrote a review for the *Leader,* no doubt the review of *Little Dorrit* which appeared there on June 28, 1857, 616-17.

lyzed the nature of this "vivid imagination," he introduced a new and controversial element into the analysis of the nature of Dickens' genius.

In Lewes' view, imagination made Dickens a seer of visions in a manner startlingly analogous to the way in which the hallucination makes a person a seer of visions. "Psychologists will understand both the extent and the limitation of the remark, when I say that in no other perfectly sane mind (Blake, I believe, was not perfectly sane) have I observed vividness of imagination approaching so closely to hallucination." (p. 144) Lewes defined hallucinations as "*revived* impressions, revived by an internal cause which have precisely the same force and clearness which the impressions originally had when produced by an external cause." (p. 144) In other words, hallucinations are subjective images which have the same vividness as images with objective counterparts. Both the sane and the insane experience hallucinations. But the insane person feels the hallucinatory image to be true even if it is inconsistent with all previous experience. It is useless to try to convince an insane patient that what he has seen or heard has no objective reality. Lewes recalled: "I once argued with a patient who believed he had been transformed into a bear; he was quite willing to admit that the idea of such a transformation was utterly at variance with all experience; but he always returned to his position that God being omnipotent there was no reason to doubt his power of transforming men into bears; what remained fixed in his mind was the image of himself under a bear's form." (p. 144) On the other hand, the sane mind is ready to recognize the purely subjective character of an image if it is inconsistent with all other experiences: "Thus if I see a black cat on the chair opposite, yet on my approaching the chair feel no soft object, and if my terrier on the hearthrug looking in the direction of the chair shows none of the well-known agitation which the sight of a cat produces, I conclude, in spite of its distinctness, that the image is an hallucination." (p. 145)

Lewes hastened to assure his reader that he did not consider Dickens insane. The mere fact that a human being has hallucinations does not make him mad. He reiterated what he had expressed in an early article "Great Wits, Mad Wits," namely, his belief that "nothing is less like genius than insanity."[91] Furthermore, he had never observed "any trace of the insane temperament in Dickens's works, or life, they being indeed singularly free even from the eccentricities which often accompany exceptional powers. . . ." (p. 145) Still Lewes insisted that hallucination helps to explain the quality of Dickens' imagination. To Dickens, "*created* images have the coercive force of realities, excluding all control, all contradiction. What seems preposterous, impossible to us, seemed to him simple fact of observation. When he imagined a street, a house, a room, a figure, he saw it not in the vague schematic way of ordinary imagination, but in the sharp definition of actual perception, all the salient details obtruding themselves on his attention. He, seeing it thus vividly, made us also see it; and believing in its reality however fantastic, he communicated something of his belief to us. . . . So definite and insistent was the image, that even while knowing it was false we could not help, for a moment, being affected as it were, by his hallucination." (p. 145)

This kind of imagination was the source of both his power and his limitations. It explains the paradox of a writer who created vividly yet falsely. Whereas discerning critics pointed out that his characters were merely caricatures, the average reader was captivated into believing in them. "An image and a name were given, and the image was so suggestive that it seemed to *express* all that it was found to *recall*, and Dickens was held to have depicted what his readers supplied." (p. 146) He generally emphasized one particular characteristic, a sharply defined physical trait, a peculiarity of speech or manner. So vividly did he describe this characteristic that the person seemed real. "His types established themselves in the public mind like personal experiences. Their falsity was unnoticed in the blaze of their illumination. Every humbug seemed a Pecksniff, every nurse a Gamp, every jovial improvident a Micawber, every stinted serving-wench a Marchioness. Universal experiences became individualized in these types. . . ." (p. 146) Dickens captured such a large audience because the generality of mankind is influenced by sensations rather than ideas.

91 "Great Wits, Mad Wits?", *Blackwood's*, LXXXVIII (1860), 302-11.

> Give a child a wooden horse, with hair for mane and tail, and wafer-spots for colouring, he will never be disturbed by the fact that this horse does not move its legs, but runs on wheels—the general suggestion suffices for his belief. . . . It may be said of Dickens's human figures that they too are wooden, and run on wheels; but these are details which scarcely disturb the belief of admirers. Just as the wooden horse is brought within the range of the child's emotions, and dramatizing tendencies, when he can handle and draw it, so Dickens's figures are brought within the range of the reader's interests, and receive from these interests a sudden illumination, when they are the puppets of a drama every incident of which appeals to the sympathies. (p. 146)

With unerring instinct Dickens engaged the sympathy of his readers by writing the "bourgeois epic." Beyond his range was the world of thought and passion. But he could make us laugh and cry "at the joys and pains of childhood, the petty tyrannies of ignoble natures, the genial pleasantries of happy natures, the life of the poor, the struggles of the street and back parlour, the insolence of office, the sharp social contrasts, east-wind and Christmas jollity, hunger, misery, and hot punch. . . ." (p. 147)

Only reflection could detect the fantastic and unreal elements in Dickens' conception of human nature. Lewes considered Mantalini, Rosa Dartle, Ledy Dedlock, Esther Summerson, Mr. Dick, Arthur Gride, Edith Dombey, and Mr. Carker to be "monstrous failures." Dickens was unaware that man is, in the words of Montaigne, "*un être ondoyant et diverse.*" Dickens' characters are reminiscent of the frogs whose brains have been taken out for physiological reasons, and "whose actions henceforth want the distinctive peculiarity of organic action, that of fluctuating spontaneity. Place one of these brainless frogs on his back and he will at once recover the sitting posture; draw a leg from under him, and he will draw it back again . . . stroke his back, and he will utter *one* croak. All these things resemble the actions of the unmutilated frog, but they differ in being *isolated* actions, and *always the same*: they are as uniform and calculable as the movements of a machine. The uninjured frog may or may not croak, may or may not hop away; the result is never calculable. . . ."

(p. 148) Dickens had no conception of the complexity of the organism. ". . . His characters have nothing fluctuating and incalculable in them, even when they embody true observations; and very often they are creations so fantastic that one is at a loss to understand how he could, without hallucination, believe them to be like reality." (p. 149) In fact, some of the dialogues are so incongruous that they "resemble the absurd and eager expositions which insane patients pour into the listener's ear when detailing their wrongs, or their schemes. Dickens once declared to me that every word said by his characters was distinctly *heard* by him; I was at first not a little puzzled to account for the fact that he could hear language so utterly unlike the language of real feeling, and not be aware of its preposterousness; but the surprise vanished when I thought of the phenomena of hallucination." (p. 149)

Furthermore, to the cultivated and critical mind Dickens represents "an almost unique example of a mind of singular force in which, so to speak, sensations never passed into ideas. Dickens sees and feels, but the logic of feeling seems the only logic he can manage." (p. 151) Lewes commented on the strange absence of thought in the novels: "I do not suppose a single thoughtful remark on life or character could be found throughout the twenty volumes. Not only is there a marked absence of the reflective tendency, but one sees no indication of the past life of humanity having ever occupied him; keenly as he observes the objects before him, he never connects his observations into a general expression. . . . Compared with that of Fielding or Thackeray, his was merely an *animal* intelligence, *i.e.*, restricted to perceptions. . . . He never was and never would have been a student." (p. 151)

Lewes then made use of what he personally knew about the novelist to reinforce the charge of intellectual inadequacy against Dickens. He recalled that Dickens' library at Doughty Street contained a collection of presentation copies of three volume novels and books of travel. Two years later it contained more of the standard works, but it still lacked any "individual physiognomy." However, Lewes admitted that in the aforementioned two-year interval Dickens had changed considerably. He talked about more important subjects than actors, periodicals and London life. He was more seriously concerned with social problems. He was too honest to affect an interest he did not feel in philosophy, science or the higher literature, but he "had already learned to look upon the world as a scene where it was the duty of each man in his own way to make the lot of the miserable Many a little less miserable; and, having learned that his genius gave him great power, he was bent on using that power effectively." (p. 152)

It would be unfair to Lewes to dwell only upon the adverse criticism in the Dickens' essay. Lewes himself took to task those critics who judged Dickens from the bias of one kind of technical estimate. They overlooked or undervalued the achievements of a powerful imagination which rendered Dickens potent to millions of readers, and they stressed only his defects which resulted from an uncontrolled imagination. While he may not have succeeded in satisfying the critical or cultivated mind, he did succeed in stirring the emotions of countless readers with unparalleled skill. "Murders are perpetrated without stint, but the murder of Nancy is unforgettable. Children figure in numberless plays and novels, but the deaths of little Nell and little Paul were national griefs. . . . Captain Cuttle and Richard Swiveller, the Marchioness and Tilly Slowboy, Pecksniff and Micawber, Tiny Tim and Mrs. Gamp, may be imperfect presentations of human character, but they are types which no one can forget. . . . The cultivated and uncultivated were affected by his admirable *mise en scène*, his fertile invention, his striking selection of incident, his intense vision of physical details." (p. 151)

That Lewes' criticism of Dickens should have aroused the ire of John Forster is not surprising. He commented on Lewes' essay in the third volume of his Dickens biography: "Since Trinculo and Caliban were under one cloak, there has surely been no such delicate monster with two voices. 'His forward voice, now, is to speak well of his friend; his backward voice is to utter foul speeches and to detract.' "[92] Forster was particularly horrified by one of the "foul speeches" in which Lewes had pointed out the relation of hallucination to Dickens' imagination. Forster's answer to Lewes doesn't warrant attention, for it is essentially an *ad*

[92] John Forster, *The Life of Charles Dickens* (Philadelphia, 1890), II, 333, 337.

hominem attack. More recently George H. Ford has reserved for Lewes' essay the attention that "the most effective attack on Dickens ever written" deserves.[93] He also believes that Lewes played the role of the "smylere with knyf under the cloke." He points out that whereas Lewes ostensibly appeared to be rebuking the critics, not Dickens, through the use of sophisticated irony and subtle shadings Lewes managed to convey the impression that Dickens' world was a "fantastic absurdity." Lewes ingeniously combined Walter Bagehot's view of Dickens as an illiterate with Hippolyte Taine's belief that Dickens' imagination was allied to madness. To illustrate Lewes' method, Ford noted how Lewes discussed Dickens' imagination as if it were a form of madness: "On one page, he assures us that he had 'never observed any trace of the insane temperament' in Dickens, but a few pages later, he describes Dickens' 'hallucinations' in the very terms he had previously applied to the insane."

Ford admits that Lewes correctly described Dickens' characters as being static. However, he maintains that Lewes' limitations as a critic stemmed not from inaccuracy but inflexibility. Ford accuses Lewes of being too rigidly committed to a particular theory of the novel. "Mrs. Podsnap is not 'real' in the sense that a minor character in George Eliot's novels is real. Her reality is of the same terrifying kind as we find in the simplified and expressive figures of Elmer Rice's play, *The Adding Machine.*" Lewes was not aware that in a poetic novel, the kind of novel Dickens wrote, reality could be conveyed through the use of static characters. But despite his sharp criticism of the Lewes essay, Ford confesses that "even when disagreeing with it, one can admire its skillful argument, and especially its tone. Like the walrus and the carpenter, Lewes weeps over the oysters he is consuming, and he assures his victim and his audience that it is all for the best." Ford even credits the Lewes article with being the most influential factor in initiating the revolution of taste which dethroned Dickens. All the following attacks on Dickens are merely variations on a theme by Lewes.

Curiously enough, Lewes himself was unaware that he had written one of the classic attacks on Dickens. Anthony Trollope

93 George H. Ford, *Dickens and His Readers: Aspects of Novel-Criticism since 1836* (Princeton, 1955), 152 ff.

recalled that Lewes was hurt by Forster's remarks because they seemed to accuse him of unfairness. According to Trollope, Lewes was "dealing with the work of a man he loved and admired,—work which he thought worthy of the thoughtful analysis he applied to it." Trollope, never very enthusiastic about Dickens' novels, considered Lewes' criticism "the best analysis we have yet had of the genius of that wonderful man, and it displays at its best not only the critical acumen of the writer, but that special lucidity of expression."[94] On the other hand, Swinburne, whose adulation of Dickens was so intense, detested Lewes, that "pseudosophical quack," for what he had written about Dickens. Ford, who considers Dickens' novels to be masterpieces, judges Lewes' estimate of Dickens to be wrong, whereas Gordon Haight, who obviously does not value Dickens as highly as Ford, regards Lewes' criticism to be "severe but fundamentally sound."[95]

It is hard to understand how Lewes could have been unaware of the effect of the tone and emphasis he employed. He meted out more severe criticism than praise, although to his credit were those passages, ignored by Forster and Ford, in which he eulogized the emotional power of Dickens' genius. At no point in the essay did Lewes deny Dickens the status of genius. But lovers of Dickens could hardly help but object to his three main points: (1) Dickens' characters are not real; (2) his novels lack intellectual or philosophic content; (3) they are dependent upon an imaginative power which can best be explained in terms of hallucination.

The first charge can be dealt with in terms of Lewes' definition of realism. As we have seen, he himself broadened the meaning of realism when he used the concept of idealism as a type of realism in poetry and drama. However, he obviously felt that Dickens' characters were neither symbolic, nor ideal, but *false*, and to answer his attack a defender of Dickens would have to deal with the limitations of Lewes' theory of realism.

As for the second charge, not only Lewes, but also the modern philosopher and critic, George Santayana, has written about Dickens' intellectual limitations. And, indeed, still other critics have been hard at work trying to refute this contention. But

94 Trollope, "George Henry Lewes," FR, XXXI (1879), 22-23.
95 Haight, "Dickens and Lewes," *PMLA*, LXXI (1956), 177.

a rather curious controversy sheds considerable light on Lewes' estimate of Dickens' intelligence. The modern reader readily interprets Krook's death from spontaneous combustion as a symbolic device used by the author to forward the chancery theme of *Bleak House*. However, Dickens wanted the reader to accept Krook's death in a literal sense. In the *Leader* and in several letters to Dickens, Lewes noted that no contemporary organic chemist of any repute accepted the idea of the spontaneous combustion of human bodies.[96] Of course, as a novelist, Dickens was not restricted to scientific truth. Still, Lewes objected to the inclusion of the Krook death scene because of the influence it would have in encouraging the belief in an erroneous conception. However, when *Bleak House* was published in book form, Dickens added a preface in which he assured his readers that he had worsted Lewes in the argument and had demonstrated, after careful investigation, that certain authorities believed in spontaneous combustion. Since Dickens obstinately refused to be impressed by the evidence offered by the great chemists of his age, and since he persisted with naive credibility in relying upon unscientific and unreliable testimony, Lewes was goaded into commenting in the *Leader*: "It is unpleasant to be forced to recur to this subject, the more so because our protest must necessarily be so ludicrously disproportionate to the effect of his [Dickens'] assertion, carried as it will be all over Europe. . . . He was at liberty to cite all the authorities in his favour, he was *not* at liberty to disregard and pass over in silence the names of Liebig, Bischoff, Regnault, Graham, Hofmann, and Owen; and against that omission we protest."[97] Lewes, the philosopher and scientist, could not admire the mind of a man who remained indifferent to scientific truth. Such indifference seemed to him to signify serious intellectual limitations.

The most controversial part of Lewes' analysis deals with the relation of hallucination to Dickens' imagination. It is easy to

[96] George Santayana, *Soliloquies in England and Later Soliloquies* (New York, 1923), 59; "Perhaps, properly speaking, he had no *ideas* on any subject. . . ." *Leader*, December 11, 1852, 1189; January 15, 1853, 64; February 5, 1853, 137-38; March 26, 1853, 303-6; September 3, 1853, 858. See also "Spontaneous Combustion," *Blackwood's*, LXXXIX (1861), 385-402 and Gordon S. Haight, "Dickens and Lewes on Spontaneous Combustion," *Nineteenth-Century Fiction*, X (1955), 53-63.

[97] *Leader*, September 3, 1853, 858.

understand the chagrin of Dickens' admirers because the word *hallucination* has a pejorative connotation and conjures up the image of an insane person. But Lewes denied that he was in any way impugning the sanity of Dickens. By 1872, the year in which he wrote the Dickens' criticism, Lewes had devoted many years to the study of psychology. It is not surprising, therefore, that he analyzed Dickens' imagination from the viewpoint of the psychologist, especially since his theory of imagination was psychologically oriented. To understand what Lewes meant by hallucination, it is helpful to supplement his remarks in the "Dickens in Relation to Criticism" with his more technical explanation in the *Physiology of Common Life* and *Mind as a Function of the Organism.* In Lewes' psychological system every sensation is considered real, regardless of whether it has an objective or external equivalent. He defined *subjective* sensations as the means by which "we *see* objects very vividly where no such objects exist; we *hear* sounds of many kinds, where none of their external causes exist; we *taste* flavours in an empty mouth; we *smell* odours, where no volatile substance is present; and we *feel* prickings or pains in limbs which have been amputated. These are actual, not imaginary, sensations."[98] We would continue to believe that every sensation had an external cause if it were not for the controlling reactions of other sensations: ". . . Sensations require constant confrontation with the reports of other senses, otherwise they would be credited as sensations, produced by actual objects. . . . A man feels prickings in his amputated fingers, but he sees that the fingers are not there, and, consequently, he knows that his sensation is deceptive."[99] Hallucinations and dreams are special kinds of subjective sensations which are not affected by other sensations. "In the state of cerebral excitement named Hallucination, this confrontation is *disregarded;* in the state of cerebral isolation named Dreaming, this confrontation is *impossible:* the first condition is one in which the cerebral activity completely domineers over the excitations from without; the second condition is one in which the cerebral activity, though feeble, is entirely isolated from external excitations—thus, in both cases the cerebral reflexes are undisturbed, uncontrolled by reflexes

[98] *The Physiology of Common Life* (Leipzig, 1860), II, 256.
[99] *Ibid.,* 256, 259.

from Sense."[100] The dream, then, is a temporary hallucination which has no connection to other series of sensations, while the hallucination itself does have some connection to other sensations, but is not in any way controlled by them. And it is important here to stress the point that Lewes knew of Dickens' preoccupation with his recurring dream visions concerning Mary Hogarth, and an unknown woman named Napier, whom he later supposedly met in real life.[101]

Lewes believed that dreams and hallucinations arise out of normal cerebral processes. Hallucinations can result from the normal process of silently articulating the words read: "Now if from our cerebral condition this normal process of silent articulation be exaggerated, we think aloud; and this may be carried so far as to produce a true hallucination; the voices heard are projected outwards, and attributed to objective sources if our reason be affected, attributed to disease if we are sane."[102] Lewes related the story of a physician who had a horrible dream at the age of five, and who years later imagined that he had actually *seen* what he had dreamt: "There are sufficient examples of hallucination, even in persons not suspected of any mental disturbance. . . . Now the difference between dreams and hallucinations is little more than that, in the one case, we dream with our eyes closed, in the other, with our eyes open."[103]

Thus it should be apparent that Lewes meant to make no vicious attack upon Dickens' sanity. He erred in using the term *hallucination* in a technical sense, expecting the ordinary reader to grasp, from the brief definition he supplied, the psychological distinctions implied. All that he seems to have meant was that *subjective* sensations were more intense in Dickens than in any other sane persons. What should concern the defenders of Dickens is not the irrelevant question of whether Lewes impugned Dickens' sanity, but the relevant question of whether Lewes' conception of hallucination has psychological validity. From a psychological viewpoint, his theory can be criticized as being too tenuous. The behavioristic school of psychology would

100 *Ibid.*, 256-257.

101 Winter Warrington, "Dickens and the Psychology of Dreams," *PMLA, LXIII* (1948), 984-1006.

102 MFO, 344.

103 "Falsely Accused," *Blackwood's,* LXXXV (1859), 220-21.

claim that subjective experience cannot be analyzed scientifically and that, therefore, Lewes' remarks on subjective sensations and the relation of hallucination to imagination are unverifiable distinctions. However, Lewes deserves credit for being one of the first critics, before the influence of Freud, to attempt a psychological explanation of the nature of genius. His essay on Dickens may infuriate Dickens' fans but it remains to this day an ingenious and thought provoking criticism.

The question of morality in the novel does not arise to any appreciable extent in Lewes' discussion of the English novelists. A characteristically Victorian reaction was elicited from Lewes by Tom Jones's relations with Lady Bellaston, when Lewes wrote: "On the question of the morality of Tom Jones we will not dwell, because we suppose that there can really be very little difference of opinion as to the insensibility of the author to the disgracefulness of Tom's relation to Lady Bellaston."[104] But Lewes confronted the issue of morality more directly in criticizing the European novelists: Balzac, George Sand, Hugo and Goethe.

We can distinguish between Lewes' early and late view of Balzac. His early judgment is similar to the one made by Henry James: "He [Balzac] had no natural sense of morality and this we cannot help thinking a serious fault in a novelist."[105] Lewes also could not forgive Balzac for his lack of moral sense. This led him to make the egregiously erroneous prediction in 1842 about Balzac's future: "Fame, we fear, is inexorably denied thee!"[106] Even when Lewes came to appreciate Balzac's achievement, he still objected to Balzac's amorality. Balzac described rascals without indignation; in fact, he described them glowingly, insensible to their vices. He seemed to approve of villainy as long as it was cunningly schemed. His characters succeed because they can manipulate men's reactions as they would mathematical data. In reality, men do not act in *straight* lines. Moreover, to claim that villainy succeeds through intellectual superiority is false and immoral. Balzac implied that only Parisian refinement can make a human being estimable. By penetrating into the secret springs of vanity, he corrupts the taste of his reader.

104 "Tom Jones," *Blackwood's*, LXXXVII (1860), 341.
105 Henry James, *French Poets and Novelists* (London, 1878), 114.
106 "H. de Balzac," *Monthly Magazine*, VII (1842), 472.

He is always unclean, describing feelings in detail which were better left unnoticed. In *La Vielle Fille* he describes the sexual desires of an old maid; in *Le Ménage de Garçon* the physical effects of incontinence. In *Béatrix*, Fanny O'Brien, the pure mother who wishes to read a letter her son has received, is described as approaching her son in the following manner: "Le mère eut en ce moment la grâce d'une courtisane qui veut obtenir une concession."[107] The second part of *Le Cousin Pons* contains a horrible caricature of human nature, made even more horrible by virtue of the profound truth which is at the basis of the exaggeration. Such a novel belongs to the school of French romance where base passion sets in motion horrible intrigues. To provide more exciting incidents for the *feuilleton* of *La Presse,* Balzac distorted his work: "He added the fish's tail to the woman's breast, having no fear of Horace and the Ars Poetica."[108]

Balzac's style is crabbed, prolix, pedantic, and usually euphuistic, except in the dialogue portions. His detailed description in *Eugénie Grandet, La Vielle Fille, La Recherche de L'Absolu,* and *Le Curé de Tours* is very effective but tedious, and reveals the prosaic mind of a pedant. Although he read a great deal to acquire the necessary knowledge, his information was essentially superficial and his intellect specious. He often erred because he had no poetic instinct or love of the beautiful. This is illustrated by *Père Goriot*, which Lewes placed in the company of Balzac's poorest novels: *L'Histoire de Treize* and *Peau de Chagrin.* Like Hugo, Balzac forgot that parental love is felt by both the brute and the man. To sympathize with such passion the reader must be made to sympathize with the parent. Goriot is a monomaniac and monomania does not invite sympathy. Goriot's love for his daughter ranges from the passion of a brute to the passion of a debauchee. Because King Lear is a noble soul he earns our sympathy, but Goriot is merely stupid.

However, Lewes' mature judgment led him to recognize Balzac's achievements in such works as *Eugénie Grandet, La Recherche de L'Absolu, Le Médecin du Campagne* which he praised as psychological studies of profound significance, unspoiled by

107 *Béatrix* (Paris, 1902), 241.

108 "Recent Novels," *Fraser's Magazine,* XXXVI (1847), 695; "Balzac and George Sand," *Foreign Quarterly Review,* XXXIII (1844), 272, 285.

his usual extravagances. Lewes came to recognize that Balzac's forte was characterization. He had great powers of observation and an astonishing knowledge of motivation. In novels without charm, with little action, with poorly constructed plots, he triumphs "because he has discovered the true source of human interest to lie in human interest."[109] Thus Lewes learned to appreciate Balzac despite his moral defection, and he even introduced the French novelist to Charlotte Brontë by sending her copies of *Modeste Mignon* and *Illusions Perdues*.[110] By 1858 Lewes no longer believed that fame was denied to Balzac. In that year he paid tribute to his genius by observing that if Balzac had written Otto Ludwig's *Zwischen Himmel und Erde*, "he would have made it disagreeable, no doubt and painful; but would so have presented the characters and the feelings, and even the external life of these slaters that we should have been forced to believe in their existence, and sympathize in their struggles."[111] In other words Balzac was a true realist.

But, while Lewes objected to Balzac's amorality, he defended George Sand and Goethe against the charge of immorality. In rushing to George Sand's defense, he played the same role he had undertaken in attempting to refute the wrong notions spread by Shelley's calumniators.[112] In fact, Lewes admired Sand's novels for the very qualities he found in Shelley's poetry—their beauty, idealism, and optimism. Society derived the impression of her immorality from her life, rather than from her books; she did not advocate libertinism or the emancipation of women; in *Lettres à Marcie* she showed her opposition to the St. Simonian doctrine of woman's mission. She was opposed not to marriage but to its abuses, and she treated adultery as a social evil. Admittedly, the very young and inexperienced female reader might be adversely influenced by such novels as *Lélia, Spiridion, Leone Leoni,* and *Jacques.* Voluptuous, she dealt with matters better imagined than described, but she was never unclean. She had a fondness for describing unconventional women, and perhaps it was her influence that led women to rebel against the conven-

109 "Balzac," *Foreign Quarterly Review,* XXXIII (1844), 293.

110 Shorter, *op. cit.*, II, 175.

111 "Realism in Art," WR, LXX (1858), 499.

112 "Balzac," *Foreign Quarterly Review,* XXXIII (1844), 281; "George Sand," *Monthly Magazine,* VII (1842), 578-91.

tions of society, but on the whole her novels had a beneficial effect.

She was accused of advocating radical theories. Disturbed by the social anarchy and injustice of the period, she did desire ardently the social improvement which she outlined. Dissatisfied with the modern version of Christianity, she looked for new and broader interpretations of the doctrine of Christ. She was democratic and believed in the greatness of the common people. For such views she hardly deserved the brand of infamy. Lewes admitted that he did not accept many of her ideas, but at the same time he respected her for her beliefs. He wrote: "The doubts which perplex the earnest loving souls of those who, like Madame Sand, feel for mankind, and yearn for social amelioration, are certainly dangerous, in as much as they disturb society; but he must be a bold man who would pronounce the utterance of these doubts an immoral act. . . . And as long as evils exist, all men are bound to signalize them; and as long as evils are signalized, so will there be works immoral in their tendency: since all works are considered such which tend to unsettle men's opinions."[113]

He disliked George Sand's later novels. *Jeanne, Isidora, Le Péché de M. Antoine,* and *Teverino* were generally more feeble, less impassioned and more moral and commonplace. He could not forget that "the author was once a great poet, uttering in harmonious language the deep experience of life. It is a sad fall this poet makes when dropping into the conventional agonies and unreal passions of the circulating library."[114] He blamed her deterioration on her attempt to rival Dumas and Sue in the *feuilletons.*[115] But when *François le Champi* was published, Lewes praised George Sand for returning to the simplicity of nature and eschewing the extravagances of exhausted invention: "In these pages we have the naiveté of La Fontaine and the rugged force

113 "Balzac," *Foreign Quarterly Review,* XXXIII (1844), 281. Lewes translated George Sand's *Le Sécrétaire Intime* in *"The State Murder: A Tale," Fraser's Magazine,* XXX (1844), 394-412; 563-71.

114 "George Sand's Recent Novels," *Foreign Quarterly Review,* XXXVII (1846), 36.

115 Lewes disliked the novels of Dumas and Sue. In the *Leader* Lewes referred to Dumas as the "Briareus of fiction." (October 22, 1853, 1023-24). See the *Athenaeum,* April 1, 1848, 333-34; "Historical Romance-Alexander Dumas," BQR, VII (1848), 181-204. In "Eugene Sue: *Les Mystères de Paris,"* BFR, XVIII (1844), 217-38, Lewes described Sue as a bad novelist who emphasized murder and crime.

of Montaigne reproduced in a most artistic manner. The style is exquisitely colloquial without ever, as it seems to us, becoming vulgar; and hits the very nice point of simplicity without insipidity. . . . These pages have a tone interpreting Nature that has an effect like that of stepping out into her secret and quiet ways from the artificial atmosphere of a fetid civilization."[116]

Lewes liked Goethe's *Werther* for the same reason he liked *François le Champi*. *Werther* also contains a beautiful and artistic representation of the simplest realities: Charlotte preparing bread and butter for the children, the scene of the ball, the children grouping around Werther asking for sugar. A masterpiece of style, nothing in German literature is the equal of *Werther* for "clear sunny pictures, fulness of life, and delicately managed simplicity."[117] Thus, in consistent fashion, Lewes praised Goethe's novels for their realism.

In discussing *Wahlverwandschaften* and *Wilhelm Meister*, Lewes offered his mature observations on morality in the novel. *Wahlverwandschaften*, he noted, neither attacks nor sanctifies marriage; in it Goethe described the truth as he experienced it, and "he necessarily presented it in a form which would permit men to draw from it those opposite conclusions which might be drawn from the reality itself."[118] Critics who object to the immorality of the theme judge art and human life abstractly: ". . . Disregarding fact and necessity, [they] treat human nature as a chess board, on which any moves may be made which the player chooses, the player himself being considered an impersonal agent, untroubled by rashness, incapable of overlooking what is palpable to the bystanders. . . ."[119] However, critics who realize that art should reveal the "wondrous complexity of impulses," understand the tragedy, by no means immoral, inherent in the conflict between passion and duty, desire and social law which Goethe portrays in the story of Eduard and Ottilie and Charlotte and the Captain. Neither can *Wilhelm Meister* be said to be immoral because it has no explicit moral aim. "It may not be written for the edification of virtue; assuredly it is not written for the propa-

[116] "George Sand's *François le Champi*," *Athenaeum*, May 20, 1848, 502.
[117] *Life of Goethe*, 153.
[118] *Ibid.*, 512.
[119] *Ibid.*

gation of vice. . . . All that can be said is that the Artist has been content to paint scenes of life, *without comment*; and that some of these scenes belong to an extensive class of subjects, familiar indeed to the experience of all but children, yet by general consent not much talked of in society. If any reader can be morally injured by reading such scenes in this novel rather than in the newspaper, his moral constitution is so alarmingly delicate, and so susceptible of injury, that he is truly pitiable. Let us hope the world is peopled with robuster natures; a robuster nature need not be alarmed."[120] Remembering Lewes' more narrow minded treatment of the moral issue in Balzac's novels, we can justly appreciate his growth as a critic when he adopted a broader view of the function of morality in a realistic novel.

However, Lewes did not praise all of Goethe's novels; he criticized them when they failed to contain realistic characterization or relied heavily on symbolism. Lewes noted that when Goethe wrote the first six books of *Wilhelm Meister*, he still preferred the "healthy objective fact" to the use of the symbol. When he resumed writing the novel after a ten year interval, he made the theme symbolical of the faulty striving of youth to attain culture. By adding the Mysterious family, he ruined what might have been a masterpiece. Profound thoughts are expressed in the last two books. Philina, "one of the most bewitching and original creations in fiction," the poetical Mignon, the weird Harper, the passionate Marian, and Wilhelm are skillfully created characters. But Lothario, the Abbé, the Doctor, Theresa, and Natalie are part of the philosopher's study, not of the fresh air of Nature. Passionless and lifeless characters, and trivial and improbable incidents combined with the absurd mystification of the Mysterious Family mar the latter part of the novel.[121]

But whatever reservations Lewes may have had about Balzac, Sand, and Goethe, in the end he praised them for their love of truth, and their realism. He reserved his strongest censure for Victor Hugo precisely because he preferred effects to truth. He described what he expected the public would want to see fantastically and hyperbolically. Like Thackeray, he employed the antithesis, but unlike Thackeray, whose contrasts grew out of a keen

[120] *Ibid.*, 404-5.
[121] *Ibid.*, 403.

observation of opposites in nature, Hugo deliberately invented an antithesis to produce a desired effect. To reveal the beauty of parental love, Hugo displayed it in such unpleasant personalities as Lucrezia Borgia and Triboulet; to describe the virtue of woman's love, he embodied it in the hearts of public courtezans, Marian de l'Orme and Tisbe. These antitheses enabled him to create striking and effective situations, but he was without passion and a sense of tragedy. Hugo's essentially picturesque imagination penetrated no further than the picture, and as a result his characters are wooden dolls.[122]

Les Travailleurs de la Mer illustrates Hugo's mastery of the picturesque. Unfortunately, it also illustrates his lack of insight into human nature, for the emotional appeal of the story is feeble. The human being is of minor importance compared to the Infinite, which under the familiar and tedious guise of the Abyss, the Unknown, the Night, the Shadows, and Immensity, is the real protagonist in this story (and many other stories by Hugo). The last scene of the novel reveals that Hugo used a story essentially to display his powers of description. When Gilliatt kills himself after Deruchette leaves with her husband, the reader cannot sympathize with his excess of self-sacrifice. His love, based on no more than the fact that she once aroused his curiosity by writing his name on the snow, is not psychologically credible. Hugo is considered imaginative because of his grandiose images and his avoidance of the commonplace. Actually, he often becomes so obsessed by an image that he disregards sense or truth. But an artist with fine imagination sees vividly and truly. "The difference between the aimless wandering of reverie, and the concentrated, regulated, orderly movements of thought, may be tested by anyone in his experience. It is easy to let the mind wander capriciously amid the evanescent suggestions of reverie, and difficult to fix the thought upon the true relations of things. If the reader who has been delighted with the *brio* of one of Victor Hugo's descriptions, and astounded at its wealth of images, will only think of the thing described, and ask himself whether it has become more vivid to him . . . he will be able to estimate aright the value of his prodigal rhetoric."[123]

122 "Victor Hugo's New Novel," FR, V (1866), 30-46.
123 *Ibid.*, 46.

In *Les Misèrables,* Hugo achieves his effect through brilliant rhetoric, incisive epigrams, and a polished, elaborate style. However, his is "not the strong, healthy, inspiring eloquence of a serious and beautiful mind, but rather the turbulent and factitious power of a strong talent loosened from all control: a debauch of diction, not a draught from Helicon."[124] Hugo's penchant for antithesis is particularly apparent in the Fantine section. The Bishop's present life is contrasted with his former life as a sinner, and he is contrasted with the cynical senator. Regarded as a sinner, the revolutionist is discovered in his death scene to be the incarnation of virtue. The Bishop is extremely kind and tender to Valjean who leaves unmoved to rob a boy. The Bishop's characterization fails because it is untrue. Meant to be good, he turns out to be "goody." "No one can believe in the Bishop of D., because all the traits of humanity have disappeared in this type of evangelical mansuetude. He exhibits none of the inconsistencies, none of the little absurdities, which are often seen in the best of men; he is never ignorant, never out of temper, never despondent, never off the moral stilts."[125] Fantine is also described falsely to carry out an antithesis. A mother who is forced into prostitution in order to feed and educate her child is a harrowing symbol of tragedy. The writer who wishes to arouse our sympathies for this pitiful victim of society must be sincere, never lapsing into the sentimental or employing misplaced rhetoric. But after Hugo carefully describes Fantine's degradation as a wretched street walker, he contends that she is sinful only in the eyes of men; in the eyes of God she is virtuous and chaste. Lewes derided this antithesis as being nothing more than silly, sentimental rhetoric. Obviously Fantine has certain virtuous qualities, but Hugo purposely contrasts her degeneration and virtue to produce an antithesis. "It is only Parisians who thus make angels; and . . . only in French literature is hell the necessary introduction to heaven. . . . It is the besetting sin of most French writers to be incapable of trusting to the truth. Victor Hugo is eminently French."[126]

It seems clear, then, from this survey of Lewes' comments on

124 "Victor Hugo's Last Romance," *Blackwood's,* XLII (1862), 181-82.
125 *Ibid.,* 175-76.
126 *Ibid.,* 179-80.

the novel that the overriding consideration for him was the theory of realism. How much he valued it is revealed in the following test he proposed for a young writer: "The first test we should apply to a young writer, in a consultation as to whether he had genuine artistic power, would not be whether his style was harmonious, his images captivating, or his command of language remarkable; we should set him to describe the brick wall opposite! Ten to one he would fail miserably. Twenty to one he would exaggerate. The attempt to describe the realities of Life is singularly ambitious, because the difficulties of Art become intensified the nearer its subject and form approach to the Actual. . . ."[127] And without question, as René Wellek noted, "Lewes seems to have been the first English critic who systematically applied standards of realism. . . ."[128] As will be shown in the following pages, the standards of realism were also applied to his drama criticism, but with a special turn of the screw.

127 *Leader,* May 31, 1851, 517.
128 R. Wellek, *Concepts of Criticism* (New Haven, 1963), 229.

5

Lewes as a Drama Critic

Lewes fell in love with the theater at an early age. This is not surprising in view of the fact that his grandfather, Charles Lee Lewes, had been a successful comedian, and his father had been an actor as well as a manager of the Theater Royal in Liverpool.[1] He was eight when he saw Edmund Kean perform in 1825; at the age of ten, he was delighted by the French theater in Nantes; at seventeen, he saw Macready perform in Byron's *Sardanapalus*, and he wrote dramas which were to be acted by boy actors. Several years later, Lewes read his play on Tasso to his friend William Bell Scott, who objected that the roles in the play were much too complex and mature for them to handle. Undaunted, Lewes boasted: "Well, do you know, young as I am, I have been all through such experiences! I have had ladies at my feet, and I have myself been next to mad with love and its fallacies!"[2]

During his lifetime he did all the things that a devotee of the dramatic arts might want to do. He wrote plays, he acted, he reviewed plays, and he wrote articles on the drama for many journals. William Archer, who collected and edited Lewes' reviews for the *Leader*, observed that "Lewes was probably the most highly-trained thinker who ever applied himself to the study of theatrical art in England."[3] From 1800 to 1854, the four major

1 *On Actors*, 15; John Lee Lewes (ed.), *Charles Lee Lewes Memoirs* (4 vols., London, 1803).

2 W. Minto (ed.), *Autobiographical Notes of William Bell Scott* (London, 1892), I, 103 ff.; *Life of Goethe*, 26; [James Sully], "George Henry Lewes," *New Quarterly Magazine*, II (1879), 357.

3 Archer and Lowe, *op. cit.*, xliii, xiv, xv. See also the following dissertations:

drama critics were Hunt, Hazlitt, Forster, and Lewes. When Lewes began reviewing for the *Leader,* Macready had just retired, leaving the stage to Anderson at Drury Lane, Charles Kean at the Princess, and Phelps at Sadler Wells. At that time, Lewes offered his opinions of the stage under the pseudonym, Vivian.

Volatile, argumentative, satirical, personal, witty, Vivian was an entertaining character. He was a gay young rake, a bachelor with a horror of marriage, who had to resist the blandishments of his Julias, Harriets, and Fannies. "There must be some extraordinary charm in 'conjugal love,' "—he wrote, "some intense fascination in legal happiness which has hitherto escaped my observation. . . . I must marry and find out that secret! If I do marry, beloved reader! (I shan't; but I put the extreme hypothesis,) I will tell you all about it, isn't that my function in this majestic universe,—to tell you 'all about' everything?"[4] He was also a serious student who liked to read the Church Fathers. "I am alone with my folios —companioned by the Fathers! . . . Basil was speaking to me in somewhat inelegant Greek of the advantages to be derived from the study of Greek writers—if I have *not* gained all the wisdom there awaiting me, I am willing to suppose the fault was mine. . . . Whatever the cause may be, certain it is that when Fanny, with the dove-like eyes, declared I must take her to the Lyceum to see the Christmas piece, I quitted my folios with immense alacrity!"[5] When Vivian questioned whether Macbeth's "fell of hair" was the correct phrase, several correspondents explained why the term was correct: "So you see," Vivian admitted, "I made an ass of myself—*mais que voulez-vous?* I can't know everything. I don't read the Eirbiggia Saga, and have only once seen, never read, Xiphilin!"[6] The indefatigable Vivian also reviewed operas and concerts, and humorously disposed of mediocre singers and composers in sarcastic passages like the following. After listening to a tiresome solo by Herr Schneider, at a concert at Exeter Hall, he wrote: "Immanuel Kant was the curse of his nation; an illustrious iconoclast, he dashed the majestic idol Time from its

---

Robert B. Doremus, "George Henry Lewes: A Descriptive Biography with Special Attention to His Interest in the Theater" (2 vols., Harvard, 1940); Edgar W. Hirshberg, "George Henry Lewes as Dramatic Critic" (Yale, 1951).

[4] *Leader,* November 27, 1852, 1145.

[5] *Ibid.,* January 1, 1853, 21.

[6] *Ibid.,* February 2, 1853, 214; February 19, 1853, 189.

pedestal, proved to his countrymen that Time did not exist . . . and from that time (which was *no* time) the Germans have severely ignored the existence of Time. Hence their immeasurableness in all things! their long books, long dinners, long pipes, long hair, long ballets, long operas, long winded orations, long epithets—their slow coaches, slow movements, slow *conversaziones*! Why should they hurry? *Tempus edax rerum*? A figment! Even those who recognize Time only think of killing it: Kant killed it! *'s ist doch wahr*!"[7] Reviewing Biletto's comic opera *White Magic*, at the Haymarket, he said of the unknown librettist: "The poet is 'anonymous'; if he is wise, he will remain so. He will pant for obscurity and deathless unrenown! . . . The tenor Mr. Harrison—the true British tenor—he sang with this throat, his nose, and his calves, and was much applauded by a delicately discriminating part of the audience. The opera succeeded although he sang in it."[8]

Lewes' justification for Vivian's jesting may be found in a letter he wrote to J.M. Kemble concerning his Goethe article: "Is jesting incompatible with earnestness, when that jesting be not employed on earnest points? Is not Folly to be laughed out if its pride of Bells? Are there not points of the ludicrous successfully mingled with the most passionate & earnest works of art the Scourging of Christ by Albrecht Dürer—the Lear of Shakspere, or the Divine Comedy of Dante—to mention the highest, or with Jean Paul & Carlyle on a lower scale?"[9]

George Bernard Shaw paid Lewes the compliment of admitting that the Shavian manner had been anticipated by Vivian. Praising Lewes for his culture, flexibility, and fun, he said:

> I consider that Lewes in some respects anticipated me especially in his free use of vulgarity and impudence whenever they happened to be the proper tools for his job. He had a rare gift of integrity as a critic. When he was at his business,

7 *Ibid.*, June 18, 1853, 597. Lewes was, however, very partial to Beethoven. He wrote in the *Leader*, May 24, 1851, 492-93: "I am somewhat of a fanatic about Beethoven. He moves the heights and depths of my soul as no other artist—poet, painter, or musician—ever moved them." For other samples of Lewes' music criticism, see the *Leader*: June 22, 1850, 306; July 6, 1850, 355; May 31, 1851, 518; June 14, 1851, 564; August 16, 1851, 782.

8 *Ibid.*, March 20, 1852, 282.

9 Lewes' Letter to J.M. Kemble, March 23, [1844?], Beinecke Library, Yale University.

> he seldom remembered that he was a gentleman or a scholar. In this he showed himself a true craftsman, intent on making the measurements and analyses of his criticism as accurate, and their expression as clear and vivid, as possible, instead of allowing himself to be distracted by the vanity of playing the elegant man of letters, or writing with perfect good taste, or hinting in every line that he was above his work. In exacting all this from himself, and taking his revenge by expressing his most labored conclusions with a levity that gave them the air of being the unpremeditated whimsicalities of a man who had perversely taken to writing about the theatre for the sake of the jest latent in his own outrageous unfitness for it, Lewes rolled his stone up the hill . . . kicking it at random hither and thither in pure wantonness. In fact, he reminds Mr. William Archer of a writer called Corno di Bassetto [i.e., G. B. Shaw] who was supposed—among other impostures—to have introduced this style of writing. . . . But these articles of Lewes's are miles beyond the crudities of Di Bassetto, though the combination of a laborious criticism with a recklessly flippant manner is the same in both.[10]

Behind the flippant tone adopted by Vivian was the serious concern of a lover of good drama. Vivian castigated what he called the "Fast School of Criticism" which preferred only sensational amusement and disliked poetry and psychology in plays. The following is a typical passage by Vivian which combines serious reflection with levity.

> I once had a maternal uncle (had, alas! vixit!) whose views on the drama were freely communicated to me in the high and buoyant days when five-act tragedies in swelling verse were the dream and occupation of my life. He resided in Bungay, where he adorned a large domestic circle with all the virtues of a citizen, and earned the eternal gratitude of mankind by his improvements in soap!
>
> In soap! Imagine Vivian in connection with saponaceous commerce! But biography has no delicacy, and facts are shattering to all illusions; and the fact is as I state. This free-spoken uncle was an anticipation of the Fast School of Critics.

[10] Shaw, *Our Theater in the Nineties* (London, 1932), II, 161–62.

> He snored at five-act dramas, and was merciless to mine. Shakespeare was his personal enemy. I think I see him now, rubbing his fat fingers through his scanty hair, as he authoritatively delivered himself of this favourite remark: "*Hamlet* sir? If *Hamlet* were produced to-morrow, Hamlet would be d-----d, sir." After uttering that he would relapse into his chair, complacent, authoritative, obese.[11]

But Lewes was not concerned with the theater *merely* as Vivian. He had a deeper involvement with it than with any of the other literary forms he criticized. His theory of the drama grew out of an extensive preoccupation with the theatrical world. He considered the actual experience of writing plays to be invaluable to the drama critic. Critics, he wrote, "cannot recognize their own deficiencies. They will sometimes (not always) admit that unless a man has studied the means and methods of painting, he is an imperfect judge of pictures, but they will not admit that one who had never studied the mechanism of a drama is an imperfect judge of dramas."[12] Critics too often lack the technical and special psychological knowledge indispensable for good criticism. "Their observations, for the most part, turn upon the general conditions, not on the special conditions, and are consequently on a par with those made about pictures by amateurs unacquainted with the laws of perspective, composition and colour—insensible to the exigencies, and limits of the art. Their criticisms may be valuable and suggestive in elucidating questions of literature, but the drama as a special form of literature requires a more technical estimate.[13]

Lewes must have acquired a good deal of this special knowledge by writing plays. Of the five extant manuscripts of Lewes' unacted plays, one was written as early as 1843, *Pretension: or the School for Parvenues,* a comedy in five acts. The four other plays in manuscript form are *The Miser's Niece,* a comedy in two acts, n.d.; an unfinished melodrama, *Marguerite,* n.d., *Drat That Dick: A Philosophical Farce* [1852?], and *The Fox Who Got the Grapes,* 1854.[14] His tragedy, *The Noble Heart,* written in 1841, was first

11 *Leader,* June 19, 1852, 594.
12 "Shakespeare in France," *Cornhill,* XI (1865), 54.
13 *Ibid.,* 35.
14 Beinecke Library, Yale University.

performed on April 16, 1849 in Manchester, three times more in Manchester, three times in Liverpool, and on February 19, 1850 it was produced at the Olympic Theater in London. He himself recalled how his manager compared him to Shakespeare on the evening before the play opened, and how the next morning *The Noble Heart* was damned by the critics.[15] The bombastic quality of its verse resembles Elizabethan rant, but Lewes could easily have found the same tendency towards pompous and didactic declamation in the Spanish drama. Indeed he may have consciously tried to rework a favorite Spanish theme. In Calderon's *A secreto agravio secreta vengenza,* the husband who has killed his wife and her lover is rewarded by the king with another wife. But Lewes expressed antipathy for the moral code in the Spanish tragedy which considers the act of dishonoring someone a greater crime than murder.[16] In *The Noble Heart,* the husband gives up his wife to her lover in a noble gesture of renunciation. Juanna does not know that Leon, her betrothed, is the son of the rich and noble Don Gomez de le Vega. While Leon is away, she marries Don Gomez to save her father from financial ruin. When Don Gomez discovers that Juanna and Leon were betrothed secretly and still love each other, he magnanimously annuls his marriage and retires to a hermitage. No such charitable action would be forthcoming from a character in a Spanish drama; in fact, the father would have to kill the son. Unfortunately, *The Noble Heart* is unredeemed by the virtues of the great Spanish plays.

Using the pseudonym of Slingsby Lawrence, Lewes wrote several melodramas in collaboration with Charles Mathews. *A Chain of Events,* adapted from Anicet-Bourgeois' and Masson's *La Dame de la Halle* in eight acts, was performed at the Lyceum on April 12, 1852. In this play, the villain Gaspard attempts to deceive the peasant George Michel into believing that Michel is the lost heir of the Marquis de Melcy of Paris, as marketwoman, water carriers,

15 "The Miseries of a Dramatic Author," *Cornhill,* VIII (1863), 511. Most of Lewes' plays are reprinted in T.H. Lacy's *Acting Edition of Plays* II, V, VI, X, XV, XXI, XXII, XXIV. Lewes used the pseudonym Frank Churchill for *Taking by Storm*; see Lacy, VI.

16 *The Spanish Drama, Lope de Vega and Calderon* (London, 1846), 121-22. For reviews of *The Noble Heart,* see *the Examiner,* February 23, 1850, 117; *Times* (London), February 19, 1850, 6; *Spectator,* February 23, 1850, 180, and *Literary Gazette,* February 23, 1850, 149.

singers, millers, soldiers, peasants, noblemen, firemen, waiters, children, and masqueraders move confusingly across the stage. Another melodrama, *A Strange History,* in nine acts, adapted from Anicet-Bourgeois' and Masson's *Marianne,* was produced on March 29, 1853. It concerns the unjust imprisonment of a Swiss girl Christine who is falsely accused of a theft. Many years later the true thief is discovered and Christine is reunited with her husband and children. Lewes himself wrote still another melodrama, *Captain Bland,* which was first performed at Wallach's Theater in New York on May 30, 1864. Captain Bland, the villain, escapes from prison and is foiled in his attempts at blackmail. In his Diary (November 30, 1860) Lewes correctly referred to this play as an "unfortunate piece."[17] He had sold it originally to Alfred Wigan of the Olympic Theater, with the express provision that he was not to be identified as the author. Fortunately, it was never produced in England.

Lewes was under no illusion as to the actual merit of these melodramas. But we should be grateful for their existence because they led Vivian to indulge in humorous depreciation of the lucky but "over-estimated writer," Slingsby Lawrence. Concerning the *Chain of Events* Vivian wrote: "My favorite theatre, the Lyceum, terrified me by announcing a dramatic story in eight acts. In eight acts! Why not in eighty? I couldn't in cold blood be asked to assist at *that,* until I knew whether the eight acts were amusing, and as the authorship was whispered to be claimed for my intimate enemy, Slingsby Lawrence, I preferred sending my *critique* blond, the Screech Owl . . . because if I abused the piece it would be supposed that I was moved by personal motives."[18] Vivian also complained of having to sit through another long play, *A Strange History,* in nine acts. He recalled that Martial had advised a poet to make necessary erasures in his work: "'One erasure,' Martial answered, 'will suffice.' Slingsby Lawrence and Charles Mathews might think of this. . . . Oh angry Lawrence, one must have story, character, dialogue—three things in which this piece is unfortunate."[19]

[17] A prompter's copy of *Captain Bland* is in the New York Public Library. See Edgar W. Hirshberg, "*Captain Bland* on the New York Stage," *New York Public Library Bulletin,* LVII (1953), 382-88.

[18] *Leader,* April 17, 1852, 377.

[19] *Ibid.,* June 5, 1852, 547.

Lewes was considerably more adept at adapting French comedies and writing farces. He served as a kind of stock author for the Lyceum, at a time when Charles Mathews and Madame Vestris were instrumental in making French comedy popular on the English stage. John Hollingshead has described for us what Lewes did when he received the script of Adolphe D'Ennery's *Mercadet*, based upon Balzac's *Le Faiseur*, on a Saturday morning at the end of September, 1851. He retired to a room at the top of the theater in the company of six shorthand writers: "He dictated, a la Masaniello, to each and all in turn . . . the 'flimsy' was copied from shorthand into slips of English; the slips were sent down to the stage every half-hour to the actors who were there, learning these fragments with one eye, while they were rehearsing, so to speak with the other. This work went on through Saturday and Saturday night, a part of Sunday and Sunday night, and a greater part of Monday, and the result, the three-act comedy of the "Game of Speculation" was produced at the Lyceum Theatre on the same Monday night, spoken and acted to perfection. . . . Was the dialogue slip-shod? No. . . . Was it badly adapted? No."[20] Years later, Hollingshead, manager of the Gaity Theater, tried to adapt the play, but "it was no good. Mr. George-Henry-Lewes-Slingsby-Lawrence had cut the ground from under us with his forty-eight hour's adaptation, his phonographic echo of Balzac."[21]

Another one of Lewes' adaptations was praised by the *Times* reviewer: "We would almost give the adapter, Mr. Slingsby Lawrence, the credit of an original production. *The Lawyers* is a thoroughly English piece, the dialogue is written with English vigor and the abuses of the Bar are satirized with a perfect feeling for the professional peculiarities of this country. And it is not the coloring alone that is original. The adapter has altered the plot of the Gymnase piece in several essential particulars. . . ."[22] Produced in 1853, *The Lawyers* was adapted from *Les Avocats* by P.F.P. Dumanoir and L.F. Nicolai and first performed at the

20 John Hollingshead, *My Lifetime* (London, 1895), I, 65-66.

21 *Ibid.*, 66. Actually, Lewes took 13 hours to write his adaptation, and the play was first performed on Thursday, October 2, 1851. See Hirshberg, "George Henry Lewes as Dramatic Critic," 61 ff.

22 *Times* (London), May 20, 1854, 5. This review was quoted in the *Leader*, May 21, 1853, 501-2.

Théâtre Gymnase in 1852. It still reads rather well today, and reveals Slingsby Lawrence's remarkable ability to Anglicize a French comedy.

Other plays by Lewes are: *Wanted a She-Wolf,* based upon Dumas' Romulus; *Sunshine through the Clouds,* a translation of Madame de Girardin's *Le Joie Fait Peur; Taking by Storm* (written by Frank Churchill), a version of the comedy *Tambour Battant* by A. Decourcelle, T. Barrière, and L. Morand; *Give a Dog a Bad Name,* adapted from *Quand On Veut Tuer Son Chien* by T. Barrière and J. Lorin; *A Cozy Couple,* an adaptation of O. Feuillet's *Le Village; Buckstone's Adventure with a Polish Princess,* billed as an original farce; *Stay at Home,* a version of P.E. Piestre's and E.P. Basté's *Un Mari qui Se Dérange.* In *Taking by Storm,* Backhuysen Buff, the marine painter, "takes by storm" Fanny Seabright and they marry after a whirlwind courtship of one day. In *Give a Dog a Bad Name,* Dr. Dearlove convinces his wife of the folly of believing in the flattery and attentions of Horace Ogle. In *A Cozy Couple,* Tom Russelton, an old boyhood friend of Mr. Dormouse, almost convinces Mr. Dormouse that he should leave his loving wife and their comfortable home to seek excitement. In *Buckstone's Adventure with a Polish Princess,* the hero has an odd dream that he is involved with a Polish princess who is both rich and ugly. Hardly more than second rate farces, these pieces were probably sufficiently diverting when well acted and well staged.

Lewes must have learned one very important fact about the drama by writing these plays and adapting them for public performance. In an early article, he had defined the drama as a "form of poetry occupying a distinctive place in the national literature [and] . . . expressing the generalized reflection of the epoch on human life."[23] But he soon came to understand that no other literary form must cater to an audience in the direct manner of the play: "The drama is not merely poetry nor literature, it is an *applied form* of this."[24] Its special purpose is to entertain an audience using many devices such as scenery, spectacle, beautiful verse, and strong passions. A writer who has the tech-

23 "The Rise and Fall of the European Drama," *Foreign Quarterly Review,* XXXV (1845), 292.

24 *Selections from the Modern British Dramatists* (Leipzig, 1867), I, 7.

niques required to create a play which interests an audience is a *playwright*. But the dramatist, in Lewes' sense, needs more than this kind of theatrical excellence. The dramatist offers an audience more than mere amusement or entertainment; he appeals to our curiosity, to our love of sensuous impressions, to our sympathy for mankind, while he expresses great ideas in beautiful imagery. The greatest dramatists, such as Shakespeare and Molière, had both theotrical and dramatic skill; they could amuse through stories skillfully presented, and they could inspire and challenge the audience to experience new feelings and ideas. Indeed, the dramatist has to have many talents: "It is not enough for a man to be a great poet, a great inventor, a great humorist—it is not enough for him to have insight into character, and power of representing it in action—it is not enough for him to have command over brilliant dialogue and striking situation—there must also be added to these, a peculiar instinct for dramatic evolution, peculiar art of construction and ordonnance, [sic] which will combine all these qualities so as to meet psychological and theatrical exigencies."[25]

Perhaps more than any other writer, the author of a tragedy must have all of these skills. Since tragedy is "passion manifest in action" it has two requirements: "a collision of elemental passions, from whence the tragic interest should spring; and the construction of its materials into the dramatic form."[26] The writer of tragedy is not only faced with the difficult problem of analyzing the operation of passions in human beings, but he must also represent these passions as they evolve within a framework of organically related situations. While it is relatively easy to suggest powerful dramatic situations, it is difficult to show them evolving naturally from the characters and circumstance of the play: ". . . To make them consistent with human motives—*this* is the problem for the artist and only he deserves the name who can satisfactorily solve that problem. . . . Art consists in evolving from inwards organically; not in mechanical juxtaposition of materials."[27]

Lewes made use of the philosophic concept of reasoned realism, to explicate the modus operandi of revealing truth in the theater;

[25] *Ibid.*

[26] "Strafford and the Historical Drama," WR, XLI (1844), 121; *Life of Goethe,* 304.

[27] *The Spanish Drama,* 208.

this involves his favorite distinction between realism and idealism. The simple, uncritical spectator naively accepts what is presented on the stage; the prosaic viewer objects to the fact that what he sees is not like life. But the understanding critic knows that a play is to be judged "first in its representation of the real, the truth of the characters and events; and secondly in its artistic truth, which has reference not only to the effect, but also to the means by which the effect is reached. Without for a moment believing that men and women off stage speak and act in this way, he sees that this is the way of artistically representing their emotions and actions, under the conditions of the theatre."[28] Thus the dramatist, unlike the novelist or poet, has to convey the truths of life under theatrical conditions. This is his special dilemma. In a play, life is idealized: "In a play we have no accurate reproduction of what does occur, or ever did occur, but a reflection of the elementary motives, incidents, passions, *under artistic conditions*. . . . The conditions of Art necessitate the omission of much that is real, because it is too unwieldy for expression, while much also is transposed and altered, because the reality would be unsuitable for the desired end. Thus all is selected and arranged according to the internal conditions of theatric representation, and not according to the internal conditions of the life represented."[29] But even though the painted canvas is not the sky and the goblets are not really made of gold, and the wine is water, the wounds bloodless, and the gods merely mortals, "the real world is represented; the facts of life are there, both the facts of common experience and the facts of imaginative experience. The idealism is founded on realism."[30] Thus Lewes emphasized the fact that drama has a special way of conveying reality. The actor on the stage is not the real person. As an applied form of literature, the drama necessitates a study not only of the form in which it is written, but also of the conditions which bring it to life on the stage.

Lewes devoted a good deal of attention to the histrionic art, both as a critic and as an actor. As late as 1851 he referred to acting as "an art in which I have a personal ambition."[31] In 1849,

28 FC, II, 133.
29 FC, II, 132; *Leader,* February 22, 1851, 182.
30 FC, II, 132-33.
31 *Leader,* March 8, 1851, 228.

presumably after he had appeared as Shylock at the Manchester Theater Royal on March 10, he is supposed to have said, "As Macready is about retiring, and the young men you have here for the past few seasons, Brooke and Barry Sullivan, are popular, but, in my opinion, not equal to taking a leading position, much less of assuming our departing tragedian's mantel, I have been seriously thinking of taking to the stage permanently, and have every reason to be pleased with my initial effort."[32] We must make due allowance for the fact that this remark was quoted by the biased Barry Sullivan who played Bassanio to Lewes' Shylock, and who judged Lewes to be a poor actor. However, although Sullivan may have exaggerated to indicate Lewes' conceit, the remark does reveal that Lewes was really interested in acting. He had acted in Garrick's *The Guardian* at the Whitehall Theater in 1841. When Dickens asked Lewes to participate in his amateur theatricals, he told Lewes: "[You] are, I am told, an excellent actor."[33] In 1848, Lewes performed the role of Sir Hugh Evans in *The Merry Wives of Windsor* and Wellbred in *Everyman in his Humour* at the Haymarket. On March 10, 1849, he appeared as Shylock at the Manchester Theater Royal.

For his performance in this Shakespearean role, he was both glowingly praised and strongly censured. He evidently anticipated Sir Henry Irving in playing Shylock as a sympathetic character. As one critic noted, "[Mr. Lewes] has a purpose to give a new interest to Shylock by raising him from the position of the sordid, malignant Jew, to that of a man with less devilish intents —the vindicator of his race—one whose bitterness and revenge are excited by the scorn and insults to which he is exposed by his Gentile enemies."[34] However, Lewes was criticized for playing the Jew as if he were a Church divine: "But there was too much of repose, almost of gentleness, in his general manner, which marred rather than added to the effect of his outbursts, by making

[32] Robert M. Sillard, *Barry Sullivan and his Contemporaries: A Histrionic Record* (London, 1901), I, 189.

[33] Sotheby & Co. Catalogue, June 27, 1923, item 610, as quoted by Gordon S. Haight in "Dickens and Lewes," *PMLA*, LXXI (1956), 169, n. 4.

[34] *Manchester Guardian*, March 7, 1849, 6. See also Charles Hiatt, *Henry Irving: A Record and Review* (London, 1899), 172-82. For contemporary views of Lewes' acting ability, see *Times* (London), May 16, 1848, 8; *Spectator*, May 20, 1848, 487; *Dramatic Omnibus*, November 24, 1849, 3.

them appear forced and unreal."[35] On the other hand, the drama critic of the *Examiner and Times* thought highly of Lewes' Shylock: "It was an intense and thoughtful performance. . . . There was a freshness and purity of manner, a high refinement, in the whole mode of his acting, which would not at first fall with telling effect on a public accustomed to the conventional exaggerations."[36]

Lewes performed the role of Don Gomez in his own play, *The Noble Heart,* in Manchester on April 16, 19, 24, and 27, 1849 and in Liverpool on May 14, 16, and 18, 1849. Although as late as 1855, we find him playing the part of Buckstone at the Royal Haymarket, his concern with acting clearly became a secondary consideration, as his philosophic and scientific interests absorbed him more and more to the gradual exclusion of other involvements. Probably he was aware of his limitations as an actor. Furthermore, he considered the art of acting to be inferior to the other arts. He felt that the actor's genius is generally overrated, whereas his training is underrated. Often he is identified with a particular character and assigned the praise that properly belongs to the dramatist. In reality an actor may have little or no intellectual power of his own.

In 1851 Vivian noted that an actor has to have (1) conceptual intelligence, that is, the ability to understand the character, (2) representative intelligence, the mimetic power of imitating the peculiarities of a character, and (3) physical advantages, such as deportment, voice, physical power, etc.

> All the intellect in the world, all the representative intelligence in the world, could not enable a man with a weak voice limited in its compass, unless compensated by some peculiar effects in tone, to perform Othello, Macbeth, Shylock, etc. with success. Whereas a noble presence, a fine voice, and a moderate degree of representative intelligence, with no appreciable amount of conceptual intelligence, have sufficed to draw the town ere now, and make even critics believe a great actor has appeared.[37]

[35] William Archer, "George Henry Lewes and the Stage," FR, LXV (1896), 217.
[36] *Ibid.*, 218.
[37] *Leader,* February 8, 1851, 132-33.

For this reason Lewes denied that Thackeray's characterization of Miss Fotheringay, the good but ignorant actress, was a caricature. Actors can be ignorant and yet read parts competently. Intelligence is not necessarily a prerequisite of good acting. The talent of the actor is exaggerated because he is judged only by the effect he produces, not by the means he uses. The dramatist works for him, creating his role, supplying him with poetry, pathos, tenderness, eloquence, and sublimity. In addition, he is aided by costumes, scenery, lights, music, and other fascinating stage effects. Without them, he is nothing. In spite of his own love of acting, Lewes denied that the actor is as intelligent as the author or the artist, but agreed that he usually receives greater financial rewards and attains greater fame than they do. Lewes seemed, in this disparaging judgment, to be drawing upon personal experiences with actors.[38]

The volume *On Actors and the Art of Acting* was published in 1875 at the suggestion of Anthony Trollope who urged Lewes to collect many of the critical notices he had written. It contains penetrating observations on the nature of acting and invaluable assessments of the dramatic genius of some of the most famous actors in the history of the drama. Sir John Gielgud labelled it "*the* handbook of actors."[39] Lewes had occasion to observe what historians of the drama have described as the transition from the so-called classical or traditional style of acting to the romantic and realistic schools. It is, of course, difficult to know exactly what these terms connoted to different critics: Edmund Kean's acting, for example, was described at various times by all three terms. In *On Actors and the Art of Acting*, which represents Lewes' most mature statement on the subject, he carefully enunciated what seemed to him, after a lifetime of experience, to be the most valid concept of acting.

In acting, perhaps more than in any of the other arts, classifications are indistinct. In *On Actors and the Art of Acting* Lewes told of his attempt to make a reader understand that his defense of naturalism did not make him an opponent of realism. One writer has recently accused Lewes of being a reactionary because

38 See p. 148 in this book for Lewes' comments on Macready.
39 GE VI, 156-57, n. 9.

he was opposed to realistic acting.[40] But it is difficult to see how this concept of "natural" acting can be misunderstood, since it is not only explicated in various issues of the *Leader,* but it is clearly explained in the *Actors* volume.

To illustrate his views on natural acting, Lewes referred to Fielding's remarks in *Tom Jones* on Garrick's Hamlet. Partridge's observations have been considered complimentary to Garrick, but Lewes believed that Fielding intended a sarcasm rather than a compliment in the lines: "He the best player! Why, I could act as well as he myself. I am sure, if I had seen a ghost, I should have looked in the very same manner, and done just as he did. . . . If that little man upon the stage is not frightened, I never saw any man frightened in my life." (p. 101) Would a frightened Partridge have acted in the same way as a frightened Hamlet? On the assumption that Partridge correctly indicated Garrick's manner, Garrick's manner was a false representation of Hamlet's nature. Fielding implied that Garrick's acting was "natural" but, according to Lewes, Garrick's presentation of Hamlet was not natural. The saddened prince might have been awed by the appearance of his father's ghost, but he would not have experienced the vulgar terror of a vulgar nature. Natural acting means "truthful presentation of the character indicated by the author, and not the foisting of commonplace manner on the stage. . . ." (p. 104) Hamlet must not act like a servant or like any one particular prince, but like an ideal prince. He is not stupid, feeble, or coarse, but pensive, dreamy, and accomplished. He would not be frightened by the ghost in the same way as a servant or a Partridge. Garrick's Hamlet "was not natural, consequently not ideal, for ideal treatment means treatment which is *true to the nature of the character represented under the technical conditions of the representation.*" (p. 108)

Since naturalness is simply truthfulness, the manner, delivery, and gestures of actors in a play about ordinary life will differ considerably from those in poetic tragedy or comedy. Kean as Shylock, Bouffé in *Père Grandet,* and Rachel in *Phèdre* were all

40 M. Glen Wilson, "George Henry Lewes as Critic of Charles Kean's Acting," *Education Theater Journal,* XVI (1964), 367. The following references to *On Actors and the Art of Acting* are incorporated into the text and appear within parentheses.

natural. Actors make the mistake of playing ideal characters as ordinary men, and ordinary men as ideal characters. Since the actor's art is one of representation, the greatest difficulty he faces is to make ideal characters seem real, and he does not accomplish this by depicting the character as ordinary or vulgar. The actor must use natural expressions which convey real feelings. But these natural expressions, like the language of poetry or poetic prose, must be purified of the imperfections of conversational speech. The actor's speech must be "measured, musical, and incisive. . . . If the language depart too widely from the logic of passion and truthfulness, we call it bombast; if the elevation of the actor's style be not sustained by natural feeling, we call it mouthing and rant; and if the language fall below the passion we call it prosaic and flat; as we call the actor tame if he cannot present the character so as to interest us. The most general error of authors, and actors, is turgidity rather than flatness. . . . But it by no means follows, as some persons seem to imply, that because exaggeration is a fault, tameness is a merit. Exaggeration is a fault because it is an untruth; but in art it is as easy to be untrue by falling below as by rising above naturalness." (p. 103)

Shakespeare, in the advice that Hamlet gives to the players, showed his understanding that art involves calculation. A good actor never relies upon inspiration. He deliberately decides upon an interpretation and plays the role every night without varying gesture or tone. He might be viewed as a mechanical performer, but he knows that "trusting to the inspiration of the moment is like trusting to a shipwreck for your first lesson in swimming." (p. 99) The actor could hardly stand the psychological strain of really feeling the same emotion every night; it would disturb his intellectual equilibrium and hamper his acting. As Lessing observed, passion must be expressed symbolically; the ugly facial distortions of grief and the harsh, screaming sounds of anger are inadmissible in the drama just as they are inadmissible in sculpture. Dealing with the perplexing antinomy, "If the actor really feels, he cannot act, but he cannot act unless he feels," Lewes said that the actor must be in an emotional state which is capable of furnishing him with the necessary elements for expression, but which is at the same time so controlled that it does not blot out his consciousness of performing. In this sense his passion is sympathetic and ideal rather than personal.

In other words, the actor makes the decision as to how to play his role. Since there are all kinds of characters, tragic, heroic, noble, vulgar, he must decide upon the appropriate interpretation so that his acting will seem natural or real. Natural acting is realistic acting. Thus for the actor, as for the writer, achieving the effect of reality becomes the prime aim. Verisimilitude can be effected through a variety of techniques appropriate to the kind of character. "The test of an actor's genius," Lewes wrote, "is not fidelity to nature, but simply and purely his power of exciting emotions in you respondent to the situation—ideal when that is ideal, passionate when that is passionate, familiar when that is familiar, prosaic when that is prosaic."[41] When he offered his views of the many actors he saw, he was concerned with whether the methods they employed were appropriate for the kinds of roles they played.

Of the famous actors of poetic drama, Edmund Kean, Charles Kean, Rachel, and Macready, Lewes considered Edmund Kean and Rachel to be the greatest artists. He wrote of Edmund Kean: "[He was] incomparably the greatest actor I have seen, although even warm admirers must admit that he had many and serious defects." (p. 13) Kean never abandoned himself to the impulse of the moment. He knew that in art all effects are prearranged; so he rehearsed carefully all details until he was satisfied with the way he had regulated them, and then he never changed them in his performances. He was remarkable for the intensity of his passion and for his expression of subsiding emotion. Although he was too fond of abrupt transitions, "passing from vehemence to familiarity, and mingling strong lights and shadows with Caravaggio force of unreality—nevertheless his instinct taught him what few actors are taught—that a strong emotion, after discharging itself in one massive current, continues for a time expressing itself in feebler currents. . . . In watching Kean's quivering muscles and altered tones you felt the subsidence of passion." (pp. 18-19)

However, Kean had a limited range of miming power. He was

[41] *Leader*, February 8, 1851, 132.

physically suited only for tragic roles and could not handle simple or long narratives. Because his elocution had to be sustained by strong emotion to be effective, he was always ready to startle his audience into applause with abrupt, inappropriate transitions. Even his Othello, his masterpiece, was a "patchy performance . . . slovenly, spasmodic and false" in the first and second acts. But in the rest of the play, Kean's artistry has seldom been equalled: "In the successive unfolding of these great scenes he represented with incomparable effect the lion-like fury, the deep and haggard pathos, the forlorn sense of desolation, alternating with gusts of stormy cries for vengeance, the misgivings and sudden reassurances, the calm and deadly resolution of one not easily moved, but who, being moved, was stirred to the very depths." (p. 17) Lewes remembered how Kean, puny besides Macready, could by the sheer force of his personality appear commanding and tall. When roused by Iago's insinuation in the third act, Kean "moved towards him with a gouty hobble, seized him by the throat, and, in a well-known explosion, 'Villain! be sure you prove,' etc., seemed to swell into a stature which made Macready appear small. On that very evening, when gout made it difficult for him to display his accustomed grace, when a drunken hoarseness had ruined the once matchless voice, such was the irresistible pathos —manly, not tearful—which vibrated in his tones and expressed itself in look and gestures, that old men leaned their heads upon their arms and fairly sobbed." (pp. 15-16)

Kean played Richard III with a feline type of gaiety. "Who can ever forget," Lewes asked, "the exquisite grace with which he leaned against the side-scene while Anne was railing at him, and the chuckling mirth of his 'Poor Fool! what pains she takes to damn herself!' It was thoroughly feline—terrible yet beautiful. He had tenderness, wrath, agony and sarcasm at command. But he could not be calmly dignified; nor could he represent the intellectual side of heroism. He was nothing if not passionate." (p. 20) Kean's Shylock was a marvelous performance in which the passionate recrimination and wild justice of argument in his "Hath not a Jew eyes?" was the most impressive thing yet done on the stage.

Harold Clurman has observed that Lewes' "description and discussions of Rachel's acting might well be the envy of actors and theater people for all time."[42] Lewes wrote glowing accounts of her great acting ability. Rachel was limited in the range of characters she could portray effectively, but she was incomparable in the difficult tragic roles. She deteriorated greatly in her later years, but in her best days she was "the panther of the stage; with a panther's terrible beauty and undulating grace she moved and stood, glared and sprang. There always seemed something not human about her. She seemed made of different clay from her fellows—beautiful but not loveable. . . . She was very much as a woman what he [Edmund Kean] was as a man. If he was a lion, she was a panther." (p. 31) With irresistible power she represented scorn, triumph, rage, lust, and merciless malignity. Graceful, powerful, and dignified, she had little womanly tenderness, and "you always felt in her presence an indefinable suggestion of latent wickedness." (p. 31) She proved to ignorant Englishmen that the "cold" tragedies of Racine were vitally passionate and dramatic; she was unsurpassed as Phèdre: "What a picture she was as she entered! You felt that she was wasting away under the fire within, that she was standing on the verge of the grave with pallid face, hot eyes, emaciated frame—an awful ghastly apparition." (pp. 33-34) Marvelous in Corneille's and Racine's plays, she was ineffective in modern drama and comedy. Her thrilling, flexible voice and exquisite elocution were meant for musical verse; prose she could not handle with even a minimum of success.

While Macready did not have the genius of Edmund Kean and Rachel, his marked and individual talent approached very near to genius. Inferior to Edmund Kean in Shakespearean roles, Macready had the versatility to play many roles. He had an admirable physique, an expressive face, a powerful voice, extensive in range, and intelligent but unmusical declamation. A very thorough and conscientious artist, he tried to understand the character he portrayed by almost becoming that character. Lewes recalled that backstage Macready was supposed to have worked himself into a rage before appearing for an angry scene in *The Merchant of Venice*. But Macready was incapable of handling heroic characters as Edmund Kean did; his characterizations were domestic rather than ideal, that is they were not natural. Nothing was less

[42] *New York Times Sunday Book Review*, April 28, 1957, 7.

heroic than his portrayal of Macbeth: "He stole into the sleeping-chamber of Duncan like a man going to purloin a purse, not like a warrior going to snatch a crown." (p. 41) But he was successful as Lear, King John, Richard II, Cassius, Iago, Werner, Claude Melnotte, and Virginius. Thus, unlike Edmund Kean who was unsuccessful in modern drama, Macready infused life into many roles in both old and modern plays. As for Macready's intellectual pretensions, his *Reminiscences and Diaries* confirmed Lewes in his opinion that an actor does not share intellectual parity with the author or the artist. Macready "was undeniably a cultivated, honourable, and able man, and would have made an excellent clergyman or member of Parliament; but there is absolutely no evidence that he could have made such a figure either in the Church or Senate as would compare with that which he made upon the stage." (p. 53)

Lewes' evaluation of Charles Kean was quite influential. George Bernard Shaw noted that "the one failure of Charles Kean's life that matters now is his failure to impress Lewes in anything higher than melodrama."[43] M. Glen Wilson has devoted an entire article to proving that Lewes was "a questionable authority" on Kean. He argues that Kean's acting ability should be reassessed without major dependence on *On Actors and the Art of Acting*, "the most familiar and respected commentary accessible to students of the history of acting."[44] However, even a cursory reading of Watson's *History of the Nineteenth Century Stage* reveals that other critics of that time held substantially the same view of Kean as Lewes.[45] William Archer concluded that Lewes' evaluation was severe, but just.[46]

When Charles Kean announced his intention of producing plays at the Princess Theater, Lewes looked forward to them with eager anticipation. He praised the first production of *Twelfth Night* in the *Leader* on October 5, 1850. On October 12, 1850 Lewes criticized Charles Kean's performance of Hamlet, noting, however, that Kean was a more satisfactory Hamlet than Macready. But Lewes' friendly attitude towards Kean was shortlived.

43 Shaw, *Our Theater in the Nineties, op. cit.*, II, 160.

44 "Lewes as Critic of Kean," *Education Theater Journal*, XVI (1964), 360.

45 E.B. Watson, *Sheridan to Robertson: A Study of the Nineteenth Century London Stage* (New York, 1926), 362-65.

46 Archer & Lowe, *op. cit.*, xxxix-xli.

Vivian opened hostilities against Kean on February 7, 1852. He disclosed that Kean had cut him off the Free List of the Princess Theater because he had made no reference to Kean's merits as a tragedian.[47] Vivian explained he had remained silent because he had a personal liking for Kean and chose silence instead of severe criticism. Since Kean wanted only fulsome eulogies, Vivian vowed to break his compassionate silence and express his opinions frankly. In ensuing reviews Vivian kept his promise, ridiculing Kean's inadequacies as a tragic actor. There is no question but that Lewes would have been kinder if he had withheld some of his withering sarcasm. Kean was notoriously sensitive to criticism; he was supposed to have locked up a critic in a dressing room because he called his wife's performance vulgar.[48] On March 27, 1852 Vivian wrote about Kean's inability to perform Shakespearean tragedy and his skill in such melodramas as *Pauline* and *The Corsican Brothers.* Lewes advised Kean to "frankly take position as the hero of the Blood and Bogie School and leave Poetry in unmangled repose."[49] On February 19, 1853 Vivian criticized Kean's performance of Macbeth because he made him ignoble, "one whose crime is that of a common murderer, with perhaps a tendency towards Methodism."[50] Alternating rant with calmness, he made melodrama out of tragedy by hiding the mind of the criminal. When Kean multiplied Shakespeare's witches from three to fifty, he went too far indeed!

Vivian also flayed Kean unmercifully for his archaeological preoccupations. Kean informed his audience that *Sardanapalus* had never been played properly because nothing was known of Assyrian architecture and costume, and he proudly announced that his was the firest production to contain the proper scenic effects. Lewes, who remembered Macready's Sardanapalus and Ellen Tree's Myrrha which were memorable performances without benefit of "proper scenic effect," exclaimed in exasperation: "Is the Drama nothing more than a Magic Lantern on a large scale? . . . It is a strange state of Art when the mere *accessories* become the aim and purpose of representation—when truth of

47 *Leader,* February 7, 1852, 137.

48 Archer & Lowe, *op. cit.*, xl.

49 *Leader,* March 27, 1852, 306; October 5, 1850, 666; October 12, 1850, 787; February 7, 1852, 137; February 14, 1852, 161.

50 *Ibid.,* February 19, 1853, 189.

archaeology supplants truth of human passion. . . ."[51] He later admitted that Kean was an excellent manager and created splendid and successful scenic productions, but he deplored the excessive emphasis Kean placed upon archeological details.

In his final evaluation of Kean in *On Actors and the Art of Acting*, Lewes used Kean's career as an example of what can be achieved by courageous devotion and a burning desire to learn the art of acting. Originally Kean was a "stamping, spluttering, ranting, tricky actor," but he learned to become an effective player, remarkable for the naturalness and forceful quietness with which he performed certain roles. A poor tragedian, he lacked the flexibility of conception and expression which Shakespearean characters required. Handicapped by monotonous, mechanical elocution which disassociated rhythm from meaning, and a harsh voice, Kean could not be poetic, or subtle, or real in his tragic roles. But he was a first rate melodramatic actor. The inflexibility of his face and his animal force not only made him impressive in revealing the broad, coarse outlines of an exaggerated situation, but it also enabled him to play successfully such comic parts as Ford in *The Merry Wives of Windsor*, even though, like his father, he had no real natural gaiety. Finally, Kean had more literary culture and ambition than his father, and he did improve scenic representation.

Lest there be any misconception that Lewes could only appreciate classic acting, it is instructive to turn to his comments on the comic actors. He was associated with the Vestris-Mathews team at the Lyceum in the capacity of adapter of French farces and melodramas. Both Madame Vestris and her husband Charles Mathews had earned their reputations in farcical comedy. Yet when they appeared in serious roles in *The Day of Reckoning, Lewes* praised them highly: "I declare that the acting of Vestris and Charles Mathews in the new piece gave me more unmixed delight—more exquisite enjoyment—than I have for a long time received from the English stage. All the freshness of early enjoyment came back upon me, and no boy ever relished his first play more. . . . Vestris and Charles Mathews were *natural*, nothing more, nothing less. They were a lady and gentleman such as we meet in drawing-rooms. . . . I carry away from the theatre an

[51] *Ibid.*, June 25, 1853, 620; May 3, 1856, 428.

exquisite picture on which it is delightful to dwell, which reflection tells me was perfect in its art. . . ."[52] Again writing about the two Keeleys, Lewes distinguished between the kind of realism needed for comic roles, and the kind of realism needed for poetic roles which, as we have seen, he labelled idealism. ". . . Keeley was eminently an idealist, and as capable of personating characters in high and poetic comedy as in broad farce. Mrs. Keeley was eminently a realist and her realism was always a disturbing tendency in poetic comedy." (p. 80)

Lewes did not limit his study of actors to the English stage. He not only observed many English performers—G.V. Brooke, Mrs. Glover, Isabella Glyn, Frances Ann Kemble, Barry Sullivan, Helen Faucit, Wigan, and Farren, but he also recorded his impressions of various foreign actors he saw in France, Germany, Spain, and Italy: Déjazet, Emil Devrient, Ristori, Frédéric Le Maître, Fechter, Plessy, Got, Salvini, Seydleman. Thus while his professional association as drama critic for the *Leader* ended in July, 1854, Lewes continued to go to the theater when he was on the continent as well as at home. As a result of his observations of different kinds of acting organizations outside England, he made the following interesting suggestion in *On Actors* which reads like a prophecy of the trends in the theater today. He proposed the formation of smaller theaters with smaller audiences: "It is only by a rigid adherence to the principle of specialisation that such a scheme could have a chance. The theatre must be mounted with the sole purpose of performing works of art, for an art-loving public. It must avoid spectacle, 'scenic effects,' and encroachments on the domains of melodrama and burlesque. . . . It must have one small company of well-trained and art-loving actors [what a condition!], not a large miscellaneous company attempting *all* kinds of performance." (pp. 183-84)

Thus far we have been discussing Lewes' personal involvement with the theater. But he also wrote a good deal of criticism about the drama as literature. In this connection it is important to distinguish between his earlier and later views. In an early attempt to explain the development of the drama, he employed one of the cyclical theories which were so popular in the nineteenth century. He had, of course, the precedent of Aristotle's explanation in

52 *Ibid.*, December 7, 1850, 882.

evolutionary terms of the development of tragedy, and the writings of Dionysius of Halicarnasus, Quintillian, Velleius Paterculus, Winckelmann, Herder, F. Schlegel, Hegel, Comte, the Grimms, Taine, and Spencer offered variations on the cyclical theme.[53] It would be difficult to decide exactly from which source Lewes borrowed his conception of the principle of continuity in literary growth, but most likely he was influenced by Hegel's *Lectures on Aesthetics,* since at this early period he wrote his long review of this work. Like most of these writers, he conceived of the art in terms of some evolutionary principle of growth, perfection and decline. In "The Rise and Fall of the European drama," an article he wrote for the *Foreign Quarterly Review,* he also used this kind of description to trace the stages of the growth of tragedy. He traced the origins of European drama in Aeschylus, Corneille, Marlowe, and Cervantes. The perfection of drama he found in the plays of Sophocles, Racine, Shakespeare, Lope de Vega, and Calderon, while the decline was represented by the plays of Euripides, Voltaire, Fletcher, and Moreto. Although Lessing and Alfieri were respectively the fathers of German and Italian drama, neither Germany nor Italy produced more than an imitative drama.

Lewes' analysis of the Greek dramatists outlined the characteristics he attributed to the three stages of development in tragedy. Aeschylus introduced the second actor, limited the function of the chorus, expressed profound ideas, and utilized Homeric dialogue in iambic meter. But he was not, according to Lewes, a profound artist; he invented, but he did not perfect Greek drama. Many of the elements in his plays usually attributed to genius were necessitated by the exigencies of stage production in his era. For example, Prometheus had to keep silent in the first scene of *Prometheus Bound* because only two actors were permitted on stage. As for his alleged sublimity, Aeschylus was "more simple than sublime; more *naïf* than terrible. This simplicity is often sublime; but it is often, to modern tastes at least, trivial. It is the rudeness and triviality of the infancy of art, often more interesting than the finest polish; but interesting as an indication of the condition of the human mind at that period, not as the perfection of

[53] R. Wellek, *Concepts of Criticism* (New Haven, 1963), 37-53.

art."[54] Both *Prometheus Bound* and *Agamemnon* contain rant and bombast. Most important of all, Aeschylus lacked the power of creating subtle characters.

Sophocles was the greatest of the Greek dramatists, and second only to Shakespeare. He appears in Lewes' list of the great poets along with Dante and Goethe. Sophocles excelled in depicting passion and motivation. The art of Sophocles is "so rich, so varied, so delicate, subtle, and profound." Lewes praised the "miraculous unity" of his plays, and contrasted his *Electra* with the *Choephori* to illustrate the two periods in the Greek theater: the latter representing its primitive stage, and the former representing its perfected stage.

Lewes' preference for Sophocles was consistent with his theory of the drama as an idealized reflex of human life. In his view, Euripides made noble, heroic figures human, by making them commonplace. He was the poorest of the three tragedians. Using the prologue and the deus ex machina, he avoided dramatic evolution of character and the denouement. Expressing his religious and political opinions, he wrote down to his audiences who loved his dramatic rhetoric, skeptical ingenuity, and moral aphorisms. Unquestionably a great poet who wrote passages filled with pathos and imagery, he added warmth to a drama which came into his hands "as a statue, cold, elaborate and ideal." In sum, Aeschylus was "grand and trivial," Sophocles "passionate and majestical," Euripides "passionate and familiar." But by making Greek drama more familiar, Euripides put it in the market place. Aeschylus described "demi-gods and their passions," Sophocles painted "passionate men; he made the drama human," but Euripides "degraded the drama by making it prosaic."

Thus, according to Lewes, the earliest dramatists of most nations lacked the power of characterization which the later dramatists perfected, and the decline set in when rhetorical rather than genuinely dramatic devices were employed in the theater. Whether Lewes later came to understand the shortcomings of this cyclical view is not clear, although his rejection of Comte's later views and his own mature philosophical position would

54 "The Rise and Fall of the European Drama," *Foreign Quarterly Review*, XXXV (1845), 305.

imply his rejection of any deterministic theory. Even though he retained the view that the drama had declined in England, his comments in this connection indicate that he did not think of the decline in a deterministic sense as many others did who applied the evolutionary principle to art. Whatever else he may have said about the advances of modern art, he was clearly not in the camp of the progressionist when he wrote about the drama, nor did he believe that the decline was inevitable.

Many reasons have been given to explain the inferiority of nineteenth century English drama. A. Nicoll attributes it to the materialism of the age.[55] Watson lists no less than seventeen reasons for dramatic failure in that period.[56] Lewes attempted to pinpoint the reasons for the gradual deterioration of the theater. In 1842 he pleaded for the abrogation of the monopoly of patent theaters and urged dramatists to learn more about stagecraft. He then considered the reasons for the decline to be: late dinners, bad actors, cheap literature, and personal annoyances at large theaters.[57] Thus he blamed the degeneration upon conditions essentially extraneous to the quality of the plays themselves, except in so far as the dramatists were deficient in technical knowledge of the exigencies of stage production. Therefore, he could still retain some hope for the regeneration of the drama. But by 1845 this hope had faded, primarily because he had to recognize that the intrinsic quality of the plays themselves were at fault. As long as books were too costly and generally unavailable to the public, the stage was the main source of instruction. But when the theater became primarily a source of amusement, it had to "cater to the lower appetites of a miscellaneous public. Hence the increased demand for scenery and spectacle."[58] Lewes himself learned very well how to cater to the "lower appetites of a miscellaneous public;" witness the success of his melodramatic spectacles and farces.

In the *Leader* (August 3, 1850), Lewes expressed the "black heresy," namely that, "the *greatest injury yet sustained by the*

[55] Allardyce Nicoll, *A History of Late Nineteenth Century Drama 1850-1900* (Cambridge, Eng., 1949), I, vii-viii.

[56] Watson, *op. cit.*, 136-37.

[57] "Authors and Managers: Regeneration of the Drama," WR, XXXVII (1842), 71-97.

[58] "European Drama," *Foreign Quarterly Review*, XXXV (1845), 330.

English drama was the revival of admiration for the Old English dramatists." Despite the beauty of certain parts of their work, they were justly forgotten until Charles Lamb and his friends "struck with the brilliancy of the jewels cast upon these dunghills, cried out with all the quick delight of discoverers, 'Here is a new world!' " Because of their efforts, the Elizabethans were rescued from oblivion and became the models of nineteenth century poets, but "more detestable models were never held up before a student's reverence; their very excellencies being fatal lures."[59] Lewes' review of Richard Hengist Horne's production of *The Duchess of Malfi* (November 3, 1850) revealed specifically what he disliked in Elizabethan plays. He criticized *The Duchess of Malfi*, "a feeble and foolish work" for the irredeemable mediocrity of its *dramatic* evolution of human passion. . . ."[60] Even its many memorable passages do not redeem it. Many critics object to the accumulation of horrors, but its worst defect is "the motiveless and false exhibition of human nature." The horrors are not caused by tragic motives. As a result of insulted pride, Ferdinand might wish to kill his sister, and genuine tragic motivation exists when he gives her a poinard and tells her to die. But all the fantastic tricks Webster uses—the waxen image of Antonio, the mad, howling people—are "mere madness." When the Duchess is dead, Ferdinand, who has never shown real love for her, suddenly becomes tearful and repentant. This, said Lewes, is "clumsy ignorance," not the work of a dramatist. *The Duchess of Malfi* is a nightmare not a tragedy.

In the dramas of Beaumont and Fletcher, Lewes found amusing and rapid intrigues, passages of delicacy and pathos, passionate and humorous scenes, but they, like the plays of Marlowe, lack dramatic construction and characterization.[61] Furthermore Lewes was careful to point out that even if the Elizabethans were great dramatists, it would still be wrong to imitate them. The drama is an idealized reflex of the life and atmosphere of the present, not of the modes of the past. For this reason the French critics erred when they used classical precedent to justify the form of French classical tragedy. The Greeks were never

59 *Leader*, August 3, 1850, 451.
60 *Ibid.*, November, 30, 1850, 859.
61 "European Drama," *Foreign Quarterly Review*, XXXV (1845), 308.

confined by the rules of Aristotle. Similarly, the French writers wrote for their own audiences, not for antiquity. Therefore, Racine was as justified in giving us Madame Hermione and Monsieur Orestes as Euripides was in injecting anachronisms into his *Iphigenia.*[62] Like the young Tories of 1842, who wanted to revive the old-fashioned relations between the upper and lower classes, the "Young Englandism of Art" wanted to revive the old-fashioned techniques of the drama by imitating the earlier dramatists. If, instead of imitating old forms, the modern dramatists had concentrated on creating new forms, they would have enriched the theater greatly. "To appeal to the public taste, to move the general heart of men, you must quit the study, and try to image forth some reflex of the world that all men know, speaking their language, uttering their thoughts, espousing their idealisms. This does not mean that the dramatist should be ignorant of the past; it means only that he "should not strive to revive defunct forms, but produce a nineteenth century drama; something that will appeal to wider audiences than that of a few critics and black-letters students."[63]

Vivian derogated most serious, contemporary English plays as belonging to the "Fast" or "Material" School of melodrama. Such mediocre works as Dion Boucicault's *The Corsican Brothers* and *Sextus V*, A.R. Slous' *The Templar*, and Bulwer's *Lady of Lyons* relied on spectacular stage effects and situations, ignoring poetry, psychology, and truth.[64] Lewes also found contemporary English comedies wanting. Douglas Jerrold's *The Catspaw* and *Retired from Business*, and Boucicault's *Love in a Maze* and *London Assurance* were poorly structured with stereotyped, artificial characters. Employing wit excessively, they were too influenced by Congreve, when they should have been influenced by Scribe. Lewes had no use for Scribe as a serious dramatist; but he considered him to be a model writer of comedy, displaying his realism and his exceptional skill in constructing a comedy in such works as *La Camaraderie* and *Une Chaine*. The English, advised

[62] *Life of Goethe*, 267; "The New Classical Drama in France," *Foreign Quarterly Review*, XXXVI (1845), 36.

[63] *Leader*, August 3, 1850, 451.

[64] *Ibid.*, February 22, 1851, 181-82; November 16, 1850, 812; January 11, 1851, 43; February 28, 1852, 209.

Vivian, need to learn from him the technique of constructing plays about real people in the modern world.[65]

In 1867 Lewes edited a collection of dramas called *Selections from the Modern British Dramatists,* including Bulwer's *Lady of Lyons, Money, Richelieu;* Sheridan Knowles' *Virginius, The Hunchback, The Love-Chase;* Leigh Hunt's *A Legend of Florence;* Douglas Jerrold's *Bubbles of the Day, The Prisoner of War, The Rent Day;* Talfourd's *Ion;* Boucicault's *London Assurance;* Planché's *Fortunio;* Oxenford's *Twice Killed;* and Taylor and Reade's *Masks and Faces.* These were supposedly the best contemporary plays; but as Lewes observed, the best was none too good. In his introduction to the *Selections,* he was forced to admit that the reasons for the decline could not be explained simply in terms of the changed habits of modern society and the increase of popular literature. The dramatists themselves lacked genuine talent and failed to achieve either theatrical or dramatic excellence. He criticized Browning's *Blot on the Scutcheon* as a "very clever superstructure on very rotten basis. In the worst sense, it is *written for the stage,* i.e., the poet has asked himself what *situations* could be made out of his subject, not what would be the natural consequences of the passions. He has succeeded so far. But the whole *dramatic* nature of the piece is false. The brother's love is preposterous, and his honour only fit for the Spanish stage. It failed to touch the audience, because it was *untrue;* it succeeded occasionally in rousing them because it was theatrical."[66] He directed his sharpest statements against the influence of the religious world and attacked it for the part it had played in opposing the theater:

> It is in vain for you to argue that dancing is not sinful, that concerts are not sinful, that the pit of a theater is no pit of perdition: the "religious world" sourly declares these things *are* sinful, and will never hear your protest to the contrary; or hearing it, will declare that it leads to "scoffing unbelief." In England, whatever the "religious world" objects to, is apt to be branded as "leading to Atheism. . . ." One gloomy sec-

[65] *Ibid.,* June 14, 1851, 565; May 17, 1851, 469-70; May 11, 1850, 162; May 10, 1851, 446-47; January 18, 1851, 67; March 15, 1851, 253-54.
[66] "Review of Browning," WR, XXXIX (1843), 603-4.

> tion bitterly declaims against it because it is an Amusement (and all amusement beyond the control of the priest is sinful); the other section turns away from it because it is no longer amusing. And I think this second cause the more powerful of the two; for so strong is the natural desire for amusement, that even the "religious world" will seize any flimsy subterfuge to enjoy it. Thus, people who shudder at the idea of a theatre, crowd to see an actor or actress giving a dramatic representation in a concert room; and the pale-faced clergy, with their atribiliar followers, who would consider a visit to the opera a step on the path of perdition, may be seen in great numbers listening to operatic singers and operatic music, provided they listen to it in Exeter Hall, or a provincial cathedral.[67]

The church objected to the theater as a center of vice and profligacy. "There was a time," Lewes remarked bitterly, "when such accusations were just—and that was a time when theatres flourished, and the drama occupied a considerable place in men's thoughts. It is no longer true of our theatres; they have been purified of these causes of offense—and the drama is rapidly decaying."[68] These remarks clearly indicate that he did not consider the decline in the drama to be inevitable; in the 1867 edition he placed the blame for the decline upon imitative, inferior writers and the puritanical restrictions imposed by the Christian world.

However, it would be a mistake to limit a discussion of Lewes' dramatic criticism merely to an article such as the "Rise and Fall of the European Drama," or to the 1867 edition, or to reviews in *The Leader*. His interests ranged over the whole of European drama, and he has left us what practically constitutes a survey of world drama. His writings on the drama alone would fill a volume. He has been described both as a defender of Romantic drama, and as a reactionary classicist because of his preference for poetic drama. M. Greenhut correctly observed that Lewes was familiar with and drew upon classical, neo-classical and romantic theories of drama.[69] However, Lewes himself ob-

67 *Selections from the Modern British Dramatists,* I, 10-11.
68 *Ibid.,* 11-12.
69 Wilson, "Lewes as Critic of Kean," *Education Theater Journal,* XVI (1964),

jected strongly to the use of these terms: "Racine and Alfieri, who adopt the Greek model, are to be judged according to the 'classic principle' while Shakespeare, Calderon, and Schiller are to be judged according to the 'romantic principle.' So great a contempt of facts and such substitutes of verbiage for ideas, will be found in no other classification that has even been adopted by sane men."[70] Denying emphatically that any *absolute* standard of great drama exists, he maintained "that in the drama, as in all other arts, widely differing forms may be equally admirable. . . ."[71] This relativistic emphasis is most strikingly revealed in his drama criticism: in fact, the prime value of this criticism is its appreciative explication and comparison of different kinds of drama.

In his evaluation of Greek, German, French, Spanish, Italian, and English drama, he did not necessarily judge all different forms to be "equally admirable." Lewes was not an impressionistic critic. Working with certain basic principles, his judgments could be adverse even though he tried to avoid parochial narrowness. For example, he believed that inferior drama usually results from the slavish imitation of models. The drama, above all the other arts, reflects the "spirit of the age." This spirit could involve spiritual, sensual, aesthetic, didactic, frivolous, or skeptical feelings."[72] But its growth cannot be forced. "It must spring from the soil of national manners and feelings."[73] The Germans and Italians never developed a drama of their own, unlike the English, French, and Spanish who created their own special kind of national theater. Lessing, Schiller, and Goethe tried to create a national drama, but they did not succeed, despite their very considerable achievements. Lessing wrote some remarkable plays: *Minna Von Barnhelm* is Germany's best comedy; *Miss Sara Sampson* is notable for its avoidance of sentimentality; and *Der Freigeist* is commendable for its tolerance; *Emilia Galotti* and *Nathan der Weise,* however, have been overrated.[74]

367; K.W. Hooker, *The Fortunes of Victor Hugo In England* (New York, 1938), 84; M. Greenhut, "G.H. Lewes's Criticism of the Drama," *PMLA,* LXIV (1949), 358.

70 *The Spanish Drama,* 99.

71 "Shakespeare in France," *Cornhill,* XI (1865), 42.

72 "Goldoni and Modern Italian Comedy," *Foreign and Colonial Quarterly Review,* VI (1845), 367-68.

73 "European Drama," *Foreign Quarterly Review,* XXXV (1845), 300; "Weimar and Jena," *Saturday Review* (June 7, 1856), 137.

74 "Lessing," *Edinburgh Review,* LXXXII (1845), 458 ff.

Emilia Galotti is an interesting version of the Roman story of Virginius, but it lacks integrated poetic effect. Furthermore, Lessing erred in retaining the original ending which fails to awaken modern sympathies, for it is difficult today to believe that a Christian girl would want her father to commit the sin of murder to save her honor. As for *Nathan der Weise*, it is particularly interesting to note what Lewes wrote about this drama, in view of his and George Eliot's interest in Judaism. Lewes had met the German Jew Cohn at Red Lion Square, and he described his friend Cohn as a type of "philosophic dignity" and "sweet personal worth." Evidently he liked him because he had none of the usual bigotry which Lewes associated with *all* religious creeds. But Lessing made the mistake of assuming that the Jew could be used as a symbol of tolerance. In *Nathan der Weise*, a philosophic, epigrammatic, polemical play, remarkable for its deep, generous feeling and profound thought, Lessing pleaded for tolerance by comparing Christians and Jews to the disadvantage of Christians. But Nathan, a superb character, should not have been represented as a Jew because he is not Judaic. He has none of the bigotry of the Jews who would have denounced him for his views. Lessing chose an example "of the most exclusive and fiercely bigoted of all races as the exemplar of tolerance. . . ."[75] The Jew is as intolerant of the Christian as the Christian is of the Jew. Even if, as is generally assumed, Nathan was modeled after Moses Mendelssohn and Spinoza, the objection still holds for they were not really Jews, but apostates. What Nathan really symbolizes is philosophic tolerance in contrast with general intolerance.

Despite his considerable efforts, Lessing was not able to effect a vitalizing change in the German stage, and Lewes agreed with Lessing's own evaluation of his art, namely in his *Hamburgische Dramaturgie*, that his dramatic success was the result of a critical rather than a poetic genius.

Disgusted by the poor plays that vitiated German taste, and without faith in public opinion, Goethe and Schiller directed their efforts at the cultured minority. They wanted to create an

[75] *Ibid.*, 466. See "Spinoza," FR, IV (1866), 391, where Lewes wrote "I have never seen any evidence of Jews being morally inferior to Christians."

ideal drama, but they made the mistake of preferring culture to passion and humor. Lewes believed they erred in creating a literary rather than a popular drama; they ignored the need for reconciling the demands of the audience and of art. Goethe and Schiller committed the same blunder as the Unacted Dramatists in England, "the error of supposing a magnificent dome could be erected without a basis on our common earth; the error of supposing that a Drama could be more successful as Literature, than as the reflection of a national life."[76] In their experiments with restorations of ancient drama at Weimar, they succeeded in rejuvenating the very forms of French tragedy which Lessing had ridiculed. They even tampered with Shakespeare's plays to make them more classical. Lewes cited the ludicrous example of Schiller's translation of *Macbeth* in which the three witches are transformed into three young and beautifully dressed Fates. Although Lewes considered *Wilhelm Tell* and *Wallenstein* to be Schiller's masterpieces, he described *Kabale and Liebe* as one of the worst plays ever written and he called "The Robbers" an intolerable absurdity.[77] Goethe was also guilty of similar dramatic indiscretion because he lacked dramatic genius.

In his *Life of Goethe*, Lewes showed how Goethe's own plays as well as his critical and theatrical treatment of Shakespeare reveal his deficiencies as a dramatist. Goethe's version of *Romeo and Juliet* indicates how thoroughly he misunderstood Shakespeare's art.[78] Since Lewes considered *Romeo and Juliet* to be one of Shakespeare's poorer plays, he was willing to concede that it needed revision more than other works. But instead of revising the poorer elements, Goethe eliminated the excellent opening scene in which the servants quarrel, the means of visualizing the conflict between the two houses in vivid, dramatic fashion. Instead Goethe substituted a chorus of servants arranging lamps and garlands before Capulet's house, very much in the style of a comic opera. Goethe also eliminated the Queen Mab scene and the nurse's individuality, because he objected to the farcical personalities of both Mercutio and the nurse. Moreover, he believed that

76 *Life of Goethe,* 425-26.
77 *Leader,* April 26, 1851, 396.
78 *Life of Goethe,* 434-37.

the Ghost in *Hamlet* and the witches in *Macbeth* should be imagined, not represented, yet these are vivid touches which strengthen the dramatic power of the two plays.

Again in reworking Greek tragedies, he imitated only the accidental, temporal character of Greek art. In *Iphigenia,* he imitated the simple action and slow scenic movement of the Greek play, but he did not recreate its passionate life. Agreeing with Schiller that *Iphigenia* is essentially a modern, German tragedy, moral rather than passionate, Lewes defended Goethe's right to modernize the ancient story. As a dramatic poem, it has the one great value characteristic of Greek statues: "the perfect unity of impression produced by the whole, so that nothing in it seems *made,* but all to *grow;* nothing is superfluous, but all is in organic dependence, nothing is there for detached effect, but the whole is effect."[79] Goethe's Iphigenia is a more admirable person than the Greek priestess; a noble, tender Christian, she makes Thoas discontinue the practice of human sacrifice. But, Lewes pointed out, no Greek woman would have rebelled against a religious rite—witness what Antigone endured to fulfill a burial rite. By making Thoas a generous person who loves Iphigenia, Goethe destroyed the dramatic conflict, for the audience can hardly expect much interference from him. Euripides skillfully keeps Thoas off the stage until the end of the play, and in his absence he is imagined as a fierce and terrible person.

From the viewpoint of dramatic structure, Goethe's own dramas are very weak, although they do have great literary interest. Both *Egmont* and *Gotz von Berlichingen* are not genuine dramas: *Egmont's* defects stem from the fact that Goethe began it under the influence of Shakespeare and completed it under the influnce of classical drama. As for *Gotz,* considered in reference to the age in which it was produced, it was an unusual, original, daring play, one of the first to reveal the tendencies of the Romantic school.[80] By injecting history and local color into a play which dramatizes a segment of sixteenth century life, Goethe made the subject of the Feudal Ages one of universal interest. But unfortunately, his influence in this direction was more harmful than beneficial. Historical accuracy became more important than

[79] *Ibid.,* 268.
[80] *Ibid.,* 113.

passion, and many German and French dramas suffered from this excessive emphasis on history. Thus despite the efforts of Lessing, Schiller, and Goethe, Germany did not develop a national drama.

According to Lewes, not only does imitative effort hamper dramatic achievement, but any theater dominated by an absolute religious creed is by nature inferior and limited. He used the Spanish drama as a prime example of what happens when religious dogma stifles genuine creativity. Although he had listed Calderon among the greatest dramatists in "The Rise and Fall of the European Drama," in the *Spanish Drama* he emphasized Calderon's limitations. Lewes noted that he did not wish to condemn Calderon for his religious beliefs, and he objected to the "too prevalent system of testing a foreign poet according to our national standards; and . . . the angry criticism which Calderon's opinions have sometimes drawn from Protestant writers are wholly misplaced. The Catholic poet must be judged according to Catholic opinions."[81] However, when Schlegel rated Calderon above Shakespeare because Calderon had solved the mystery of life and because his plays contained the "true solution of life's enigma," Lewes' ire was aroused by this presumptuous claim. Calderon was a Catholic for whom the Catholic Church had solved all the riddles of existence. He employed his genius in illustrating, not interpreting, the dogmas of the church. As a pious Catholic he was not permitted to question them. "Surely," Lewes observed, "it required no great effort of the mind to preach a doctrine constantly preached by the Church? Who so looks in Calderon for a solution of the riddle of life may find one, indeed; but unless he be a devout Catholic he will not estimate it highly."[82] Calderon was not a philosophic poet. Philosophy and religion are incompatible because philosophy values reason and investigation whereas religion places itself beyond the test of reason. "Was not Calderon a Catholic?" asked Lewes. "The nature of his religion forbade questioning, and forbade new interpretations of its dogmas. . . ."[83] The famous *Life is a Dream* is an ingenious "Cloak and sword" comedy with a romantic subject, but it can hardly

81 *The Spanish Drama,* 179.
82 *Ibid.,* 178.
83 "The Three Fausts," BFR, XVIII (1844), 80.

be classified as a philosophical poem. Its theme is neither profound nor philosophical. Furthermore, in such plays as *Devotion to the Cross* or the *Purgatory of St. Patrick,* the most revolting villains obtain salvation despite their acts of murder and other vile deeds because they believe in God. Nor could Lewes understand why Schlegel extolled the morality of Spanish tragedians. They had no notion of conscience in the English sense. For them "the Holy Inquisition, the Catholic Faith, and the Tribunal of Opinion; these were terrible in their vengeance, rigid in their decrees. All men knew what crimes were, and what their punishment. Both were definite, objective."[84] While the Catholic can confess his sins and forget about them after the priest acts as mediator for an outraged heaven, the Protestant has no such assurance of definite penance. The Spaniard has a very curious conception of honor; a man will die for honor's sake with the public gaze upon him, but when unobserved, will have no scruples about the kind of dirt he crawls through. Since the church takes care of his moral education, the Spaniard goes to the theater to be amused, and this explains why the drama reflects this paradoxical coupling of intense religious zeal with great moral laxity.

Years later, when Lewes was traveling in Europe, he had occasion to see the performances of several religious plays.[85] At the Gaieté in France, he saw a production of *Paradise Lost* and expressed his astonishment that the masses in the audience could derive enjoyment from such a vulgar, nineteenth century, mystery play in which Satan makes love to Eve in the style of a French novelist. Evidently the Church had conditioned them to accept this absurdity with reverence. At Antwerp, he saw a mystery play on the Life of Christ which was better than *Paradise Lost,* but it made use of such effects as a large doll lamb which "baa'd" when its head was pulled down. At Barcelona, he saw a mystery in the Catalonian dialect on The Shepherd of Bethlehem, similar to the Chester and Coventry versions, and it was a real drama with serious and comic acting and poetic quality as well as religious significance. But even though he praised this play, he viewed it as a secularist who realized that English Puritans would

[84] *The Spanish Drama,* 110.
[85] *On Actors,* 173 ff.

find all such mysteries to be blasphemous. In general, his attitude toward religious drama was far from enthusiastic.

However, Lewes did not merely derogate Calderon as a thinker. While he denied that he was a *great* dramatist, he termed him a first-rate playwright: "Great knowledge of stage-effect; great spirit and ingenuity in the working out of complicated plots; an imagination brilliant and fertile, loving to lose itself in the dark regions of terror; wonderful harmony and fluency of verse, with a facility for the production of spirited dialogue amidst a profusion of metaphors: these are no contemptible qualities, and these Calderon unquestionably possesses. . . . He has a rich and theatrical genius."[86] But again, Schlegel was wrong when he lauded Calderon as a great poet. A true poet places the greatest value on thought and passion, but in Calderon's plays, "you find none of those pregnant thoughts which frequent meditations constantly extend. . . . However brilliant may be the ornaments of his verse, it is impossible to be more meagre in the substance. I seriously declare that his poetry does not seem to me a whit richer, in thought or feeling, than that of Lope de Vega, while it is even more defaced by hyperbolical conceits and frigid 'Gongorisms.' "[87]

Whereas Calderon was generally overrated, Lope de Vega suffered from unjustified depreciation. He was not concerned with dramatic evolution of character, subtle analyses of passion, and penetrating motivations. Without depth, he was certainly no Shakespeare, Molière or Schiller. But he was a creator of the greatest farces. Unfortunately, Europeans borrowed most of his plots and they have become so familiar that they seem commonplace. But he was a remarkable playwright, with the great charm of gaiety and great skill in dramatic exposition. Such amusing plays as *Sancho Ortiz, El perro del hortelano,* and *Amar sin saber a quien* "bear the stamp of a gay and cultivated mind. . . . He seldom rises to wit; but in light banter, and uproarious farce, he has few rivals, and in his own country we believe none. . . . He is ironical, humorous, mirthful. . . . [He has] wonderful sweetness and fluency of versification, with considerable felicity of expression, and an occasional touch of poetry in the higher sense." It

86 *The Spanish Drama,* 253-54.
87 *Ibid.,* 180.

was Lope, not Calderon, who helped to effect a kind of national drama: Lope "fixed the taste of his country as Shakspere fixed ours; and in spite of all changes in taste, and an occasional reaction by the imitators of the French classical school, he is still the standard of excellence."[88]

This last comment, with its reference to Shakespeare, contains the view which serves as the basis for Lewes' discussion of the drama of different nations. Since he was an Englishman, he would naturally turn to his own drama for purposes of comparison and clarification. It should be noted, however, that he did not use it as an example of unparalleled greatness, nor did he, as we shall see below in his Shakespearean criticism, engage in idolatry of the Shakespeare who "had fixed the standard of excellence." He noted that "the idolatry of Shakespeare has certainly had the bad effect of preverting our views of every other dramatic literature."

> We not only believe our own drama to have attained the highest excellence, but we imagine that there is no other kind of excellence. Molière is pronounced Shakspearian, and is welcome; Goethe and Schiller are received on the same terms. Calderon has also, by a preposterous misconception, been declared Shakspearian, and his name is therefore mentioned with fervour. Racine and Alfieri, the two greatest dramatists of southern Europe, not having yet been admitted into this Shakspearian brotherhood, are spoken of with coldness, sometimes with contempt. The ignorance implied in this is great. Grant . . . these writers to be widely different from our national standard. . . . The real question for the student to ask is, are Racine and Alfieri great dramatists? The question of resemblance to any other dramatist is a secondary one. Each nation must necessarily vary from every other in the form of its drama; it will also vary profoundly in its representation of passions and character.[89]

What Lewes specifically had to say about Italian, French, and English drama reveals the strong relativistic emphasis of his criticism.

88 *Ibid.*, 89, 94-95. Probably Lope did not write *Sancho Ortiz*.

89 "Alfieri and the Italian Drama," BFR, XVII (1844), 357-90. All references to this essay are incorporated into the text and appear within parentheses.

The main purpose of his article on Alfieri seemed to be to give English critics the rationale for his judgment that Alfieri was not only the greatest Italian dramatist, but one of the greatest dramatists of Europe. However, the paper also stressed the point that the kind of drama a man writes depends, to a considerable degree, upon his nationality. Lewes used his subjective-objective distinction to distinguish some national characteristics. Thus the Italian, being objective, would tend to write sensuous and passionate plays, while the Englishman, being subjective, would tend to write reflective plays. He compared Alfieri's *Oreste* and Aeschylus' *Choephori,* as well as Alfieri's *Saul* and Shakespeare's *King Lear* to illustrate the way in which national resemblances are reflected in Greek, English, and Italian art. Outlining the procedure to be followed in comparing the *Oreste* and the *Choephori,* he wrote: "At every resemblance [the inquirer] should stop to examine whether it were accidental, or whether it arose from a kindred feeling either in the men or in external conditions; if in the men, then whether this were a peculiarity of the individuals, or also a characteristic of the nation. So also at every difference, the inquiry must be, whether it were national or simply the result of religious or theatrical necessities. . . . The inquirer would therefore be forced to understand the whole history of the stage, before he could answer all these points satisfactorily. . . ." (p. 380) While Greece and Italy are nations of kindred tendencies in art, a close examination of the two plays reveals very fundamental differences as well as resemblances. The Greeks, like the Italians, are objective artists, that is, they describe characters objectively by their words and deeds. However, "Italians differ from Greeks, not only as Christians from heathens, but as men of different stages of civilization: morals, customs, and even affections take different shapes in the two nations: the Greek hero becomes the modern scoundrel; Greek virtue is modern vice." (p. 382) The *Oreste* and *Choephori* are alike in their use of the unities and dialogue, and the representation of a few characters. But there is nothing in *Oreste* to equal the sculpturesque effect of the tableaux scenes in Aeschylus' play: the invocation at the tomb of Atrides, Clytemnestra bearing her breast to Orestes and bidding him strike, Orestes over the dead bodies of Aegisthus and Clytemnestra.

But the most important difference has to do with characterization, particularly of Orestes and Clytemnestra. The Greek Orestes is a hero, but judged by Christian standards, he would be an unsympathetic character. Yet we have no right to apply Christian standards. The Greeks admired Orestes' craft. He is ferocious, cold, and never for a moment questions the right to use deceit in planning vengeance. "This subtle intellectual pride, this preference of craft over force, this utter disregard of truth and admiration of successful lying, has descended to the degenerate successors of the Greeks; but it is no symptom of degeneracy, it flourished in the flourishing times of Greece. The hero of the *Odyssey,* the much-experienced Ulysses, is constantly honoured with the epithet of the *crafty.* . . . In the 'Electra' the very gods teach cunning." (p. 383)

On the other hand, Alfieri could not have drawn such an Orestes and represented him as a hero. Modern heroes may commit murder, but they cannot have petty vices. His Orestes is a passionate, noble soul who abhors deceit and who kills his mother in a moment of rage, ignorant of what he is doing. An even more striking difference is to be found in the characterization of Clytemnestra. In Aeschylus she is a grim, horrible figure, an inhuman fiend, while in Alfieri she is a more human being, comparable to Lady Macbeth and Hermione. "She is a woman of intense passions which lead her into crime; but she is never lost to shame. She loves Egisto, she loves Elettra [*sic*], she loves Oreste; with her love for Egisto is mingled the recollection of her crime; with her love for her children is mingled the dread of retribution. The ebb and flow of these contending passions are managed with wonderful skill. We pity but can hardly abhor her, for in the very depths of her abasement there are symptoms of a higher nature." (p. 384)

Thus far Lewes has described Alfieri's forte, his ability to dramatize subtle and profound passion. His comparison of the madness of Saul and King Lear also emphasizes this same ability. In *Saul,* "the passions alone are diseased;" in *Lear,* "both passions and intellect; in other words, the madness of Lear has its root in a disordered intellect; while that of Saul is the mere extravagance of the passions themselves,—the intellectual malady from which this extravagance arises being kept entirely out of view." (p. 370)

Now all men are alike in that they feel, but men differ in their capacity to think. Therefore, Shakespeare creates unique kinds of characters because he concentrates on both the emotional and intellectual nature of man, while Alfieri who depicts primarily emotional qualities creates recognizable types.

At first glance Saul and Lear seem alike; they are old, willful, passionate, and hasty in word and deed. Actually, they are very different. Lear is not only the greatest tragic figure ever conceived, in a "colossal monument of a play," but he offers us a profound lesson in moral pathology. The root of Lear's insanity is in his intellect, not in the mere violence of the passions, as it is with Saul who is constantly fluctuating between the most violent and contradictory passions of love and hate. An English audience would be sympathetic to the suffering of an unsettled intellect, but an Italian audience would pity a jealous madman. As to the question of why the intellect is stressed by the English and the passions by the Italians, "the ordinary answer would be that Shakspeare was the greatest dramatist known to the world, and Alfieri a very indifferent one; that Shakspeare had marvellous psychological knowledge and as marvellous an artistic power, while Alfieri was deficient in both." (p. 372) Lewes ridiculed such a critical attitude as false and ignorant. The difference between Lear and Saul is not the result of Alfieri's inferiority to Shakespeare, but the result of national differences in their genius. "The question," said Lewes "is not whether [Alfieri] has executed, but whether he has once attempted, what the English poet has succeeded in. A great writer like Alfieri—or indeed a far inferior writer—might have exhibited the condition of Saul's intellect; he would at any rate have attempted to do so, and made his endeavour palpable. Alfieri did not attempt it." (pp. 372-73) And therefore he should not be criticized for what he did not attempt. He clearly had his faults and limitations. He was not a great poet; he described few characters, with little variety; and he introduced no profound gems of wisdom that linger in the memory. But his plays are organically constructed with great care, and he relies mainly on the depiction of the passions. In this he is unexcelled.

Lewes' essay on Alfieri is flawed. The discussion of national differences in terms of the subjective-objective distinction is not developed in a convincing manner. But its main value lies in the way it attempts to assess the dramatic achievements of several nations with sympathy and understanding, as well as with unsentimental critical firmness.

Lewes was also disturbed by the fact that critics judged English and French plays by the same standards, despite their recognition that the dramas differed. Lewes remarked: "It is as the poppy saying to the violet, 'How blue you are! God bless me, how dreadfully blue! Why don't you become red like me?' "[90] Not only the English, but the Schlegels and Lessing were unfair to the French dramatists because they were unaware of their "peculiar merit." While the English are primarily interested in dramatic effect, the French are impressed with literary effect. "Good;" said Lewes, "But if the public be equally interested, the object of the dramatist is equally attained; and thus both French and English tragedy are, and ought to be, respectively admired."[91] The drama in England originated as a popular amusement for a large public. Since French drama was developed in the court for highly cultivated audiences, it is easy to understand why the French revealed more concern for literature and culture in their tragedies than the English. Both French and English dramatists supplied their audiences with what they preferred. "The French delight in a well-planned story, unfolded in a direct and 'logical' manner; in sustained pomp of language; in philosophic maxims and in sharp antitheses. The English delight in action, passion, and imagery. They trouble themselves very little about dignity or *bienséance.* A Frenchman's first remark on a new play is respecting its *beaux vers;* an Englishman is struck by its characters and its 'situations.' The danger which most besets a French dramatist is lengthy dialogue and descriptions; that of an English dramatist is the tendency to melodramatic exaggeration."[92]

Those who condemn French classical drama as cold, pompous, and artificial overlook the peculiar beauty and charm of the plays by Corneille and Racine. Noble characters, elevated sentiments, and beautiful versification are the elements which justify the fame of their tragedies. Of Corneille, Lewes wrote: "He made the language more suitable to the expression of serious thoughts;

90 "The French Drama; Racine and Victor Hugo," WR, XXXIV (1840), 298.
91 "Shakespeare's Critics," *Edinburgh Review,* XC (1845), 52.
92 *Ibid.,* 57.

enriched it with many new turns; gave life and vigour to the feeble and contemptible imitations of the classic model then in vogue, and by the force of passion, rhetoric, and concentrated energy, made that form of drama truly national. . . . He had astonishing vigour and a daring spirit. He is sublime, but it is in sudden flashes, not in steady conceptions."[93] Like Aeschylus, Corneille has sublimity as well as bombast and triviality. He lacks the power of characterization; his people, therefore, are dominated by opposite passions. A comparison of the *Cid* and *Andromaque* reveals why Racine is France's greatest dramatist. Racine had the genius of creating subtle human beings. Racine is "rarely intense, but seldom or ever feeble. More elegant than energetic, he is more plastic even than the generality of poets. He has a gentle soul, a fine scholarly relish of antiquity and a peculiar sensibility to the power of language, poor as his native tongue may be."[94]

Lewes never lost his admiration for French classical drama, but he was at one time quite sympathetic to the aims of the Romantic drama of France. Although it disregarded the essential characteristics of classical drama, it tried to enlarge the scope of the theater by treating not only classic myths but also medieval and modern history and other types of tragic figures besides kings and queens. Hugo, Dumas, and others vitalized a stage which had been reduced to academic dullness by Voltaire. Lewes defended their right to concentrate upon the deformed instead of the beautiful: "It is the greatest absurdity to object to the subject of the poet, provided it always be founded on human nature—it is the treatment of it on which the critic can alone pronounce. If Mss. Hugo and Dumas prefer working out their ends through the Bad to the Beautiful, it is because they feel the bent of their genius lying that way—as was the case with all our old Dramatists, who delighted in the most horrible subjects and extravagant passions. The danger is, that in their mistaking the means for the end they are as apt to sometimes confound it with the end."[95] After study-

93 *Foreign Quarterly Review,* XXXV (1845), 310. William Archer in the *Fortnightly Review* [LXV (1896), 220] gives no source for his statement that Lewes "detested" Corneille.

94 "French Drama," WR, XXXIV (1840), 299. See also *Leader,* July 20, 1850, 403; June 14, 1851, 565; August 2, 1851; 735; July 6, 1850, 355.

95 "French Drama," WR, XXXIV (1840), 323-24.

ing the reputation of Hugo in England, K.N. Hooker designated Lewes as the representative of the brave new spirit, in the age which welcomed French poetry and Hugo with "a cosmopolitan enthusiasm," because he was the first English critic to rally to a defense of Hugo's plays.[96] Most critics derided Hugo's *Marion de Lorme* as a depraved work. Consider Lewes' remarkable judgment; he called it Hugo's best play and defended the action of Marion the courtesan who gives herself to a man in order to save her lover from jail. Comparing Marion to Shakespeare's cold, selfish Isabella, he judged Marion to be more virtuous. Chastity, he said, resides in the soul; impurity results from what is in us, not from what is done to us. "This play is full of poetry and passion, and like all true *things,* is a noble tribute to the majesty of Virtue. It grapples with the elementary passions of our nature, and trusts them with the healthy morality of a keen eye, discerning the false from the true . . . ."[97]

However, when Lewes became convinced that the Romantic playwrights had mistaken means for ends and had made the deformed the ruling principle of art, he unleashed his critical scorn. He criticized Dumas, Hugo, and Scribe. He objected vehemently to Dumas' *La Dame aux Camélias* and called it an "unhealthy idealization" of prostitution, an evil too sad to be treated lightly. He wrote: "I am not prudish nor easily alarmed by what are called 'dangerous' subjects, but *this* subject I protest against with all my might. . . . The very skill with which young Dumas has treated it, makes his crime the greater, because it tends to confuse the moral sense, by exciting the sympathy of an audience. I do not place much faith in the 'danger' of love-stories teaching how to sin, according to Ovid,—*peccare docentes,*—but I do believe that the false education men receive, in the direction of sexual sentiment, is pandered to by stories such as this of the consumptive courtesan and her ignoble lover. . . ."[98] Nor was Victor Hugo any more praiseworthy as a dramatist. A man of talent, effective in the *mise-en-scène* and in striking and terrible situations, he sacrificed everything to antitheses and tirades.[99] In his

[96] Hooker, *op. cit.,* 84; Edgar W. Hirshberg, "George Henry Lewes and Victor Hugo's Reputation in England," *Language Quarterly,* I (1963), 9-11.

[97] "French Drama," WR, XXXIV (1840), 322.

[98] *Leader,* April 2, 1853, 333.

[99] *Ibid.,* March 27, 1852, 306; "Criticism in France," BFR, XVI (1844), 357 ff.

review of Scribe and Legouvé's *Adrienne Lecouvreur,* Lewes left no doubt in the mind of the reader as to where his true sympathies lay with respect to French classical and romantic drama: "To think of a small public like that of the St. James's theatre, one necessarily selected from the educated classes, actually being so dead to all the claims of Art, in its highest expression, as to prefer the vulgar frippery of *Adrienne Lecouvreur* to the chastened style and distilled essence of beauty of *Phèdre,* is quite exasperating. . . . *Phèdre* is separated from *Adrienne* by a chasm as wide, deep, and impassable as that which separates Phidias from Tussaud."[100] Everyone has a right to his own taste, but "if you *do* choose the lower style, do not talk about Art. If you really prefer that long exhibition of physical agony with which the poisoned Adrienne excites your applause to the exhibition of mental agony in Phèdre . . . we have no objection; we merely tell you that such effects are vulgar, cheap. . . ." But, Lewes concluded sadly, "why should the critic stand alone, speaking about Art to a public which does not care a jot about it, simply because it does not understand it? We are rich and can 'patronise' Art; what need therefore to feel it? We can talk about Art, vote money for it on occasion. As for our own aesthetical taste—why—'Tuppence more and up goes the donkey!'—Ay! *that* is amusing: the donkey balanced on a ladder on a human chin, and 'only tuppence!' "[101] How useless to fulminate against the "stupid, undiscriminating" public: "Enough, enough!" he cried, "I croak in vain. What is logic against a full house? I write my protest and pass on."[102]

As an Englishman and lover of the drama, he was led inevitably to the subject of Shakespeare. But his was not a bookish interest. He lived during an era when he had the fortunate opportunity to review many Shakespearean productions. In a paper written for the *Edinburgh Review* in 1849, in which he surveyed the history of Shakespearean criticism, he expressed his disapprobation of Shakespearean idolatry, just as he had disapproved of the classicist's idolatry of Homer, the Roman poets, and the Greek dramatists.

100 *Leader,* July 13, 1850, 378.
101 *Ibid.,* 379.
102 *Ibid.,* February 22, 1851, 182.

Lewes did not deny that Shakespeare was a dramatic genius, but he did deny that Shakespeare was infallible. Pope attempted to excuse the bombast in his plays on the grounds that he had addressed a vulgar audience. But Lewes believed that Shakespeare sincerely admired the bombastic passages and had a genuine affections for his puns. Furthermore, his versification was sometimes irregular. His plays were meant to be spoken not read, and his actors could make verses sound metrically correct when they read them, whereas to the reader they would seem incorrect. No doubt some of the irregularities were the result of sheer carelessness. Were Shakespeare himself alive, he would have been "exceedingly amused at our making any difficulty in acknowledging his inequalities, and at our being at so much trouble to account for them, where they cannot be explained away."[103] Unfortunately, he became a model for slavish imitation, and his defects were consecrated as beauties.

Actually he wrote some poor plays. Lewes said: "I have always considered *The Merry Wives* one of the worst plays, if not altogether the worst, that Shakespeare has left us. The wit for the most part is dreary or foolish; the tone is coarse and farcical; and the characters want the fine distinctive touches he so well knew how to give. If some luckless wight had written such a comedy in our time, I should like to see what the critics would say to it?[104] Although *King John* "contains some truly Shakespearian writing, and characters such as Falconbridge, Hubert, Arthur, Constance, and King John, the effect, on the whole, is very heavy, and the play needs some accessory attraction. Gervinus, indeed, thinks it a "tragedy of the purest water"—vom reinsten Wasser (whatever *that* may be); but he is a German, and accustomed to watery dramas. . . ."[105] The *Two Gentlemen of Verona, The Comedy of Errors,* and *The Midsummer's Night's Dream* are tedious. *Much Ado about Nothing* is such a weak comedy that it succeeds only when the very best actors perform it. Its plot centers "so constantly on the unpleasant . . . the wit is often so forced and (burn me, idolators!) feeble, that unless the insolence of youth and beauty, and the confidence and animal spirits be represented as

103 "Shakespeare," *Edinburgh Review,* XC (1849), 47. See also "Shakespeare and his Editors," WR, XLIII (1845), 69 ff.

104 *Leader,* November 29, 1851, 1142; May 21, 1853, 502.

105 *Ibid.,* February 14, 1852, 161.

such . . . [*Much Ado*] becomes mere impertinence and is unpleasant."[106] *Romeo and Juliet,* filled with life, character, and dramatic movement is "in some respects among the worst of Shakspeare's fine plays. Juvenility of style is apparent in almost every scene. The frequence of rhyme, the forced rhetoric and conceits, the lame expression, and the deficiency in that passionate and profound poetry which illuminates the great plays, prove it to be an early work. In most of the great situations we find long tirades of rhetorical *concetti* in place of the nervous language, strongly colored by passion, which Shakspeare afterwards knew so well how to employ."[107]

Reviewing the history of Shakespearean criticism in both England and France, Lewes observed that it was vitiated either by the application of arbitrary principles drawn from Greek or French drama, or by the analysis of isolated passages and particular subjects. Even the attempts at philosophic criticism were defective since they were not based upon an understanding of Shakespeare's aims. While he was eulogized as the greatest of English poets and dramatists, at the same time he was stigmatized as Nature's child, deficient in regularity and art. Critics admitted that he was equal, if not superior, to the ancients in beauty of imagery, depth of insight, passion, grace, tenderness, wit, and pathos. Nevertheless, they insisted that he lacked art: "Superior to the classics in the *effect* which he produced, he was supposed to be inferior in the means." Such critics interpreted art as the "*closest imitation of ancient models*" instead of viewing it correctly as "*the best means of attaining an end.*"[108] In effect, they really meant that Shakespeare lacked learning. To reconcile the paradox of an artist who produced the most finished effects but who was totally ignorant of art, the word *inspiration* was utilized. "Homer, indeed, might occasionally nod, Aeschylus be obscure; Euripides prosaic, and Virgil verbose and tautologous; for they were men—But Shakespeare could have made mistakes only because he had not read certain classic authors; a tincture of learning would have infallibly guarded him from every error!"[109] But an investigation of his plays reveals that he was a "very careful,

106 *Ibid.,* December 3, 1853, 1173.
107 *Life of Goethe,* 434.
108 "Shakespeare," *op. cit.,* 45-46.
109 *Ibid.,* 47.

though perhaps not a theoretical artist." He did not immerse himself in the ancients but watched humanity itself very closely. His rules were not drawn from ancient precedent, but from his own keen sense of the way in which audiences should be moved.

In Lewes' judgement, it was Coleridge who helped to foster a more intelligent understanding of Shakespeare. Admittedly, Coleridge treated Shakespeare in too fragmentary a fashion; furthermore, it is difficult to determine what is original in his writings and what he owes to the Germans. But he offered many valuable insights which served to foster the kind of idolatry which reached its culmination when Madame de Staël induced the French to admire Shakespeare. France, England, and Germany attempted to outdo each other by praising him: France extolled him as a dramatist; England lauded his poetic genius; and Germany analyzed his philosophy.

Although Lessing, Wieland, Goethe, Herder, Lenz, Merk, Gerstenber, the Schlegels, Tieck, and Schiller helped to enlarge the reputation of Shakespeare in Germany, German critics also contributed an unusual amount of nonsensical, trivial, and perverted criticism. For example, Goethe recognized Shakespeare's brilliance and imitated him in several plays, but he also accepted the paradoxical view that Shakespeare was not a great theatrical writer. Along with Charles Lamb and others, he actually maintained that Shakespeare's excellencies as a dramatic poet were so great that they failed to produce the very effects for which they were employed on the stage. William Hazlitt, for example, complained that the delightful *Midsummer Night's Dream* is dull when performed; it loses its poetry, and moreover its six foot high fairies are quite ludicrous. Lewes observed that there was nothing odd about the fairies when they were played by small children on the Elizabethan stage. This play was meant to be acted, and the conditions of the modern theater are to blame if the performance is boring.[110] To object to stage representation may seem to be a sign of delicate and refined taste, but Shakespeare would have considered Goethe's, Lamb's, and Hazlitt's statements to be very sorry compliments. In Shakespeare's time, plays were written expressly for the stage and not for the study. "Therefore, if Shakespeare put forth his strength to suit this mode of publication *and*

[110] *Leader,* March 30, 1850, 15.

failed, he was in that case a bungling artist; and the "excellencies' which caused that failure were not excellencies, but splendid faults. But the fact is, that he succeeded; and that these excellencies have converted his success with his contemporaries into immortal fame."[111] After viewing a production of *As You Like It,* at the Drury Lane in 1865, Lewes was asked by a "great writer" whether he was finally convinced that Shakespeare was to be read and not seen. Admitting that the "woodland freshness" and "quaint pleasing sadness" of this work had not been captured at Drury Lane, he insisted that Shakespeare's great plays are capable of "standing the double test" of being read and seen.[112]

To Lewes, Shakespeare's art consisted essentially "in the marvellous power with which he exhibits the most beautiful poetry in combination with the most effective modes of stage representation."[113] He was always, above all, a dramatist, not merely a dramatic poet. Unlike the critics who studied his plays in texts, Lewes generally analyzed a Shakespearean play from the viewpoint of one who had seen it performed on stage. Thus his criticism of *The Merchant of Venice* was prompted by a review of Macready's performance as Shylock; his comments on *Macbeth* were prompted by the acting of the Keans; and his remarks on *Hamlet* were called forth by the performances of Barry Sullivan, Charles Kean, Fechter, and Devrient.

Since Lewes had played the part of Shylock, he had special knowledge of the problems involved in interpreting the role. It was his judgment that both Macready and Charles Kean played Shylock incorrectly: Charles Kean represented Shylock as the personification of vindictiveness; Macready made him into an abject, sordid, irritable, argumentative Jew. But actually Shylock "whatever he may be to his oppressors, the Christians . . . is a man with a man's affections to his own tribe. He loves the memory of his lost Leah; he loves Jessica. Shakspeare has given the actor an exquisite passage wherein to indicate the husband's tenderness; and I believe that in the scene with Jessica an actor may effectively show paternal tenderness. It is true the actor must *read into* the scene that which is not expressly indicated; but precisely in

111 "Shakespeare," *op. cit.,* 63-64.
112 *Pall Mall Gazette,* March 10, 1865, 238.
113 "Shakespeare, *op. cit.,* 77.

such interpretations consists the actor's art."[114] If the paternal tenderness were omitted, the tragic structure of *The Merchant of Venice* would be changed profoundly. ". . . For observe, if Shylock is a savage, blood-thirsty wretch, the whole moral is lost; if his fierceness is *natural* to him, and not brought out by the wrongs of the Christians, all the noble philosophy of the piece is destroyed; and the only way of showing that his fierceness is that of retaliation is to show how to others he is *not* fierce."[115] We can now understand why Lewes himself played Shylock as a sympathetic character, for he felt that *The Merchant of Venice* attains the stature of great tragedy only if Shylock is humanized, whereas it becomes nothing more than a brutal melodrama if Shylock is envisioned as inhuman. As for Jessica, Shakespeare blundered seriously in conceiving her as an odious person. The tragedy is heightened by supposing Shylock to be fond of his child and bitter at her rebellion. That she should forsake her religion and home for a Christian is believable, especially if the emphasis is on how love makes her sacrifice everything. But when she robs her father, throws away her mother's turquoise for a monkey, and speaks of her father in a shocking way, she is shown to be merely frivolous and heartless. Only Shakespeare could get away with such a characterization.

Lewes' discussion of *Macbeth* was based upon a performance of the play that he witnessed at the Princess Theater on February 14, 1853. He objected to Kean's unintelligent reading of the part which divested Macbeth of his tragic stature. It is possible, Lewes admitted, to interpreted Macbeth in two different ways. He can be viewed as a border chieftain of the dark ages. "In this view, all the metaphysical meshes which entangle him would be but the excuses of his conscience, or the instruments used to serve his purpose. . . ."[116] The truer conception would regard him as a wild, but heroic king, great even in crime. Shakespeare's penchant for reflection made him transform a feudal chief into a Hamlet type of metaphysical character. Macbeth who is superstitious and more imaginative than the average man is "good, too; full of the milk of human kindness. He would be great, is not without

114 *Leader*, November 9, 1850, 787.
115 *Ibid.*
116 *Ibid.*, February 19, 1853, 189.

ambition, but is without the illness which should attend it. He desires highly, but would win holily. He has a moral conscience. And here lies the tragedy. He is no common murderer; he is criminal because great temptations overcome great struggles; the tragic collision of antagonistic principles—Ambition and Conscience—take him from the records of vulgar crime, and raise him into a character fitly employed by Art."[117]

On the other hand, Lewes praised Ellen Kean for not divesting Lady Macbeth of tragic stature. She came closest to interpreting the part as he conceived it. He had formerly compared Lady Macbeth and Antigone; both "are fierce and restless till the deed is done; in both women the fierceness is spasmodic—it is feminine vehemence concentrated in one absorbing project. When all is over both relapse into weakness. Lady Macbeth has troubled dreams which break her agonised heart; Antigone dies despairing."[118] Obviously Lewes did not regard Lady Macbeth as a demon; instead he saw her as a woman who deliberately involves herself in a monstrous crime and then feels the remorse and despair, which, despite her ferocity, link her to the rest of humanity.

Lewes saw many performances of *Hamlet*. *Hamlet,* he once observed, has all the elements for several "Fast Dramas,"[119] that is, it is a melodrama as well as a philosophical poem. It is "a theatrical paradox, for it makes Skepticism, Reverie, Reflection, *dramatic.* Here the *activity* of thought supplies the place of action and hurries the audience along with it. The peculiarity of Hamlet is its indissoluble union of refinement with horrors, of thought with tumult, of high and delicate poetry with gross theatrical effects."[120] Shakespeare's special achievement in this play, "a tragedy of thought," is that reverie is made interesting. Hamlet is a "great *meditative* soul struggling against circumstance."

Of all of Shakespeare's characters, Hamlet is the most fascinating and the most challenging to actors. However, if a modern writer were as vague about Hamlet's character as Shakespeare, he would be judged guilty of committing an unpardonable

117 *Ibid.*

118 *Ibid.*, May 4, 1850, 137. See also "The Antigone and its Critics," *Foreign Quarterly Review*, XXXV (1845), 61, 69.

119 *Leader*, June 19, 1852, 594.

120 *Ibid.* See also *Life of Goethe*, 454.

dramatic crime. Hamlet may be mad, and yet, with a terrible consciousness of his madness, he may "put an antic disposition on" as a kind of relief to his feelings. On the other hand, he may merely pretend to be mad so that he will be excused for any unusual action which might betray his knowledge of his father's murder. The actor is not expected to solve this problem, nor is he supposed to depart too widely from the text or to misinterpret what Shakespeare has written plainly. What he cannot ignore is the language of the text, "namely, that Shakspeare meant Hamlet to be in a state of *intense cerebral excitement,* seeming like madness. His sorrowing nature has been suddenly ploughed to its depths by a sorrow so great as to make him recoil every moment from the belief in its reality. The shock, if it has not destroyed his sanity, has certainly *unsettled* him. Nothing can be plainer than this. Every line speaks it."[121] Lewes noted the irreverence with which Hamlet addresses his father's ghost, in the cellarage scene. Actors usually omit these lines, but they are significant, for from the moment the ghost departs, Hamlet is a changed man. His scenes should be pervaded by a vague horror, and he should be agitated both by the desire for vengeance and doubt as to whether he has actually had hallucinations. Even when he pretends to be calm, the disturbed state of his mind should be apparent. Lewes saw English, French, and German actors perform the role of Hamlet, and they were all generally self-possessed when they were not in a rage, pretending madness. They overlooked the psychological modification or evolution of his character.

The same mistaken conception of Hamlet's nature led actors to misinterpret the "to be or not to be" soliloquy. They wrongly used it as an oratorical display. Undoubtedly, it is a great speech, but Lewes remarked, "I think Shakspeare's genius was too eminently dramatic to have committed so great an error as to substitute an oration for an exhibition of Hamlet's state of mind. The speech is passionate, not reflective; and it should be so spoken as if the thought were *wrung* from the agonies of a soul hankering after suicide as an escape from evils, yet terrified at the dim sense of greater evils after death."[122] Such a reading of the soliloquy not

[121] *On Actors,* 122 ff.
[122] *Ibid.,* 125 ff.

only gives it greater dramatic force, but it also serves as an appropriate introduction to the following scene with Ophelia. In the Ophelia scene actors tend to look towards the door, to show that they suspect the presence of the king or some other person, and thus they hope to make the strange wildness of the prince intelligible by representing it as one of Hamlet's assumed extravagances. Shakespeare gives no warrant for this interpretation. If it is recognized that Hamlet is in a state of feverish excitement during the delivery of the soliloquy, his wildness in the Ophelia scene is readily understandable as revealing his true feelings. His wildness is no more unnatural than the way in which he receives the confirmation of his doubts by the effect of the play upon the king. In that scene, he needs no reason to assume madness since he is alone with his friend Horatio, and yet his conduct is far from normal. Actors omit the significant passages in these parts of the play because they are afraid of seeming comical. Lewes believed such passages, when properly delivered, to be terrible in their grotesqueness and highly relevant.

Thus Lewes employed what might be characterized as one of the modern approaches to Shakespearean criticism which generally views the Shakespearean play primarily as an *acting* play. Finally, it should be noted that the relativistic emphasis of his thought, combined with his broad knowledge of the drama of many nations, enabled him to make the kind of balanced judgment that is the mark of a genuine critic.

6

Conclusion

It is not difficult to assess Lewes' place in the history of philosophy. What G. Grazzi-Bertazzi wrote, in 1906, is substantially a very just estimate:

> No one can deny that Lewes for the versatility of his mind, for the originality of his scientific and philosophic views, and especially for the vigorous power of his critical spirit, has the right to occupy a very important place especially in the history of scientific psychology, as well as in the history of the philosophic sciences in general, that is, logic, gnosis, and metaphysics, on a level with J. S. Mill, Spencer, Bain, Taine, Ardigo, Wundt, with whom he collaborated in the growth of the psychological and philosophical sciences, leaving behind a patrimony of positive ideas, organized along large lines, ideas which have many points of affinity with those of the above mentioned contemporaries, and, not rarely, points of indubitable superiority.[1]

1 *Esame Critico Della Filosofia de George Henry Lewes* (Messina, 1906), 10: *"E pure nessuno può negare che il Lewes, per la versatilità, dell'ingegno, per l'originalità delle vedute scientifiche e filosofiche, e sopratutto per la forza vigorosa dello spirito critico, abbia il diritto di occupare un posto assai importante nella storia della psicologia scientifica in specie, delle scienze filosofiche in generale, cioè della logica, della gnoseologia e della metafisica, all pari con I. St. Mill, con Spencer, con Bain, con Taine, con Ardigo, con Wundt, coi quali collaborò all'incremento delle scienze psicologiche e filosofiche, lasciando un patrimonio de idee positive, organizzate e grandi linee, le quali hanno molti punti di affinita con quelle dei suoi contemporanei, sopracitati, e, non rare volte, punti di superiorita indiscutibili."*

But how are we to assess Lewes' place in the history of criticism? George Eliot has told us that his "scientific and philosophical work . . . is the part of his life's labour which he most valued."[2] Perhaps this explains why he never bothered to collect his voluminous criticism. Thus, while any reader today can turn to the five volumes of his *Problems of Life and Mind* for a complete view of his philosophy, he has no comparable edition of his criticism to use. At the end of the nineteenth century, Archer published some of his dramatic criticism from the *Leader;* and in 1965, a representative sampling of his criticism was compiled for the Regents Critics Series.[3] But these are by no means definitive collections, and without doubt, the inaccessibility of many of Lewes' writings, hidden away in nineteenth century journals, has not helped to stimulate interest in his work. Furthermore, George Saintsbury's negative judgment in his *History of Criticism* must have exerted considerable influence in damaging Lewes' reputation as a critic. However, what David Daiches aptly describes as Saintsbury's "elegant amateurism" has fallen into disrepute, and we look today to more analytic historians of criticism.[4]

Every once in a while someone calls attention to Lewes' special achievement. George Bernard Shaw described Lewes as "the most able and brilliant critic between Hazlitt and our own contemporaries."[5] R. L. Brett notes that "his claim to rank as the most important critic between Coleridge and Arnold is a considerable one."[6] However, these judgments do not seem to have been noticed by Wimsatt and Brooks, for they do not even mention Lewes in their history of literary criticism.[7] René Wellek does pay some attention to Lewes in his *History*, although whatever praise is given is offered begrudgingly: "Lewes did not have . . . an unphilosophical or provincial mind. . . . He became the

[2] GE, VII, 198.

[3] Alice R. Kaminsky (ed.) *Literary Criticism of George Henry Lewes* (Lincoln, Neb., 1964).

[4] David Daiches, *Critical Approaches to Literature* (Englewood Cliffs, N.J., 1956), 284-86.

[5] Shaw, *Our Theater in the Nineties op. cit.*, III, 155. For a more recent reference to Lewes as an authority on acting, see Kenneth Tynan, *Curtains* (New York, 1961), 352, 399-400.

[6] R.L. Brett, "G.H. Lewes: Dramatist, Novelist, and Critic," *Essays and Studies*, II (1958), 120.

[7] W.K. Wimsatt and C. Brooks, *Literary Criticism: A Short History* (New York, 1967).

first English exponent of the theory of realism in the novel. . . ."[8] Moreover, Wellek's bibliography reveals that he has read very little of Lewes' criticism, and he shows his limited knowledge of Lewes' theory when he incorrectly states that Lewes attempted to put criticism on a scientific basis.

Wellek takes the traditional position that Arnold is the most important critic of the latter half of the nineteenth century. But curiously enough, a good deal of his discussion of Arnold's critical theories is devoted to an enumeration of their deficiencies: Arnold had a racist view of literature, unredeemed by the concept of *volksgeist* or national spirit; his theory of poetry, with its notions of the real estimate, and touchstones, is limited, contradictory, and didactic; he wrote one essay on the novel, largely *reportage* on Tolstoy; and disliked *Madame Bovary* and the French realistic novel; he had no appreciation of the great Victorian writers, and wrote slightingly not only of them but of most of the Romantics; half of his criticism was primarily concerned with religion. At the end of his analysis, Wellek praises Arnold's great critical spirit, but it does not help to mitigate the negative effect of the evaluation.[9]

It is not the curious contradiction between the context and the conclusion of Wellek's essay that interests us here, but the standards that are used to judge Arnold. In the light of these standards, what should Wellek have said of Lewes, who years before Arnold wrote his essay on the "Function of Criticism" had made the same plea for an unprejudiced, urbane, flexible criticism? Furthermore, Lewes practiced what he preached when he displayed a broad range of sympathy for literary achievements in America and Europe. It is not necessary to minimize Arnold's achievements or those of other critics in the nineteenth century to appreciate Lewes' merits. But it is important to understand the special contribution that he made, a contribution which has been too long ignored. Lewes' period has been called "the age of idealogy." Perhaps it should be remembered more accurately as the time when the great antithesis of modern civilization was most vociferously argued; the battle lines of Christian super-

[8] René Wellek, *A History of Modern Criticism: 1750-1950, the Later Nineteenth Century* (New Haven, 1965), IV, 149-52.

[9] *Ibid.*, 155-80.

naturalism versus scientific naturalism seemed to be clearly drawn. The controversy involved the realms of art and education; the issues of classical versus scientific education and of art versus science were hotly debated. Science had great prestige and the religious world feared the waning of its influence. We have seen that Lewes was a scientific naturalist and his views on education clearly put him on the side of Huxley. But as a man who lived in two cultures, Lewes would have considered the Arnold-Huxley, Shelley-Peacock, Snow-Leavis controversies about science and art quite pointless. He denied that truth is the exclusive property of either the artist or the scientist; both art and science are vital means of enlarging man's knowledge. In fact, the method of philosophic and scientific inquiry seemed to him to apply equally well to artistic inquiry. Just as he had sought verification of hypotheses in his scientific speculation, so he sought corroboration of critical theories through the study of known artistic effort. Lewes used the following analogy: "To understand Nature, we must observe her manifestations, and trace out the laws of the coexistence and succession of phenomena. And in the same way, to understand Art, we must patiently examine the works of art; and from a large observation of successful efforts, deduce general conclusions respecting the laws upon which success depends."[10] Thus in criticism, as well as in philosophy or science, his method was empirical, and all the important emphases of his criticism grew out of his commitment to naturalism.

We can now understand the sense in which Lewes' contribution to criticism is of special significance merely from a historical point of view. The major mid-Victorian figures, Arnold, Carlyle, Ruskin, Newman, were clearly not empiricists and had religious or metaphysical beliefs. Macaulay, who refused to review poetry for the *Edinburgh Review,* was primarily an historian and politician; John Stuart Mill, like Carlyle, relinquished his interest in literature at a very early stage. As for the minor critical theorists, E.S. Dallas and Walter Bagehot, neither one had Lewes' philosophic or scientific knowledge and neither one wrote as extensively as Lewes. Thus Lewes was clearly the only example in this

[10] "Shakespeare's Critics: English and Foreign," *Edinburgh Review,* XC (1849), 68.

period of a scientific naturalist who had a genuine and professional absorption in the field of criticism. His approach and methodology served to enrich and supplement the critical experience of his age. If, in our sputnik age, Arnold's stress on the absolute values inherent in literature is still meaningful, then surely Lewes' relativistic approach should be equally meaningful.

While the relativist position has attained respectability in philosophical and scientific circles, it is still suspect in the literary world because it seems to lead to what L.C. Knights derogates as a "spineless kind of subjectivism."[11] Cleanth Brooks has argued that "once we are committed to critical relativism, there can be no stopping short of a complete relativism in which critical judgments will disappear."[12] Isaiah Berlin's comment, like Brooks' statement, ignores the middle ground: "If everything is relative . . . , nothing can be judged to be more so than anything else."[13] In this connection, other aestheticians have distinguished different kinds of theories—cultural, biological, logical, sociological, and psychological relativisms which do not necessarily lead to subjectivism. The views of George Boas, John Dewey, Bernard Heyl, Stephen Pepper, Frederic Pottle, and Wayne Shumaker, to name only a few, testify to the strong appeal of critical relativism in modern theory.[14]

Lewes' position should not be misunderstood. He was not a radical relativist, or subjectivist. His rejection of absolutes did not imply universal tolerance for *all* critical beliefs. He believed in the developmental nature of thought, in what he called the "Law of Continuity." In accordance with this law, we are "for ever

[11] L.C. Knights, "On Historical Scholarship and the Interpretation of Shakespeare," *Sewanee Review,* LXIII (1955), 230, 234. See also B.C. Heyl, "The Critic's Reasons," *Journal of Aesthetics and Art Criticism,* XVI (1957), 169-79.

[12] Cleanth Brooks, *The Well Wrought Urn: Studies in the Structure of Poetry* (New York, 1947), 234. See also R. Wellek, *Concepts of Criticism* (New Haven, 1963), 1-20.

[13] Isaiah Berlin, *Historical Inevitability* (Oxford, 1957), 62.

[14] George Boas, *Wingless Pegasus: A Handbook for Critics* (Baltimore, 1950); George Boas and Harold H. Wrenn, *What is a Picture?* (Pittsburgh, 1964); John Dewey, *Art as Experience* (New York, 1934); Bernard Heyl, *New Bearings in Esthetics and Art Criticism* (New Haven, 1943); Stephen C. Pepper, *Principles of Art Appreciation* (New York, 1949); Frederick A. Pottle, *The Idiom of Poetry* (Bloomington, 1963); Wayne Shumaker, *Elements of Critical Theory* (Berkeley, 1952).

seeing some new fact, some new quality, and again recombining it with others, so as to bring together in a living synthesis objects that at first seemed wide as the poles asunder."[15] In art, in philosophy, in science, in all intellectual inquiry, this synthesizing process involves the formulation of warranted judgments which are subject to change in the light of enlarged experience and knowledge. A warranted judgment is a relative judgment because the developmental nature of thought precludes the possibility of fixed, final certainties. The scientist recognizes that his so-called laws are subject to revision, and yet he is no more a "spineless subjectivist" than the critic who changes his mind about a work of art. Even for traditionalists like T.S. Eliot, and Matthew Arnold, absolute judgments often turn out to be no more than tentative opinions relative to time and place. It is hard to believe that any critic has not at one time or another experienced the kind of reversal of judgment that Lewes described in the following lines: "After dinner we [Lewes and George Eliot] fairly broke down with Leigh Hunt's Autobiography & tried his book on Byron with no better success. How strange it is thus to outlive one's admiration, & to find intolerable what a few years before seemed admirable."[16] Lewes also changed his mind about Balzac, Charlotte Brontë, Calderon, Fielding, Hugo, and Keats, but he always tried to criticize in terms of defensible principles which reflected his awareness of the aesthetic presuppositions of different nations and different ages. This did not mean that all critical principles were defensible. He clearly preferred the theory of realism, but, as a believer in the developmental nature of thought, he had to acknowledge that no theory could offer eternal truths. Bernard Heyl, in explaining the kind of relativism that he favors, describes what is in essence Lewes' own theory: "What is indubitably required is a relativism which comprehends no values apart from human valuations, yet which recognizes the necessity for and justifies the existence of sound judgments of better and worse. These, however, cannot ever be considered absolute or fixed, for they depend both upon philosophical assumptions and upon empirical criteria which will vary somewhat from individual to individual, from culture to culture. But this only means that an

15 MFO, 493-94.

16 Lewes' *Diary*, March 2, 1859.

amount of wholesome elasticity and variety is as inevitable and desirable in criticism as it is in human nature."[17]

Lewes was the first English critic in the nineteenth century to use standards of realism consistently. Realism was a popular term for many years, particularly in American criticism, but in the view of some modern critics, it signifies an inadequate theory. Benedetto Croce has rejected realism as a meaningless rhetorical equivocation.[18] Albert Camus describes it as an "impossible aesthetic because art is never really realistic.[19] But even Harold Osborne, who also believes that realism is a pseudo-concept, is forced to admit that "the old problems of Realism still walk the stage in modern dress. They are nowadays debated in terms of artistic symbolism and artistic truth, but they are at bottom the same old problems still. Their presentation has been changed and their contexts widened, but their importance for practical criticism is as great as it ever was."[20] Like the proverbial cat, the theory of realism has many lives and reappears in critical discussions under many guises.[21]

The particular guise under which it appeared in Lewes' philosophy was Reasoned Realism. He used his double aspect theory to eliminate the traditional distinction between realism and idealism. Generally idealism is supposed to refer to that which is superexperiential, whereas realism refers to that which is experiential. But Lewes reinterpretated idealism to signify a *type* of realism which is founded upon experience, and he placed falsism in opposition to both realism and idealism. This monistic type of reconciliation might be castigated as representing no more than a glib and oversimplified verbalism. But Lewes was not a naive realist; truth for him did not merely reside in the depiction of external phenomena. He was as opposed to cinematographic realism as Proust and Camus, but he denied that realism necessitates detailism. From the viewpoint of practical criticism, his Reasoned Realism served him well, for it gave him the latitude

17 Heyl, *op. cit.*, 154-55.

18 B. Croce, *Aesthetic* trans. D. Ainslie (London, 1909), 69-73. See also Wellek, *Concepts of Criticism*, 255.

19 Albert Camus, *The Rebel*, tr. A. Bower (New York, 1954), 238 ff.

20 Harold Osborne, *Aesthetics and Criticism* (New York, 1955), 69.

21 Harry Levin, *Contexts of Criticism* (New York, 1963), 67-75; Eric Auerbach, *Mimesis*, tr. W.R. Trask (Princeton, 1953).

to judge the representation of disparate realms of reality in literature. Interestingly enough, one of the greatest novelists seemed to have worked with the same conception as Lewes. Dostoevski is supposed to have written that he had "quite different conceptions of reality and realism than our realists and critics. My idealism is more real than their realism. . . . [T]hey call me a psychologist: mistakenly. I am rather a realist in a higher sense, i.e. I depict all the depths of the human soul.[22] This is exactly the sense in which Lewes conceived of idealism, as the means by which "the depths of the human soul are represented."

He used this double aspect theory to invalidate the metaphysical dualisms of mind and body, man and animal, man and environment, matter and force, cause and effect. The theory suffered, as we have noted, from *simpliciste* monism. But its most salutary influence is to be found in his psychology, where the subjective-objective distinction led him to insist on the relevance of both introspective and objective analysis of behavior. Although he avoided overstressing the biological factor, he carefully studied the physiology of the human organism. His extensive research in this area led Raymond St. James Perrin to assert that Lewes was "perhaps the best equipped man of his time to deal with the problems of Psychology."[23] H. Warren in his *History of Association Psychology* rated Lewes' associationism very highly.[24] It is, therefore, ironic that his psychological theory of imagination should have been ignored.

It would not have appealed to those who were influenced by the Romantics. In differing ways Wordsworth, Coleridge, Shelley, and Keats expressed their faith in the creatvie power of imagination to lead man to a knowledge of divine truths. Lewes scrupulously admitted into his theory of imagination what his own observation of mental phenomena had revealed to him, and it may well seem to be too prosaic an explanation to those who would like to hypostatize imagination as a revelation of the "eternal Infinite I am." But at least Lewes tried to rely upon observable psychological data, whereas many theories of imagina-

22 Dostoevski's remarks to A.N. Maykov and N.N. Strakhov as quoted by Wellek, *Concepts of Criticism, op. cit.*, 232.

23 R.St.J. Perrin, *The Evolution of Knowledge* (New York, 1905), 273.

24 Warren, *op. cit.*, 138.

tion are very often no more than elaborate mystifications. Even I.A. Richards, who was so impressed by Coleridge, as an avowed materialist had to reinterpret Coleridge's conception of imagination in terms of a "refreshed atomism," using the language of the associationist.[25] Perhaps as M. H. Abrams believes, we will never decide the issues involved in the question of mental cognition,[26] but it is quite clear that Lewes' views more nearly approximate those favored by modern scientific psychology than do the famous transcendental conceptions of the romantics.

If a philosopher is anything at all, he is a lover of wisdom, and Lewes as we would expect, placed a high valuation on intellect or vision. Although he disapproved of any didactic theory of literature, and objected to the presence of excessive speculation in a work of art, he denied that art exists merely to provide amusement. Art has cognitive value, and reflects the experience and knowledge of the creator. This is why Lewes gave the actor the lowest status among artists; a kind of parasite, he feeds upon the intellect of others without making any real contribution of his own. In his evaluation of writers, he praised the superior ones—Shelley, Goethe, Shakespeare, George Sand, Balzac, Eliot, and Thackeray—for their interest in ideas as well as feelings. Lewes' own keen, insatiable intellectual appetite led his interests to range over an unusually wide area, and even a cursory glance at his bibliography reveals the impressive range of his writing activities.

Versatility arouses suspicion because it is associated with dilletantism, but even the most insignificant of his articles are interesting because they contain examples of his intelligence and what Archer aptly called, his "sparkling common sense." There are few men who can review operas as well as dramas, who can write authoritatively about the fields of literature, philosophy and science, who can move with ease from a discussion of the mental condition of babies, to the question of Imaginary Geometry and the Truth of Axioms, to the subject of the dancing of the Greek Chorus, Slavery in America, African Life, and Hereditary Influence in Animals and Humans. Yet Lewes' versatility served him particularly well in his role as critic; it enabled him to use

[25] I.A. Richards, *Coleridge on Imagination* (Bloomington, 1960), 18-19, 70, 78-85.

[26] M.H. Abrams, *The Mirror and the Lamp: Romantic Theory and the Critical Tradition* (New York, 1958), 182-83.

a variety of critical approaches, very much in the way that R.S. Crane recommended when he pleaded for a new pluralism to counter the limited method of the new critics.[27] Sometimes, as in the Fielding paper, Lewes preoccupied himself with the concerns of the formalist, dealing with plot, and structure in the novel; sometimes he combined historical, biographical and exegetical analysis as in the Goethe biography. In parts of the Shelley paper, particularly in his analysis of *The Cenci* and elsewhere, he often employed *explication de texte* in the manner of the contextualist stressing always the significance of organic relationships. His Dickens essay employs what is perhaps the first genuine psychological interpretation of the genius of Dickens. As a drama critic he utilized extensive and elaborate comparative evaluation.

A critic, no matter how versatile and profound, cannot escape making errors of judgment, especially when he is involved in criticizing new writers over a long period of time and formulating opinions without precedent to guide him. Lewes was not perturbed that he might have overestimated certain writers, for he wrote: "I would rather make a mistake in overrating than in underrating; although as a critic I desire to make no mistake either way."[28] While he did not hesitate to criticize well-established reputations, he was often guilty of being too charitable to young, contemporary poets; he treated Alexander Smith, Gerald Massey, William Allingham, Robert Buchanan, and Owen Meredith much too generously.[29] But the sympathy which led Lewes to encourage young poets also enabled him to recognize the artist with genuine talent. Thus when George Meredith published his first volume of poems, Lewes wrote of them: "A nice perception of nature, aided by a delicacy of expression, gives to these poems a certain charm not to be resisted; and, although they betray no depth of insight nor of feeling . . . yet they rise from out the mass of verses by a certain elegance and felicity of expression which distinguish them."[30] However, he did overrate George Sand

27 R.S. Crane, *The Languages of Criticism and the Structure of Poetry* (Toronto, 1953), 140-94; *Critics and Criticism*, ed. R.S. Crane (Chicago, 1952).

28 "Robert Buchanan," FR, I (1865), 446.

29 *Leader*, June 25, October 8, November 5, 1853, 617, 976, 1072; March 4, 1854, 211-13; "Poems of Alexander Smith," WR, LIX (1853), 522-34; *Leader*, March 26, 1853, 306-7; *Leader*, June 16, 1855, 579-81.

30 *Leader*, July 5, 1851, 635.

and Elizabeth B. Browning, as well as a number of other contemporary writers, and he underrated Robert Browning and Balzac. He did not quite succeed in liberating himself from the moral confines of his age; although he professed distaste for any moral or didactic interpretation of art, in his earlier articles he worried too much about the amorality of the French novel. Although he denied that art could be governed by laws, he used the word *law* to describe literary principles, revealing the limitations of his critical vocabulary. Inevitably some inconsistencies creep into his writings; for example, he categorized Shakespeare as a subjective poet in one article and elsewhere referred to him as an objective artist.[31] To write as Lewes did in the double capacity of journalist and critic is to involve oneself in a certain amount of hack work. His dramatic criticism for the *Leader* illustrates both the advantages and disadvantages of being a reviewer who has to meet deadlines. At its best it has the kind of fresh perception which only first hand experience with the theater can produce; at its worst it lacks the theoretical approach of his longer essays which elucidate more thoughtfully the aesthetic presuppositions of dramatic art. His writings on the poets will strike the modern reader as being less original than his analyses of novelists and dramatists. It would be foolish to expect total consistency of performance from someone who wrote for more than fifty years, and, indeed, Lewes' early work was often less satisfactory than his later efforts.

However, he was always scrupulous about fulfilling his writing obligations, and even in his earliest years, he labored to perfect his style. In 1842 he wrote to Macvey Napier on the subject of his proposed revision of his article on Dramatic Reform: "I am at all times anxious to alter and to receive criticism, however severe, as Mr. John Mill, who knows this, will confirm. . . . Aiming high I am the more conscious of failure, and thankfully accept any counsels how to better reach the mark; fastidious about style, I am the more sensible of faults."[32] In 1859 Lewes aptly diagnosed the defects of his style: "Latterly I have taken to rewrite almost

31 "Character and Works of Goëthe," BFR, XIV (1843), 119; "Alfieri and the Italian Drama," BFR, XVII (1844), 369.

32 *Selections from the Correspondence of the Late Macvey Napier*, ed. M. Napier (London, 1879), 413.

everything except quite unimportant articles. This I formerly never did—or only quite by exception. But I find it necessary: the defect of my style is its want of largo: it is too brief, allusive, hurried. In re-writing the defect is in some degree remedied."[33] But if his style lacks "largo," it has the not-to-be scoffed at virtue of clarity and avoids the eccentricities and prolixities of a more ornate style.

Lewes' knowledge of many languages and literatures, coupled with his philosophic, scientific, and psychological interests, gave him a special vantage point from which to judge. He was a philosophical critic in the best sense of the word, very often playing the role of intellectual gadfly, and maverick, questioning the time honored beliefs of the traditionalists, and the new ideas of the positivists. Carlyle, Ruskin, Arnold, Pater, and Morris made their estimable contribution to the world of letters in the nineteenth century, but not one of them shared his interests in philosophy and science or his commitment to scientific, relativistic pragmatism. To assess his role as a critic seems in the end not to be so difficult. Besides the historical estimate, we might venture to approximate a "real" estimate. To read all that he has written is to be in the company of a wise and witty human being whose judgments will more often than not strike us today as being just, and on the highest level, penetratingly relevant.

[33] Lewes' *Diary,* February 20, 1859.

Bibliography

The Writings of George Henry Lewes

This bibliography accounts for almost all of Lewes' known writings, books, and articles, except for fugitive pieces which have not been identified, or which I may have overlooked. As indicated below, not all of Lewes' contributions to the *Pall Mall Gazette, Fortnightly* and *Westminster Reviews, Cornhill* and the *Leader* have been itemized separately.

The Author.

BOOKS

A Biographical History of Philosophy. 2 vols. London: Charles Knight, 1845; *The History of Philosophy from Thales to Comte* (3rd ed.), 2 vols. London: Longmans, Green, 1867; *The Biographical History of Philosophy from its Origin in Greece down to the Present Day*. New York: D. Appleton, 1868; *The History of Philosophy from Thales to Comte* (4th ed.), 2 vols. London: Longmans, Green, 1871; *A Biographical History of Philosophy*. New York: D. Appleton, 1885.

Aristotle: A Chapter in the History of Science. London: Smith, Elder, 1864.

Comte's Philosophy of the Sciences. London: H. G. Bohn, 1853.

Dramatic Essays, John Forster, George Henry Lewes. eds. William Archer and Robert W. Lowe. London: Walter Scott, 1896. (Reprints Lewes' essays from the *Leader*, 1850-1854.)

Female Characters of Goethe from the Original Drawings of William Kaulbach with Explanatory Text by G. H. Lewes. (2nd ed.) New York: Stroefer & Kirchner, 1867.

Introductory Essay, The Ethics of Aristotle, tr. D.P. Chase. London: Walter Scott, *n.d.*

On Actors and the Art of Acting. London: Smith, Elder, 1875; New York: Henry Holt, 1878; New York: Grove Press, 1957.

Problems of Life and Mind. 5 vols. London: H. Trubner, 1874-79. First

Series: *Foundations of a Creed.* 2 vols. 1874, 1875; Second Series: *The Physical Basis of Mind.* 1877; Third Series: *The Study of Psychology.* 1879, *Mind as a Function of the Organism.* 1879.

Ranthorpe. London: Chapman & Hall, 1847.

Rose, Blanche, and Violet. London: Smith, Elder, 1848.

Sea-Side Studies at Ilfracombe, Tenby, the Scilly Isles, and Jersey. Edinburgh: Blackwood, 1858.

Selections from the Modern British Dramatists. 2 vols. Leipzig: F.A. Brockhaus, 1867.

Studies in Animal Life. London: Smith, Elder, 1862.

The Life of Goethe. (3rd ed.), London: Smith, Elder, 1875; (4th ed.), London: Smith Elder, 1890.

The Life of Maximilien Robespierre with Extracts from His Unpublished Correspondence. London: Chapman & Hall, 1849.

The Physiology of Common Life: 2 vols. Leipzig: B. Tauchnitz, 1860.

The Principles of Success in Literature: ed. Fred. N. Scott. (3rd ed.), Boston: Allyn & Bacon, 1894. (Reprints articles by Lewes which first appeared in Volumes I and II of the *Fortnightly Review*, 1865.)

The Spanish Drama, Lope de Vega and Calderon. London: Charles Knight, 1846.

PLAYS

LOST

(Manuscripts and printed texts not available.)

Stay at Home, performed in 1856

Wanted a She-Wolf, [1854?]

PRINTED

(Volume numbers refer to Thomas Hailes Lacy's *Acting Edition of Plays,* unless otherwise indicated.)

Buckstone's Adventure with a Polish Princess. Slingsby Lawrence. XXII.

A Chain of Events. Slingsby Lawrence and Charles Mathews. XXI.

A Cozy Couple. Slingsby Lawrence. XXIV.

The Game of Speculation. Slingsby Lawrence. V.

Give a Dog a Bad Name. Slingsby Lawrence. XXIV.

The Lawyers. Slingsby Lawrence. II.

The Noble Heart. Boston: W.V. Spencer [1858?]

A Strange History. Slingsby Lawrence and Charles Mathews. X.

Sunshine Through the Clouds. Slingsby Lawrence. XV.

Taking by Storm. Frank Churchill. VI.

UNPUBLISHED

Drat that Dick! by Slingsby Lawrence. [1852?]

The Fox Who Got the Grapes. 1854

Marguerite. n.d.
The Miser's Niece. n.d.
Pretension or The School for Parvenues. 1843

MANUSCRIPTS

At the Beinecke Library, Yale University

Journals: X. July 24, 1856-March 31, 1859.
XI. April 1, 1859-January 1, 1866.
XII. June 1, 1866-May 6, 1870.
Diaries: 8 vols. 1869-1876.
Letter to J.M. Kemble, March 23, [1844].
Thoughts of G. H. Lewes, 18-page notebook

At the New York Public Library

Captain Bland. Prompter's Copy, 1864.
Literary Receipts Book. Berg Collection.

Lewes' Contributions to Periodicals

Besides the periodicals listed below, Lewes also contributed to the following (See his *Literary Receipts Book,* GE, VII, Appendix II.): *All the Year Round, Atlas, Constitutional Review, Historical Register, Jerrold's Magazine, Knights Weekly Magazine, Literary Gazette, Morning Chronicle, Popular Science Review, Spectator, Topic, Universal Review.*

Athenaeum

(Reviews)

"*Journal of Dramatic Art and Literature,*" MLX (1848), 185-86.
"*Literary Impostures Unveiled,*" MLXVI (1848), 333-34.
"John Conington's translation of the *Agamemnon* of Aeschylus and J. W. Donaldson's translation of the *Antigone* of Sophocles," MLXXII (1848), 478-79.
"George Sand's *François le Champi,*" MLXXIII (1848), 502-3.
"Thackeray's *Vanity Fair,*" MLXXXV (1848), 794-97
"E. Lynn's *Amymone,*" MLXXVII (1848), 853-55.
"Louis Reybaud's *Jerome Paturot's Search after the Best of All Republics,*" MXC (1848), 927-28.
"J. F. Cooper's *The Bee-Hunter,*" MXCI (1848), 950-53.
"Guizot's *Democracy in France,*" MCVIII (1849), 67-68.
"Dante's *Divine Comedy, the Inferno,* translated by E. A. Carlyle," MCXV (1849), 246-47.
"Schlegel's *Aesthetic and Miscellaneous Works,* MCXVII (1849), 295-96.
"George Borrow's *Lavengro,*" MCCXV (1851), 159-60.
"George Borrow's *Lavengro,*" MCCXVI (1851), 188-90.
"*Iliad* translated by T. A. Buckley," MCCXXV (1851), 428-30.

Bentley Miscellany

"Memoir of Sir E. Bulwer Lytton, Bart.," XXIV (1848), 1-10.

Blackwood's Edinburgh Magazine

Portions of *Sea-side Studies* . . . first appeared in *Blackwood's*, 1856-57. Most of *The Physiology of Common Life*, Vol. I also appeared in this magazine.

"Lesurques, or the Victim of Judicial Error," LIII (1843), 24-32.
"The Great Tragedian," LXIV (1848), 345-58.
"Metamorphoses," LXXIX (1856), 562-78, 676-91; LXXX (1856), 61-76.
"New Facts and Old Fancies about Sea Anemones," LXXXI (1857), 58-74.
"Phrenology in France," LXXXII (1857), 665-74.
"Hunger and Thirst," LXXXIII (1858), 1-17.
"People I Have Never Met," LXXXIII (1858), 183-89.
"Food and Drink," LXXXIII (1858), 325-43, 402-15, 515-25.
"Blood," LXXXIII (1858), 687-702.
"Circulation of the Blood: Its Course and History," LXXXIV (1858), 148-64.
"Respiration and Suffocation," LXXXIV (1858), 296-312.
"Animal Heat," LXXXIV (1858), 414-30.
"A Pleasant French Book," LXXXIV (1858), 675-87.
"Falsely Accused," LXXXV (1859), 208-22.
"Only a Pond," LXXXV (1859), 581-97.
"Novels of Jane Austen," LXXXVI (1859), 99-113.
"Voluntary and Involuntary Actions," LXXXVI (1859), 295-306.
"Another Pleasant French Book," LXXXVI (1859), 669-80.
"A Word about Tom Jones," LXXXVII (1860), 331-41.
"Great Wits, Mad Wits?", LXXXVIII (1860), 302-11.
"Seeing is Believing," LXXXVIII (1860), 381-95.
"Theories of Food," LXXXVIII (1860), 676-87.
"Uncivilized Man," LXXXIX (1861), 27-41.
"Spontaneous Generation," LXXXIX (1861), 165-83.
"Recent Natural History Books," LXXXIX (1861), 334-51.
"Spontaneous Combustion," LXXXIX (1861), 385-402.
"Life in Central Africa," LXXXIX (1861), 440-53.
"Mrs. Beauchamps' Vengeance," LXXXIX (1861), 537-54 (Adapted from *The Fox Who Got the Grapes.*)
"Mad Dogs," XC (1861), 222-40.
"How the World Treats Discoverers," XC (1861), 545-54.
"Mr. Buckle's Scientific Errors," XC (1861), 582-96.
"Fechter in *Hamlet* and *Othello*," XC (1861), 744-54.
"A Box of Books," XCI (1862), 434-51.
"Victor Hugo's Last Romance," XCII (1862), 172-82.

British and Foreign Review

"Hegel's Aesthetics: Philosophy of Art," XIII (1842), 1-49.

"The Character and Works of Göthe," XIV (1843), 78-135.
"The Modern Metaphysics and Moral Philosophy of France," XV (1843), 353-406.
"The State of Historical Science in France," XVI (1844), 72-118.
"The State of Criticism in France," XVI (1844), 327-62.
"Alfieri and the Italian Drama," XVII (1844), 357-90.
"The Three Fausts," XVIII (1844), 51-92.
"Eugene Sue: *Les Mystères de Paris*," XVIII (1844), 217-38.

British Quarterly Review

"Life and Works of Reid," V (1847), 445-69.
"Friends in Council," VI (1847), 134-55.
"Browning," VI (1847), 490-509.
"Historical Romance-Alexandre Dumas," VII (1848), 181-204.
"Charles Lamb-His Genius and Writings," VII (1848), 292-311.
"John Forster's *Life of Goldsmith*," VIII (1848), 1-25.
"R. Monckton Milne's *Life of Keats*," VIII (1848), 328-43.
"Charles Lamb and his Friends," VIII (1848), 381-95.
"Macaulay's *History of England*," IX (1849), 1-41.
"Giordano Bruno: His Life and Works," IX (1849), 540-63.
"Benjamin D'Israeli," X (1849), 118-39.
"Ticknor's *History of Spanish Literature*, XI (1850), 200-29.
"The Thirty Years' Peace," XI (1850), 355-71.
"Sedgwick on Cambridge Studies," XII (1850), 360-82.
"Modern French Literature," XIII (1851), 561-78.
"History by Modern Frenchmen," XIV (1851), 405-37.
"The Art of History: Macaulay," XXIII (1858), 297-325.

Classical Museum

"Was Dancing an Element of the Greek Chorus?" II (1845), 344-67.

Contemporary Review

"Lagrange and Hegel: the Speculative Method," XXIV (1874), 682-95.

Cornhill Magazine

Lewes edited the *Cornhill* from 1862-1871. Besides his editorial contributions, his *Studies in Animal Life* appeared in this magazine in 1850.

"The Use and Abuse of Tobacco," VI (1862), 605-15.
"The Mental Condition of Babies," VII (1863), 649-56.
"Was Nero a Monster?" VIII (1863), 113-28.
"The Miseries of a Dramatic Author," VIII (1863), 498-512.
"Shakespeare in France," XI (1865), 33-51.

Edinburgh Review

"Dramatic Reform: Classification of Theatres," LXXVIII (1843), 382-401.
"Lessing," LXXXII (1845), 451-70.
"Algazālli's Confessions: Arabian Philosophy," LXXXV (1847), 340-58.
"Strauss's Political Pamphlet: Julian the Apostate and Frederick William IV," LXXXVIII (1848), 94-104.
"Shakespeare's Critics: English and Foreign," XC (1849), 39-77.
"Currer Bell's 'Shirley'," XCI (1850), 153-73.

Foreign and Colonial Quarterly Review (*New Quarterly Review*)

"Goldoni and Modern Italian Comedy," VI (1845), 333-68.

Foreign Quarterly Review

"The Spanish Drama: Lope de Vega and Calderon," XXXI (1843), 502-39.
"Augustus William Schlegel," XXXII (1843), 160-81.
"St. Marc Girardin's *Lectures on the Drama*," XXXIII (1844), 59-78.
"Balzac and George Sand," XXXIII (1844), 265-98.
"German and English Translations from the Greek," XXXIII (1844), 459-77.
"Buchez and Danou on the Science of History," XXXIV (1844), 325-46.
"Mignet's Historical Essays," XXXIV (1844), 387-401.
"The Antigone and its Critics," XXXV (1845), 56-73.
"Michelet on Auricular Confession and Direction," XXXV (1845), 188-98.
"The Rise and Fall of the European Drama," XXXV (1845), 290-334.
"The New Classic Drama in France," XXXVI (1845), 32-39.
"Abelard and Heloise," XXXVI (1846), 257-92.
"Leigh Hunt on the Italian Poets," XXXVI (1846), 333-54.
"Pictures of the English by the French," XXXVI (1846), 474-86.
"George Sand's Recent Novels," XXXVII (1846), 21-36.

Fortnightly Review

Up until 1866, Lewes signed *Editor* after his articles; after that year, he used his name. Besides the papers listed below he wrote "Varia," "Causeries," Reviews, and the sections on Public Affairs.

"Heart and Brain," I (1865), 66-74.
"Robert Buchanan," I (1865), 443-58.
"Mr. Grote's Plato," II (1865), 168-83.
"Victor Hugo's Latest Poems," III (1865-66), 181-90.
"Criticism in Relation to Novels," III (1866), 352-61.
"August Comte," III (1865-66), 385-410.
"Spinoza," IV (1866), 395-406.

"Victor Hugo's New Novel," V (1866), 30-46.
"Comte and Mill," VI (1866), 385-406.
"Causeries," VI (1866), 759-61.
"The Reign of Law," II, New Series (1867), 96-111.
"Mr. Darwin's Hypothesis," III (1868), 353-73, 611-28; IV (1868), 61-80, 492-501.
"Dickens in Relation to Criticism," XVII (1872), 141-54.
"Imaginary Geometry and the Truth of Axioms," XXII (1874), 192-200.
"Spiritualism and Materialism," XXV (1876), 479-93, 707-19.
"On the Dread and Dislike of Science," XXIX (1878), 805-15.

Fraser's Magazine

"The State Murder: A Tale," XXX (1844), 394-412, 563-71.
"On the History of Pantomimes," XXXIII (1846), 43-45.
"Morell's History of Modern Philosophy," XXXIV (1846), 407-15.
"A Grumble about the Christmas Books," by M.A. Titmarsh, XXV (1847), 111-26.
"The Condition of Authors in England, Germany and France," XXXV (1847), 285-95.
"Life-in-Death," XXXVI (1847), 108-12.
"Recent Novels: French and English," XXXVI (1847), 686-95.
"A Charming Frenchwoman," XXXVII (1848), 509-18.
"The Life and Works of Leopardi," XXXVIII (1848), 659-69.
"The Story of a Great Discovery," LII (1855), 352-56.
"Professor Owen and the Science of Life," LIII (1856), 79-92.
"Dwarfs and Giants," LIV (1856), 140-53, 286-93.
"Life in its Simpler Forms," LV (1857), 194-203.
"A Precursor of the *Vestiges*," LVI (1857), 526-31.
"The Physician's Art," LVII (1858), 94-104.
"Murders at Deutz," LVIII (1858), 411-22.
"Carlyle's Frederic the Great': Criticism of the Work by the Author of 'The Life of Goethe,'" LVIII (1858), 631-49.

Hood's Magazine

"A Word to Young Authors," III (1845), 366-76.
"Philosophy of Plagiarism," III (1845), 464-69.

Leader

I-VIII, 1850-1857. Lewes' personal file of his contributions to the *Leader* from March 30, 1850 to April 8, 1854 is at the Yale University Library. He also wrote less regularly for the *Leader* between March, 1855 and June, 1857. Listed below are specific items used in the preparation of this work.

1850

March 30, *16-18*

April 6, *42-44*
13, *67-68*
27, *111, 114-15*

May 4, *137, 139-41*
11, *161-62, 163-65*
18, *187-89*
25, *211-13*

June 1, *236-37*
8, *260-61*
15, *258, 284-85*
22, *303-4, 306*

July 6, *355*
13, *378-79*
20, *400, 403*
27, *427*

August 3, *451*
17, *496-97*
24, *519-20*
31, *544-45*

October 5, *666*
12, *692, 787*

November 2, *763*
9, *787*
16, *812*
30, *856-57, 859, 860*

December 7, *878, 880-82*
21, *929-30*
28, *953*

1851

January 11, *43*
18, *67*

February 8, *132-33*
22, *182*

March 8, *228, 253-54*
15, *248-50*
22, *274-75*
29, *301*
31, *518*

April 12, *347-48*
26, *396*

May 10, *446-47*
17, *469-70*
24, *492-93*
31, *517-18*

June 14, *564, 565*
21, *587-88, 589-90*
28, *613-14*

July 5, *635*
12, *662*

August 2, *734-35*
16, *782*

September 6, *855*
13, *879*
27, *925*

November 1, *1045*
8, *1067-69*
22, *1115*
29, *1142*

1852

January 17, *60*

February 7, *137*
14, *161-62*
28, *209*

March 13, *258*
20, *282*
27, *305-6*

April 17, *377*
31, *330*

June 5, *546-47*
12, *569*
19, *590, 594*
26, *617*

July 3, *636-38, 642*
10, *663*

October 2, *950*

November 6, *1071-72*
20, *1116*
27, *1141-42, 1145*

December 11, *1189*
18, *1211, 1214-15*
24, *1240*

1853

January 1, *21*
8, *41*
15, *64*
22, *88-91*

February 5, *137-38, 142*
12, *162-63*
19, *189*
26, *214*

March 26, *303-6*

April 2, *333-34*

May 7, *451*
14, *473*
21, *501-2*

June 4, *549*
18, *596-97*
25, *617, 620*

July 2, *644, 646*
23, *717*
30, *740-41*

August 6, *762*

September 3, *858*
17, *905-7*

October 1, *953-54, 957*
8, *976*
22, *1023-24, 1028*

November 5, *1072*
19, *1123*
26, *1146-47*

December 3, *1169-71, 1173*
24, *1240*
31, *1265*

1854

January 14, *40*

February 18, *164*
25, *188-89*

March 4, *211-13*
26, *301-7*

May 27, *498-99*

1855

June 16, *579-81*

1856

March 8, *232*

May 3, *428*

1857

May 9, *449*

May 23, *497*

June 28, *616-17*

July 4, *641*

London Chronicle

Review of Thackeray's *Book of Snobs* (March 6, 1848), 3.

London Quarterly

"Spirit Rappings and Table Movings," I (1853), 109-30.

Lowe's Edinburgh Magazine

"Walter Savage Landor," I (1846), 28-34.
"Leigh Hunt's Recent Works," I (1847), 234-41.

Mind

"What is Sensation," I (1876), 157-61.
"The Uniformity of Nature," I (1876), 283-84.
"Consciousness and Unconsciousness," II (1877), 156-67.

Monthly Magazine

"Charles Paul de Kock," VII (1842), 134-42.
"Professor Bibundtucker's Remains," VII (1842), 148-52.
"H. de Balzac," VII (1842), 463-72.
"George Sand," VII (1842), 578-91.

Bibliography

Monthly Repository

"Hints Toward an Essay on the Sufferings of Truth," XI (1837), 311-19.
"Thoughts for the Thoughtful," XII (1838), 56-58.

Nature

"Instinct," VII (1873), 437-38.
"Sensation in the Spinal Cord," IX (1873), 83-84.
"Vivisection," IX (1873), 144-45.

Once a Week

"The Tail of a Tadpole" (July 2, 1859), 15-17.
"Spontaneous Generation" (July 23, 1859), 66-70.
"Stale Bread" (August 27, 1859), 175-76.
"The Chameleon's Colour" (September 24, 1859), 248-50.
"The Dust in a Sunbeam" (January 14, 1860), 50-53.

Pall Mall Gazette

I-IV, 1865-1866. Lewes' articles are signed with an *L*. He revised those entitled "Retrospects of Actors" and incorporated them into his *On Actors and the Art of Acting*. The following is the specific item referred to in the text: "Review of *As You Like It*," March 10, 1865, 238.

Penny Cyclopedia

"Spinoza," XXII (1842), 350-53.
"Spinozism," XXII (1842), 353.
"Subject," XXIII (1842), 185-86.
"Substance," XXIII (1842), 197-98.

St. Paul's Magazine

"Dangers and Delights of Tobacco," III (1868), 172-84.

Saturday Review

"Chevreul on Fact and Philosophy (December 29, 1855), 162-63.
"Supersition and Science" (January 12, 1856), 193-94.
"Miss Murray on Slavery in America" (January 12, 1856), 194-195; "Miss Murray's Letters on America" (January 26, 1856), 237-38.
"Catchpenny Science" (January 19, 1856), 214-15.

"*The Shaving of Shagpat*" (January 19, 1856), 216.
"A Mesmeric Quack" (February 2, 1856), 262-63.
"M. Flourens and his New Science" (February 9, 1856), 282.
"Roger's Table Talk" (February 16, 1865), 300-301.
"A Genevese Professor" (February 16, 1865), 306.
"Sir A. Alison on German Literature" (February 23, 1856), 326-27.
"Herbert Spencer's *Principles of Psychology*" (March 1, 1856), 352-53.
"The New School of Materialism in Germany" (March 8, 1856), 368-69.
"The History of Ancient Philosophy" (April 5, 1856), 460-61.
"Influence of Science on Literature" (April 12, 1856), 482.
"Weimar and Jena" (June 7, 1856), 137.
"Dr. Kitto" (October 25, 1856), 578-79.
"Review of Southwood Smith's *The Philosophy of Health*" (11th ed.), (February 4, 1865), 148-49.

Westminster Review

"French Drama," XXXIV (1840), 287-324.
"Shelley," XXXV (1841), 303-44.
"Modern French Historians," XXXVI (1841), 273-308.
"Authors and Managers: The Regeneration of the Drama," XXXVII (1842), 71-97.
"The Roman Empire and its Poets," XXXVIII (1842), 33-58.
"Recent Tragedies," XXXVIII (1842), 321-47.
"Errors and Abuses of English Criticism," XXXVIII (1842), 466-86.
"Spinoza's Life and Works," XXXIX (1843), 372-407.
"Charges against Niebuhr," XL (1843), 335-49.
"Strafford and the Historical Drama," XLI (1844), 119-28.
"Niebuhr and the Classical Museum," XLI (1844), 178-83.
"Prize Comedy and the Prize Committee," XLII (1844), 178-83.
"Shakespeare and his Editors," XLIII (1845), 40-77.
"Historical Romance: *The Foster Brother* and *Whitehall*," XLV (1846), 34-55.
"Grote's History of Greece: The Homeric Poems," XLVI (1846), 381-415.
"A Review of *Jane Eyre*," XLVIII (1848), 581-84.
"A Review of *Shirley*," LII (1850), 407-18.
"Julia von Krudener, as Coquette and Mystic," LVII (1852), 161-82.
"Shelley and the Letters of Poets," LVII (1852), 502-11.
"Contemporary Literature of France," LVII (1852), 697-703.
"The Lady Novelists," LVIII (1852), 129-41.
"Contemporary Literature of France," LVIII (1852), 306-13, 614-30.
"Goethe as a Man of Science," LVIII (1852), 479-506.
"Contemporary Literature of France," LIX (1853), 317-26.
"*Ruth* and *Villette*," LIX (1853), 474-91.
"Poems of Alexander Smith," LIX (1853), 522-34.

"French Literature: Summary," LIX (1853), 634-49.
"Life and Doctrine of Geoffroy St. Hilaire," LXI (1854), 160-90.
"The Physiological Errors of Teetotalism," LXIV (1855), 94-124.
"Lions and Lion Hunting," LXV (1856), 205-17.
"Hereditary Influence, Animal and Human," LXVI (1856), 135-62.
"Alchemy and Alchemists," LXVI (1856), 279-95.
"Suicide in Life and Literature," LXVIII (1857), 52-78.
"African Life," LXIX (1858), 1-28.
"Realism in Art: Recent German Fiction," LXX (1858), 488-518.
"The Life of a Conjuror," LXXII (1859), 91-111.

Miscellaneous References

Abrams, M.H. *The Mirror and the Lamp: Romantic Theory and the Critical Tradition.* New York: Norton, 1958.

Archer, William. "George Henry Lewes and the Stage," *FR,* LXV (1896), 216-30.

Arnold, Matthew. *The Letters of Matthew Arnold,* ed. G.W.E. Russell. 2 vols. New York: Macmillan, 1895.

Auerbach, Erich. *Mimesis: the Representation of Reality in Western Literature,* tr. W.R. Trask. Princeton: Princeton University Press, 1953.

Babkin, B.P. *Pavlov.* Chicago: University of Chicago Press, 1949.

Bain, Alexander. *John Stuart Mill: A Criticism: with Personal Recollections.* London: Longmans, Green, 1882.

Barzun, Jacques. Introduction to *Goethe's Faust.* New York: Rinehart, 1955.

Batho, Edith and Dobrée, Bonamy. *The Victorians and After, 1830-1914.* London: Cresset, 1938.

Bennett, Joan. "Unpublished George Eliot Letters," *The Times Literary Supplement* (May 16, 1968), 507.

Berlin, Isaiah. *Historical Inevitability.* London: Oxford University Press, 1957.

Bickersteth, G.L. (ed.). *The Poems of Leopardi.* Cambridge: Cambridge University Press, 1923.

Blanchard, F.J. *Fielding the Novelist: A Study in Historical Criticism.* New Haven: Yale University Press, 1926.

Blind, Mathilde. *George Eliot.* Boston: Little Brown, 1904.

Boas, George. *Wingless Pegasus: A Handbook for Critics.* Baltimore: Johns Hopkins Press, 1950; Boas, George and Wrenn, H.H. *What is a Picture?* Pittsburgh: University of Pittsburgh Press, 1964.

Bourl'honne, P. *George Eliot: essai de biographie intellectuelle et morale 1819-1854.* Paris: H. Champion, 1933.

Bowra, C.M. *Sophoclean Tragedy.* Oxford: Clarendon Press, 1944.

Brett, R.L. "George Henry Lewes: Dramatist, Novelist and Critic," *Essays and Studies,* XI (1958), 101-20.

Brick, Allen R. "Lewes's Review of Wuthering Heights," *Nineteenth Century Fiction,* XIV (1960), 355-59.

———. "The Leader: Organ of Radicalism." Dissertation, Yale University, 1957.

Brooks, Cleanth. *The Well Wrought Urn: Studies in the Structure of Poetry.* New York: Harcourt Brace, 1947.

Brown, A.W. *The Metaphysical Society.* New York: Columbia University Press, 1947.

Browning, Oscar. *Life of George Eliot.* London: Walter Scott, 1890.

Bull, Patricia M. "Sincerity: The Rise and Fall of a Critical Term," *Modern Language Review,* LIX (1954), 1-11.

Bullett, Gerald. *George Eliot: Her Life and Books.* New Haven: Yale University Press, 1948.

Burke, Edmund. *The Works of the Right Honorable Edmund Burke.* (3rd ed.), I. Boston: Little Brown, 1869.

Camus, Albert. *The Rebel.* tr. A. Bower. New York: Alfred Knopf, 1954.

Carlyle. T. *On Heroes, Hero-Worship, and the Heroic in History.* Boston: Ginn, 1901.

Casey, Weldon. "George Eliot's Theory of Fiction," *Philological Papers West Virginia University Bulletin,* IX (1953), 20-32.

Clurman, Harold. "Review of Joanna Richardson's *Rachel,*" *New York Times Book Review* (April 28, 1957), 7.

Cooke, George W. *George Eliot, A Critical Study of her Life, Writings, and Philosophy.* (2nd ed.) Boston: Houghton Mifflin, 1883.

Crane, Ronald S. *The Languages of Criticism and the Structure of Poetry.* Toronto: University of Toronto Press, 1953.

———. (ed.). *Critics and Criticism.* Chicago: University of Chicago Press, 1952.

Croce, B. *Aesthetic.* tr. D. Ainslie. (2nd ed.) London: MacMillan, 1929.

Cross, J.W. (ed.). *George Eliot's Life as Related in Her Letters and Journals.* Cabinet Edition. 3 vols. Edinburgh and London: Blackwood, [1885].

Daiches, David. *Critical Approaches to Literature.* Englewood Cliffs, New Jersey: Prentice-Hall, 1956.

Davis, Kenneth W. "George Henry Lewes's Introduction to the Blackwood Circle," *English Langauge Notes,* I (1963), 113-14.

Dewey, John. *Art as Experience.* New York: Minton, Balch, 1934.

Dickens, Charles. *The Letters of Charles Dickens.* ed. W. Dexter. London: Nonesuch Press, 1938, II.

Doremus, Robert B. "George Henry Lewes: A Descriptive Biography with Special Attention to His Interest in the Theater." 2 vols. Dissertation, Harvard, 1940.

Dostoevski, F. *Crime and Punishment.* tr. C. Garnett. New York: Grosset & Dunlap, 1927.

Dramatic Omnibus. November 24, 1844. 3.

Duffy, Sir Charles Gavan. *Conversations with Carlyle.* New York: Charles Scribner, 1892.

Eliot, George. "The Natural History of German Life: Riehl," *WR,* LXVI (1856), 51-79.

Ellis, Havelock. Introduction to Lewes, *The Life and Works of Goethe,* (Everyman ed.), London and New York: Dent, 1908.

Espinasse, Francis. *Literary Recollections and Sketches.* London: Hodder & Stoughton, 1889.

Euwema, Ben. "The Development of George Eliot's Ethical and Social Theories." Dissertation, University of Chicago, 1934.

Everett, E.M. *The Party of Humanity: The Fortnightly Review and Its Contributors, 1865-1874.* Chapel Hill: University of North Carolina Press, 1939.

Examiner. February 23, 1850. 117.

Ferri, Louis. *La Psychologie de l'association depuis Hobbes jusqu'à nos jours.* Paris: Germer Baillière, 1883.

Ford, George H. *Dickens and His Readers: Aspects of Novel-criticism since 1836.* Princeton: Princeton University Press, 1955.

Forster, John. *The Life of Charles Dickens.* Philadelphia: J.B. Lippincott, 1890, II.

Friedenthal, Richard. *Goethe: His Life and Times.* Cleveland: World Publishing, 1965.

Fulton, J.F. "The Progress of Science: Ivan Petrovitch Pavlov," *Scientific Monthly,* XLII (1936), 375-77.

Gary, Franklin. "Charlotte Brontë and George Henry Lewes," *PMLA,* LI (1936), 518-42.

Grant Duff, Sir Mountstuart E. *Notes from a Diary: 1873-1881.* London: John Murray, 1898, II.

Grassi-Bertazzi, G. *Esame Critico della Filosophia di George Henry Lewes.* Messina: Trimarchi, 1906.

Greenhut, Morris. "George Henry Lewes and the Classical Tradition in English Criticism," *Review of English Studies,* XXIV (1948), 126-37.

———. "George Henry Lewes as a Critic of the Novel," *Studies in Philology,* XLV (1948), 491-511.

———. "G.H. Lewes's Criticism of the Drama," *PMLA,* LXIV (1949), 350-68.

Haight, Gordon S. "Dickens and Lewes on Spontaneous Combustion," *Nineteenth Century Fiction,* X (1955), 53-63.

———. "Dickens and Lewes," *PMLA,* LXXI (1956), 166-79.

———. "Review of 'George Eliot, George Henry Lewes, and the Novel.'" *The Victorian Newsletter,* X (1956), 2-3.

———. (ed.). *The George Eliot Letters.* 7 vols. New Haven: Yale University Press, 1955.

Hanson, Lawrence and Elisabeth. *The Four Brontës.* London: Oxford University Press, 1949.

———. *Marian Evans & George Eliot: A Biography.* London: Oxford University Press, 1952.

Harrison, Frederic. "G.H. Lewes," *Academy,* XIV (1878), 543-44.

———. *The Philosophy of Common Sense.* New York: MacMillan, 1907.

Heyl, Bernard C. "The Critic's Reasons," *The Journal of Aesthetics*, XVI (1957), 169-79.

———. *New Bearings in Esthetics and Art Criticism*. New Haven: Yale University Press, 1943.

Hiatt, Charles. *Henry Irving: A Record and Review*. London: George Bell, 1899.

Hirshberg, Edgar W. "George Henry Lewes as Playwright and Dramatic Critic." Dissertation, Yale University, 1951.

———. "*Captain Bland* on the New York Stage," *New York Public Library Bulletin*, LVII (1953), 382-88.

———. "George Henry Lewes and Victor Hugo's Reputation in England," *Language Quarterly*, I (1963), 9-11.

———. "George Eliot and her Husband," *English Journal*, LVI (1967), 809-17.

Hollingshead, John. *My Lifetime*. (2nd ed.) London: Sampson Low, Marston, 1895, I.

Holyoake, G.J. *Bygones Worth Remembering*. London: T. Fisher Unwin, 1905, I.

———. *Sixty Years of an Agitator's Life*. 2 vols. London: T. Fisher Unwin, 1892.

Hooker, K.W. *The Fortunes of Victor Hugo in England*. New York: Columbia University Press, 1938.

Huxley, Thomas Henry. "Science," *WR*, LXI (1854), 254-70.

Hyde, William J. "George Eliot and the Climate of Realism," *PMLA*, LXXII (1957), 147-64.

James, Henry. *French Poets and Novelists*. London: MacMillan, 1878.

———. *Partial Portraits*. London: MacMillan, 1911.

James, William. *Psychology*. New York: Henry Holt, 1905.

Kaminsky, Alice R. "George Eliot, George Henry Lewes, and the Novel," *PMLA*, LXX (1955), 907-1013.

———. (ed.). *The Literary Criticism of George Henry Lewes*. Lincoln: University of Nebraska Press, 1964.

———. "The Philosophy of George Henry Lewes," reprinted with permission of the Publisher from *Encyclopedia of Philosophy*, Paul Edwards, editor, Vol. IV, 452-454. Copyright © U.S.A. 1967 by Crowell Collier and Macmillan, Inc. Copyright © in Great Britain and under International Copyright Union 1967 by Crowell Collier and Macmillan, Inc.

Kaminsky, Jack. "The Empirical Metaphysics of George Henry Lewes," *Journal of the History of Ideas*, XIII (1952), 314-32.

Kitchel, Anna T. *George Lewes and George Eliot: A Review of Records*. New York: John Day, 1933.

Knights, L.C. "On Historical Scholarship and the Interpretation of Shakespeare," *The Sewanee Review*, LXIII (1955), 223-40.

Knowlson, T. Sharper (ed.). *Principles of Success in Literature*. London: Walter Scott, [189?].

Kreyenberg, Dr. Gotthold. *A Concise Examination of the Value and the Merits of G. H. Lewes' Celebrated Inquiry into the Life and Works of Goethe*. Graudenz: n.p., 1866.

Layard, George S. *Mrs. Lynn Linton: Her Life, Letters, & Opinions.* London: Methuen, 1901.

Letter to Dr. Robert Vaughn, May 8, 1852, Beinecke, Yale.

Levin, Harry. *Contexts of Criticism*. New York: Atheneum, 1963.

Lewes, Agnes. "Lope de Vega's *Gatomachie*," *WR*, XL (1843), 75-101.

———. "Beaumarchais & Sophie Arnould," *WR*, XLII (1844), 146-60.

———. "Augustin Thierry: *Récits des Temps Merovingiens*," BFR, XVII (1844), 270-303.

———. "Pride of a Spoiled Beauty," *Fraser's*, XXX (1846), 46-57, 180-192.

———. "John Sebastian Bach," *Fraser's*, XXXIV (1846), 28-41.

———. "Scenes in the Wilds of Mexico," *Fraser's*, XXXV (1847), 15-28, 169-82, 270-84, 401-11, 538-47, 668-83; XXXVI (1847), 156-68.

———. "A Spanish Bullfight," *Lowe's Edinburgh Magazine*, I (1847), 373-81.

Lewes, Charles Lee. *Memoirs*. ed. John Lee Lewes. 4 vols. London: Richard Phillips, 1805.

Linton, Mrs. Eliza Lynn. *The Autobiography of Christopher Kirkland*. I. London: Richard Bentley, 1885. I.

———. *My Literary Life*. London: Hodder & Stoughton, 1899.

Literary Gazette. February 23, 1850. 149.

Times (London). December 7, 1842, 5; May 16, 1848, 8; Feb. 19, 1850, 6; May 20, 1854, 5.

Manchester Guardian. March 7, 1849, 6.

McCarthy, Justin. *Reminiscences*. New York: Harper, 1899, I.

Merz, J.T. *A History of European Thought in the 19th Century*. London: Blackwood, 1914. III.

Mill, John Stuart. "What is Poetry?" *Monthly Repository*, VII (1833), 60-70.

———. "The Two Kinds of Poetry," *Monthly Repository*, VII (1833), 714-24.

———. Letter to Macvey Napier. February 18, 1842. British Museum, Add. Mss. 34, 622.

Morgan, C. Lloyd. *Mind at the Crossways*. London: William & Norgate, 1930.

———. *The Emergence of Novelty*. London: William & Norgate, 1933.

Napier, Macvey (ed.). *Selections from the Corresondence of the Late Macvey Napier*. London: MacMillan, 1879.

Natorp, Paul. *Allgemeine Psychologie nach Kritischer Methode*. Tubingen: J.C.B. Mohr, 1912, I.

Needham, H.A. *Le Développement de l'esthetique sociologique en France et en Angleterre au XIXe siècle*. Paris: Honore Champion, 1926.

Nicoll, Allardyce. *A History of Late Nineteenth Century Drama, 1850-1900*. 2 vols. Cambridge: Cambridge University Press, 1949.

Norton, Charles E. *Letters.* ed. S. Norton and M.A. DeWolfe Howe. Boston and New York: Houghton Mifflin, 1913, I.

Ogden, C.K., Richards, I.A., and Wood, J. *Foundations of Aesthetics.* 2nd ed. London: Allen & Unwin, 1925.

Osborne, Harold. *Aesthetics and Criticism.* New York: Philosophical Library, 1955.

Pall Mall Budget, (December 7, 1878), 15.

Parlett, Mathilde. "The Influence of Contemporary Criticism on George Eliot," *Studies in Philology,* XXX (1933), 103-32.

Peirce, Charles Sanders. *Collected Papers: Principles of Philosophy.* eds. Charles Hartshorne and Paul Weiss. Boston: Harvard University Press, 1931, I.

Perrin, Raymond St. James. *The Evolution of Knowledge.* New York: Baker & Taylor, 1905.

Poe, Edgar Allan. *His Life, Letters, and Opinions.* ed. John H. Ingram. London: John Hogg, 1880, II.

Pond, E.J. *Les Idées morales et religieuses de George Eliot.* Paris: University of France Press, 1927.

Pottle, Frederick. *The Idiom of Poetry.* Bloomington: Indiana University Press, 1963.

Pritchett, V.S. *The Living Novel.* New York: Reynal & Hitchcock, 1947.

Report of the Twenty-Ninth Meeting of the British Association for the Advancement of Science Held at Aberdeen in September (1859, 1860).

"Recent Novels," *Fraser's,* XXXVIII (1848), 33-40.

"Review of *Ranthorpe and Rose, Blanche, and Violet,*" BQR, VII (1848), 332-46.

Ribot, Theodule. *English Psychology.* London: Henry S. King, 1873.

Richards, I.A. *Coleridge on Imagination.* Bloomington: Indiana University Press, 1960.

Robert, First Earl of Lytton. *Personal and Literary Letters.* ed. Lady Betty Balfour. London: Longmans, 1906, II.

Rose, Blanche, and Violet. Jane Welsh Carlyle Presentation Copy. 3 vols. Berg Collection, New York Public Library.

Saintsbury, George. *A History of Criticism and Literary Taste.* New York and London: Blackwood, 1917, III.

Santayana, George. *Soliloquies in England and Later Soliloquies.* New York: Charles Scribner, 1923.

Scott, William Bell. *Autobiographical Notes.* ed. W. Minto. 2 vols. New York: Harper, 1892.

Shaw, George Bernard. *Our Theater in the Nineties.* London: Constable, 1932, II, III.

Shorter, Clement (ed.). *The Brontës Life and Letters.* 2 vols. London: Hodder & Stoughton, 1908.

Shumaker, Wayne. *Elements of Critical Theory.* Berkeley: University of California Press, 1952.

Siegfried, Heinrich. *An G.H. Lewes eine Epistel.* Berlin: George Reimer, 1858.

Sillard, Robert M. *Barry Sullivan and his Contemporaries: A Histrionic Record.* London: T. Fisher Unwin, 1901, I.

Sorley, W.R. *A History of English Philosophy.* Cambridge, Cambridge University Press, 1937.

Spectator. May 20, 1848. 487; Feb. 23, 1850. 180.

Spencer, Herbert. *An Autobiography.* 2 vols. New York: Appleton, 1904.

———. *Facts and Comments.* New York: Appleton, 1902.

———. "Philosophy of Style," WR, LVIII (1852), 435-59.

Stephen, Sir Leslie. "George Henry Lewes," *DNB,* II (1937-1938) 1044.

———. *The Life and Letters.* ed. F.W. Maitland. New York: G. Putnam, 1906.

Stevenson, Lionel (ed.). *Victorian Fiction: A Guide to Research.* Cambridge, Mass.: Harvard University Press, 1964.

[Sully, James]. "George Henry Lewes," *New Quarterly Magazine,* II (1879), 356-76.

———. *My Life and Friends.* London: T. Fisher Unwin, 1918.

Tennyson, Hallam. *Alfred Lord Tennyson: A Memoir by His Son.* New York: Macmillan, 1898. II.

Thackeray, W.M. "Thorns in the Cushion," *Roundabout Paper,* No. V, *Cornhill Magazine,* II (1860), 124.

———. *The Letters and Private Papers of William Makepeace Thackeray,* ed. Gordon N. Ray. Cambridge: Harvard University Press, 1946. II.

Toyoda, Minoru. *Studies in the Mental Development of George Eliot.* Tokyo: Kenkyusha, 1931.

Trollope, Anthony. *An Autobiography.* London: Williams & Norgate, 1946.

———. "George Henry Lewes," *FR,* XXXI (1879), 15-24.

Tynan, Kenneth. *Curtains.* New York: Atheneum, 1961.

Walker, Hugh. *Literature of the Victorian Era.* Cambridge: Cambridge University Press, 1921.

Warren, Alba H. *English Poetic Theory 1825-1865.* Princeton: Princeton University Press, 1950.

Warren, Howard C. *A History of the Association Psychology.* New York: Charles Scribner, 1921.

Warrington, Winter. "Dickens and the Psychology of Dreams," *PMLA,* LXIII (1948), 984-1006.

Watson, Ernest Bradlee. *Sheridan to Robertson: a Study of the Nineteenth-Century London Stage.* New York: B. Blom, 1963.

White, Newman Ivy. *Shelley.* New York: Alfred A. Knopf, 1940, II.

Wellek, René. *A History of Modern Criticism: 1750-1950, The Later Nineteenth Century.* New Haven: Yale University Press, 1965.

———. *Concepts of Criticism.* New Haven: Yale University Press, 1963.

Willey, Basil. *Nineteenth Century Studies.* New York: Columbia University Press, 1949.

Williams, B.C. *George Eliot: A Biography.* New York: MacMillan, 1936.

Wilson, M. Glen, Jr. "George Henry Lewes as Critic of Charles Kean's Acting," *Education Theater Journal,* XVI (1964), 360-67.

Wimsatt, William K. and Brooks, Cleanth. *Literary Criticism: A Short History*. New York: Random House, 1967.

Index